Imaginary bodies

D0145750

'A major intervention in feminist theory, taking up the critical distinction between sex and gender, and relating it to fundamental distinctions that have orchestrated the history of philosophy: mind and body, nature and culture, passion and reason . . . Gatens argues that the sex/gender distinction as currently construed in feminist theory fails to take into account the psychoanalytic notion of the imaginary body; she explores the idea of the body image as a "double", an other, or a complement. She discusses the metaphorical – and metonymical – uses to which the body is put in the "body politic" and asks *whose* body is allowed to stand for others. She subjects the social contract theorists to scrutiny, particularly Hobbes and Locke, and she draws productively on Spinoza. The arguments that Gatens develops and the parallels she introduces are compelling, bringing a well-informed historical perspective to a thorough knowledge of feminist theory, philosophy and psychoanalysis.'

Tina Chanter, *University of Memphis*

'The essays draw on Nietzsche, Freud, Lacan, Deleuze as well as contemporary feminist theory. But they converge on a challenging reading of Spinoza which highlights his theory of the imagination . . . It is a strength of this book that, while making an original and important contribution to social theory, it engages directly with the challenge of constructively reconceptualizing contemporary issues in pressing need of intelligent debate – domestic violence, rape, sexual bias among the judiciary.'

Genevieve Lloyd, *University of New South Wales*

Moira Gatens is Senior Lecturer in Philosophy at the University of Sydney. She is the author of *Feminism and Philosophy: Perspectives on Difference and Equality.*

Imaginary bodies

Ethics, power and corporeality

Moira Gatens

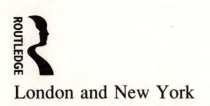

London and New York

First published 1996
by Routledge
11 New Fetter Lane, London EC4P 4EE

Simultaneously published in the USA and Canada
by Routledge
29 West 35th Street, New York, NY 10001

© 1996 Moira Gatens

Typeset in Times by
J&L Composition Ltd, Filey, North Yorkshire
Printed and bound in Great Britain by
TJ Press (Padstow) Ltd, Padstow, Cornwall

British Library Cataloguing in Publication Data
A catalogue record for this book is available from the British
Library.

Library of Congress Cataloguing in Publication Data
A catalogue record for this book has been requested.

ISBN 0–415–08209–9 (hbk)
ISBN 0–415–08210–2 (pbk)

Contents

Preface

> There is no closure of discourse, discourse only ever being a compro-
> mise – or bricolage – between what it is legitimate to say, what one
> would like to contend or argue, and what one is forced to recognize.
>   Michèle Le Dœuff, *The Philosophical Imaginary*[1]

This collection of essays investigates social, political and ethical understandings of sexed bodies. In what ways is the human body represented in
Western culture? Specifically, what are the unacknowledged philosophical
underpinnings of dominant representations of sexual difference? The
notion of woman as 'lack', as 'deformity', or deficiency, appears in the
work of ancient philosophers, such as Aristotle,[2] and in the work of
twentieth-century thinkers, such as Jacques Lacan.[3] Many feminists have
argued that these representations of women cannot be dismissed as superficial bias on the part of (predominantly) male theorists. Rather, it has been
suggested that these representations have a metaphysical basis in Western
thought that is not easily removed without destroying the coherence of the
philosophical system concerned.[4] Yet the problem cannot be confined to
the domain of metaphysics, since the deep structural bias against women
has effects that are felt at the levels of epistemology, moral and social
theory, and political theory. This, in turn, has material effects on the
manner in which we conduct ourselves ethically and politically.

The nine essays collected here were written between 1983 and 1994.
Although they may be read independently of each other, they do share a
preoccupation with the question of how to theorize human embodiment
without losing the sexual, political or ethical particularity of different
bodies. The coherence of the collection lies in these central concerns, to
which I found myself returning again and again but from new perspectives.
The essays attempt to work on two interrelated fronts. First, they are
concerned with representations of the human body, which, contrary to
popular opinion and anatomical textbooks, is unrepresentable. Human
bodies are diverse and, even anatomically speaking, the selection of a
particular image of the human body will be a selection from a continuum
of differences. Many anatomical depictions which purport to represent the

human body turn out to be depictions of white male bodies – with the bodies of others called upon to illustrate specific capacities: the female reproductive system, for example. Philosophical accounts of what it is to be human almost invariably mirror these anatomical representations, that is, woman is treated only insofar as she is not-man. Several of the essays here treat philosophical views on 'Man' and the place of 'woman' within them. Particular attention is paid to accounts of male and female embodiment, since philosophers have typically ignored the corporeal aspects of being human.[5] This has had detrimental effects on notions of women and femininity, since these notions have been closely associated with the body, nature and emotion. As a result, women's status as (fully) 'human' has sometimes been in question.[6] Hence, one central concern of the collection is philosophical representations of human embodiment.

I am not concerned with physiological, anatomical, or biological under-standings of the human body but rather with what will be called *imaginary* bodies. An imaginary body is not simply a product of subjective imagina-tion, fantasy or folklore. The term 'imaginary' will be used in a loose but nevertheless technical sense to refer to those images, symbols, metaphors and representations which help construct various forms of subjectivity. In this sense, I am concerned with the (often unconscious) imaginaries of a specific culture: those ready-made images and symbols through which we make sense of social bodies and which determine, in part, their value, their status and what will be deemed their appropriate treatment. I am not proposing a theory of the imaginary. Moreover, I doubt if such a global theory is plausible. Hence, I am certainly not using the concept 'imaginary' as a substitute for a theory of ideology.

In her account of Luce Irigaray's employment of the notion of the imaginary, Margaret Whitford cites the work of Merleau-Ponty, Althusser, Castoriadis and Lacan as probable influences. No doubt aspects of their diverse conceptions of the imaginary will be seen to resonate in these essays. However, the notion of imagination has long been central to philosophical accounts of human being and so Descartes, Hume and Spinoza must in turn be acknowledged as important influences on these twentieth-century philosophers. Spinoza, as we will see shortly, has had a marked, if largely unacknowledged, effect on contemporary notions of the imagination and the imaginary. Summarizing Irigaray's project up to and including *Speculum of the Other Woman*, Whitford writes:

Irigaray begins with an analysis of the imaginary of Western philoso-phical and psychoanalytic discourse (*Speculum*), aiming to show that the conceptualization of sexual difference in this discourse is governed by an imaginary which is anal, that is to say, which interprets sexual difference as though there were only one sex, and that sex were male (women are defective men).[7]

At this stage of Irigaray's work, she confines herself to the philosophical and psychoanalytic imaginary.

There are some similarities between Irigaray's early work and Michèle Le Dœuff's *The Philosophical Imaginary*. Le Dœuff's thesis is that the philosophical imaginary – which forms part of the unacknowledged induction into philosophy – is not incidental to the types of practice in which philosophers, understood as a corporate body, engage. She seeks to show the centrality of the image and metaphor to the philosophical enterprise, suggesting that

> imagery and knowledge form, dialectically, a common system. Between these two terms there is a play of feedbacks which maintains the particular regime of the discursive formation. Philosophical texts offer *images through which subjectivity can be structured* and given a marking *which is that of the corporate body*.[8]

Several of the essays here attempt to extend this notion of the 'structuring function' of philosophical texts to include various 'social' texts: legal texts, texts in political theory, feminist texts and social practices in so far as they function like texts. I must stress, however, that I do not hold a notion of a social imaginary but rather social imaginaries. It is for this reason that I do not think that the concept of the imaginary is analogous to that of ideology. This is, perhaps, the point at which I part company with aspects of Irigaray's project. In her later work, she too extends her use of 'imaginary' to the social *per se*. According to Whitford,

> Irigaray . . . suggest[s], [in later work,] that the imaginary is not confined to philosophers and psychoanalysts, but is a social imaginary *which is taken to be reality*, with damaging consequences for women who, unlike men, find themselves 'homeless' in the symbolic order.[9]

An unavoidable consequence of positing a unitary notion of *the* social imaginary is that it will come to stand in contrast to a notion of 'reality', as the passage above shows. The 'imaginary' is then doing the work that the notion of ideology did in new left politics of the 1960s and 70s, with sexual difference displacing the role of class struggle.

In spite of Whitford's protestations that Irigaray's work cannot be dismissed as 'utopic', the deployment of a 'reality'/'imaginary' distinction inevitably leads to a contrast between a less than satisfactory present and an idealized future. Thus, Whitford argues that according to Irigaray 'radical transformations in the social imaginary *could* take place, and that a new and previously unimaginable configuration could take shape'.[10] To acknowledge the diversity in, and dynamism of, our social imaginaries allows one to focus on those aspects of present social imaginaries which are contradictory or paradoxical. This, in turn, allows one to see that the system of linked social imaginaries is constantly being transformed and refigured. Whilst agreeing that representations of sexual difference are central to social imaginaries, I do not think it helpful to reduce the complexity and variety of social imaginaries to a univocal sexual imaginary. To do so leaves the notion of the imaginary open to precisely those objections that may be made to Marxist and post-Marxist notions of ideology.

In a recent paper David Couzens Hoy has sketched the objections that may be put, from a poststructuralist perspective, to the concept of ideology.

> First, the appeal to distorted consciousness is unhelpful if there is no consciousness that is not distorted. Second, the idea of a group consciousness is a fiction, and the idea of consciousness needs to be replaced with other ideas such as 'mentality', 'discourse', '*habitus*', or 'the background' that capture the sense in which the structures of social behaviour often are below the threshold of conscious decision-making. Third, if the ideas of distortion and consciousness are abandoned, one can live with the recognition that there is no single way that 'society' need be perceived globally and no utopia in which all would describe it univocally.[11]

The essays in this book trace a path away from a politics of (true and false) consciousness and toward notions more akin to *habitus* or 'the background'. Some of the early essays are marked by a strong investment in psychoanalytic discourses and notions such as 'body image'. These psychoanalytic notions proved less useful in contexts where I was concerned to draw parallels between the sexed bodies of men and women, on the one hand, and corporate bodies such as the body politic or legal corporations, on the other. In later essays, I argue that an insistence on ontological sexual difference leads into the *cul de sac* of essentialism, where sexual difference is privileged over all other differences. My interest in ethics and politics led me away from psychoanalytic theory to the work of Spinoza. Drawing upon Deleuze's readings of Spinoza, I have used Spinoza's notion of imagination in order to develop a notion of embodiment that posits multiple and historically specific social imaginaries.

A second major concern of these essays is to identify the resonances of imaginary understandings of human embodiment in relation to accounts, in political theory, of another kind of body: the body politic. It will be argued that this body shares several features with the masculine imaginary body. It is important to draw out the connections between the supposed moral and political autonomy of rational man and the supposed autonomy of the political body. Women, it will be shown, have a very tentative and derivative relation not only to 'Man' but especially to the product of his fecund reason: the political body. This has dire repercussions not only for women's political status and participation but also for their legal, ethical and social existence.

The relations between women and men, women and politics, women and the body politic, women and ethics, and women and the law display disconcertingly similar patterns; which is to say that social imaginaries 'link up'. They link up, however, not to form a coherent and unchallengeable front. On the contrary, different aspects of contemporary liberal sociabilities jostle against each other, create paradoxes of all kinds, and present opportunities for change and political action. Many legal, political and ethical accounts of women involve recurring images of women's incompleteness, which in turn are implicitly used to justify women's differential treatment. Moreover, in a context of male privilege, female 'incompleteness' invariably amounts to male–female complementarity. Complementarity, in a situation of domination and subordination, leads to women being conceived as both conceptually and actually dependent on men. These assumptions about men and women, however, are sometimes challenged by economic and political changes in women's status.

Imaginary aspects of everyday consciousness may well be thought by some to be undeserving of serious philosophical treatment. As Le Dœuff has observed, in another context, '[t]he images that appear in theoretical texts are normally viewed as extrinsic to the theoretical work, so that to interest oneself in them seems like a merely anecdotal approach to philosophy.'[12] Much feminist theory has been criticized in precisely these terms, that is, for taking an 'anecdotal approach' to philosophy. The opinions of the 'Great Philosophers' on women, for example, have often been dismissed as merely anecdotal and of no relevance to their serious philosophical writings. There are two responses which one should make to this sort of objection.

First, whether we care to acknowledge it or not, we are historical beings whose language, stock of images and social practices constitute an unconscious dimension of our cultural heritage. Many of us utter 'bless you' when another sneezes, exchange rings – to be worn on a specific finger – on marriage, automatically mark children with the patronym, and so on, without having the faintest idea *why* we do these things, or of the historical meanings borne by such actions. These are embodied habits, the origins of which have been long forgotten, and have now become second nature.[13] These are precisely the terms in which Pierre Bourdieu speaks of the notion of *habitus*. Moreover, he sees this notion as capable of explaining how it is that our social institutions appear to be resilient to change.

According to Bourdieu, *habitus* is our

> embodied history, *internalized as a second nature* and so forgotten as history – [it] is the active presence of the whole past of which it is the product. As such, it is what gives practices their relative autonomy with respect to external determinations of the immediate present . . . The *habitus* is a *spontaneity without consciousness or will* . . . [*Habitus* is also the means] through which agents partake of the history objectified in institutions, [it] is what makes it possible to inhabit institutions, to appropriate them practically, and so to keep them in activity,

continuously pulling them from the state of dead letters, reviving the sense deposited in them, but at the same time imposing the revisions and transformations that reactivation entails.[14]

It is precisely this 'spontaneity without consciousness or will' which requires philosophical analysis, not least because of its pervasive and largely unquestioned influence on the conduct and quality of our lives.

Second, philosophy itself has much to answer for in relation to the character of the images and representations which dominate the everyday consciousness.[15] As much as some philosophers would like to believe that they inhabit a plane beyond that of the 'person on the street', philosophers are themselves 'persons on the street'. Not only has philosophy contributed to the historical cache of everyday consciousness, philosophers do not, and cannot, put aside their own historical specificity when they philosophize. If the work of philosophers such as Genevieve Lloyd and Michèle Le Dœuff is to have its deserved effect, then philosophers will begin to accept responsibility for the particular passions and imaginings that characterize their particular philosophies.

The essays are collected under three sections. Part I contains essays which explore the manner in which particular images, employed in philosophy and psychoanalysis, serve to capture, curtail and contain women's sexual, social and political possibilities. Chapter 1 criticizes the distinction between sex and gender that has been central to feminist theory since the early 1970s. I argue that it is a distinction that has tended to track dualistic conceptions of body and mind. The notion of a sexed 'body image', which takes account of the meaning of the materiality of the body is introduced in order to think beyond 'degendering' or 'regendering' proposals for social change.[16] However, the individualism of psychoanalytic theory is not very helpful when one comes to consider corporate bodies.[17] In Chapter 2 I attempt to think about women's relation to Hobbes' leviathan, that giant 'artificial man' who functions to keep men safe from the perils of the state of nature. The writing of that chapter raised questions concerning the legal treatment which women receive from the liberal state. Whether or not it is coherent to speak of a woman's body as *anatomically* 'lacking', is irrelevant to the imaginary apprehension of women's bodies as 'begging the question' of their completion by a man and/or child. Whether the social context is that of a woman in a courtroom or in a job interview, the effects of dominant attitudes toward women's social value and the social meaning of women's bodies are discernible in the treatment they receive. Protesting the anatomical 'completeness' of a woman's body will do little to change these attitudes since they are not, in any straightforward way, receptive to rational argument. Chapter 3 offers an analysis of these attitudes, at the site of their operation, by considering the imaginary components of our beliefs concerning sexual difference and bodily integrity. The effects of such beliefs are no less 'real' or 'material' simply because their bases are to be found in the affective power of images, symbols, fictions and representations. This in turn raised issues of an ethical nature: why is it that the right to bodily integrity – so fundamental to liberal polities – appears to be of little concern to the law in the case of women?

Part II signals a rupture in the circulation of discourses about women due to the unsettling effects of a significant number of women's voices being deployed in discourses 'on' women. Part of the power or force exerted by feminist writers derives from the challenge that they pose to dominant social imaginaries. This section considers not only the critical examination of dominant discourses on women but further, tentative efforts to use existing philosophies to construct alternative accounts of present political and social possibilities. I have long believed that Spinoza's monism has much to offer feminist theory[18] and Chapter 4 represents an attempt to spell out the way in which his writings may be productively employed in the task of developing a feminist philosophy of the body. Chapter 5 asks how feminist theory may be aided by an analysis of embodiment that focuses on the different powers and capacities of sexed bodies. Further, would such an approach allow us to acknowledge historical differences in female and male embodiment without thereby essentializing sexual difference? Chapter 6 engages with the issue of essentialism in the context of recent feminist political theory in order to ask: what are the consequences for our political present and future of adopting essentialism either as an ontological fact of human embodiment or as a strategy?

The final section treats the imaginary as fully part of social and political life in an attempt to work outside the real/imaginary distinction. Chapter 7 – in some ways a reprise of Chapter 2 – offers a critical reading of modernist narratives around the social contract and women's sociopolitical status. I argue for understanding some forms of postmodernism as acknowledging context and embodied history rather than as a descent into relativism. Chapter 8 uses Spinoza's writings on law and politics to ask the Deleuzian question: what forms of sociability are open to us in the present? I argue that a Spinozistic perspective allows a new consideration of questions such as how one makes sense of the notion of responsibility within a deterministic philosophy. The final chapter draws together some of the concerns that dominate the entire collection. How do sexual imaginaries influence those relations between the sexes that are governed by institutions, such as law? What is the relation between historical practices which have become embodied in our institutions and feminist theorizations of the political which attempt to think beyond the present?

Philosophy has tended to concern itself with reason and truth rather than passion and those 'errors' which, as Nietzsche suggested, make a particular form of life possible. It is in the last section that the influence of Spinoza is most pronounced. His writings on politics and the centrality of imagination to political life loom large. In contrast to many philosophers, Spinoza does not dismiss imagination or passion as unworthy of philosophical analysis.

Human life, unavoidably, entails a large and ineradicable component which is imaginary. His theory of the imagination is succinctly captured in proposition 1 of part IV of the *Ethics*: 'Nothing positive which a false idea has is removed by the presence of the true insofar as it is true.' In the scholium to this proposition, Spinoza continues:

> an imagination is an idea which indicates the present constitution of the human body . . . For example, when we look at the sun, we imagine it to be about 200 feet away from us. In this we are deceived so long as we are ignorant of its true distance; but when its distance is known, the error is removed, not the imagination, i.e., the idea of the sun, *which explains its nature only so far as the body is affected by it. . . . And so it is with the other imaginations* by which the mind is deceived, whether they indicate the natural constitution of the body, or that its power of acting is increased or diminished: *they are not contrary to the true, and do not disappear on its presence.*[19]

The sun has reasonably stable ways of affecting the human body and these are unlikely to change. However, the 'other imaginations' to which Spinoza refers include the diverse powers which human bodies possess for affecting and being affected by each other. These human powers are historically and culturally variable, and one of the important means by which they may be altered is through changes in our understanding of self and others. I do not suppose that anything written in these pages will be sufficient to remove the damaging sexual imaginaries in which we currently live. At the same time, bringing these imaginaries into focus may well contribute to the process of altering both the affects of which we are capable and the ways in which we may affect others.

*   *   *

A collection that spans twelve years incurs many debts. I cannot acknowledge them all here. However, I wish to express special thanks to Sue Roe who, as consultant editor for Routledge, first approached me with the idea of collecting my essays on philosophy and the body. My present editor, Adrian Driscoll, has been both patient and helpful. Linnell Secomb provided me with excellent and good-humoured research assistance. Special acknowledgement must go to Barbara Caine, Rosalyn Diprose, Elizabeth Grosz, Genevieve Lloyd, Paul Thom, David West and Anna Yeatman, all of whom have graced me with both their friendship and their generous criticisms at various times over the last decade. I remain deeply grateful to Paul Patton for the support, humour, encouragement and friendship he has extended to me over many years. His keen critical sense has saved me from many blunders and embarrassments. To him I dedicate these essays.

Notes

1 Trans. Colin Gordon, London, Athlone 1989, p. 19.
2 For an excellent appraisal of Aristotle's views on women see A. Saxonhouse, 'Aristotle: Defective Males, Hierarchy, and the Limits of Politics', in M.L. Shanley and C. Pateman, eds., *Feminist Interpretations and Political Theory*, Cambridge, Polity Press, 1991.
3 There are a number of excellent and critical readings of Lacan's views on women. See J. Gallop, *Feminism and Psychoanalysis*, London, Macmillan, 1982; E. Grosz, *Jacques Lacan: A Feminist Introduction*, London, Routledge, 1990; R. Braidotti, *Patterns of Dissonance: A Study of Women in Contemporary Philosophy*, Cambridge, Polity Press, 1991, and T. Brennan, *History After Lacan*, London, Routledge, 1993.
4 Among those who make this claim are G. Lloyd, *The Man of Reason: ' Male' and ' Female' in Western Philosophy*, London, Methuen, 1984; J. Grimshaw, *Feminist Philosophers: Women's Perspectives on Philosophical Traditions*, Brighton, Wheatsheaf Books, 1986; and M. Gatens, *Feminism and Philosophy: Perspectives on Difference and Equality*, Cambridge, Polity Press, 1991.
5 There are a number of feminist philosophers who have argued this point. See S. Bordo, *The Flight to Objectivity: Essays on Cartesianism and Culture*, Albany, SUNY, 1987 and *Unbearable Weight: Feminism, Western Culture and the Body*, Berkeley, University of California Press, 1993; J. Butler, *Bodies That Matter: On the Discursive Limits of 'Sex'*, New York, Routledge, 1993; and D. Fuss, *Essentially Speaking: Feminism, Nature and Difference*, New York, Routledge, 1989.
6 For an excellent summary of historical attitudes to women see I. Maclean, *The Renaissance Notion of Woman*, Cambridge, Cambridge University Press, 1980. For a more contemporary view of women's questionable 'humanity' see D. Haraway, *Primate Visions: Gender, Race and Nature in the World of Modern Science*, New York, Routledge, 1989.
7 Margaret Whitford, *Luce Irigaray: Philosophy in the Feminine*, London, Routledge, 1991, p. 69.
8 Le Dœuff, *The Philosophical Imaginary*, p. 19, my emphasis.
9 Whitford, *Luce Irigaray*, p. 69, my emphasis.
10 Whitford, ibid., emphasis in original.
11 David Couzens Hoy, 'Deconstructing Ideology', *Philosophy and Literature*, vol. 18, no. 1 (1994), p. 7. Pierre Bourdieu, *The Logic of Practice*, trans. Richard Nice, Stanford, Stanford University Press, 1990, p. 53, defines *habitus* as: 'systems of durable, transposable dispositions, . . . principles which generate and organize practices and representations that can be objectively adapted to their outcomes without presupposing a conscious aiming at ends or an express mastery of the operations necessary in order to attain them.'
12 Le Dœuff, *The Philosophical Imaginary*, p. 2.
13 For a recent feminist appraisal of the importance of 'habit' see R. Diprose, *The Bodies of Women: Ethics, Embodiment and Sexual Difference*, London, Routledge, 1994.
14 Pierre Bourdieu, *The Logic of Practice*, pp. 56–7, my emphasis.
15 This point has perhaps been made most forcefully by M. Le Dœuff, *The Philosophical Imaginary*, and G. Lloyd, *The Man of Reason*.
16 Of course, since the first publication of Chapter 1, Judith Butler's work on gender has revolutionized the field of 'gender studies'. See *Gender Trouble: Feminism and the Subversion of Identity*, New York, Routledge, 1990 and *Bodies that Matter*.
17 Notwithstanding Freud's 'anthropological' papers, including *Civilization and*

its Discontents, *The Future of an Illusion* and *Moses and Monotheism*. See Chapter 7 for an appraisal of these texts.

18 See my doctoral dissertation, 'Dualism and Difference: Theories of Subjectivity in Modern Philosophy', University of Sydney, 1986, where the issue of sexual difference is considered from a Spinozist perspective.

19 *Ethics*, pt. IV, prop. 1, scholium, my emphasis.

Acknowledgements

Earlier versions of Chapters 2, 3, 4 and 5 were published in *Cartographies: Poststructuralism and the Mapping of Bodies and Spaces*, ed. R. Diprose and R. Ferrell (Sydney, Allen & Unwin, 1991), *Australian Feminist Studies*, no. 10 (Summer 1989), *Crossing Boundaries*, ed. B. Caine, E. Grosz and M. de Lepervanche (Sydney Allen & Unwin, 1988) and in *Destabilizing Theory: Contemporary Feminist Debates*, ed. M. Barrett and A. Phillips (Cambridge, Polity Press, 1992) respectively. I would like to thank the publishers and editors for permission to reprint these essays.

Part I

1 A critique of the sex/gender distinction*

In recent years the sex/gender distinction has gained ever greater currency in texts and papers concerned with sexual politics. This distinction is used in both confused and confusing ways and it is the purpose of this essay first to clarify what the theoretical basis of this distinction is, second, to ascertain whether or not it is a valid or coherent distinction and finally to consider the political effects of its use by various political groups. This tripartite task will involve overlapping considerations of feminism's relation to socialist and homosexual politics. The tale of the uncomfortable alliance between feminist and socialist politics[1] and feminist and homosexual politics[2] has recently surfaced in a way that is potentially productive for all parties. A critical appraisal of past and continuing alliances is the least one expects from radical theorists who value dialectical and historical analysis. It is in this spirit that the question of the viability of analyses located at the intersection of 'sex' and 'class' can be addressed. The difficulty of reconciling sex and class, or feminism and Marxism, despite the intervention of a third party, psychoanalysis,[3] has been well demonstrated.[4]

In this context, the introduction or 'spot-lighting' of gender, as an analytical tool which purportedly yields high explanatory returns (as opposed to the barren category of 'sex') offers occasion for comment. Over the past five years or so, feminist theory of an Anglo-American orientation has taken up the notion of 'gender' with considerable interest and mixed intent.

Influential journals and texts such as *m/f, Ideology and Consciousness, Feminist Studies, The Reproduction of Mothering, The Mermaid and the Minotaur* and *Women's Oppression Today* share, if nothing else, this

* During the 1970s and into the early 1980s the sex/gender distinction became central to feminist theory. My aim (when I wrote this essay, over ten years ago) was to offer a critique of the distinction using the notion of the imaginary body. Although my views on sex and gender have developed since the first publication of this essay, I think it is worth republishing here since it forms the basis of the thought of many of the essays in this collection. The reader will need to bear in mind, however, that much of what I say here bears on the political context, as I saw it, in 1983.

enthusiasm for the notion of 'gender' as a central explanatory and organizing category of their accounts of the social, familial and discursive construction of subjectivity.[5] In general, the favouring of the category 'gender'
over the category 'sex' is defended in terms of the 'dangers of biological
reductionism'. Theorists who favour analyses based on gender argue that it
is indispensable to see 'sex as a biological category and gender as a social
one'.[6] Additionally, it would appear that the role of prior or current
political commitment to any one of a variety of 'left' politics played a
decisive role in this preference for 'gender'.[7] Given that the category
'gender' commands considerable theoretical centrality in contemporary
feminist and socialist-feminist theorizing as compared with its peripheral
employment in the early 1970s,[8] it is appropriate, at this time, to critically
reassess its credentials.

It is in the area of political analysis and practice that the recent proliferation of the sex/gender distinction becomes most worrying. The distinction has been used by groups as diverse as Marxists, (usually male)
homosexual groups and feminists of equality.

Clearly, these three groups display distinct political and theoretical
motivations, yet the effect of their use of the sex/gender distinction is to
encourage or engender a neutralization of sexual difference and sexual
politics. This neutralizing process is not novel; it can be traced to nineteenth-century liberal environmentalism where 're-education' is the catchcry of radical social transformation. Much of contemporary radical politics
is, perhaps unwittingly, enmeshed in this liberal tradition. A feminism
based on difference rather than on an a priori equality is representative
of a decisive break with this tradition.

What I wish to take to task in these uses of gender theory is the
unreasoned, unargued assumption that both the body and the psyche are
postnatally passive *tabulae rasae*. I will challenge the notion that the mind,
of either sex, is initially a neutral, passive entity, a blank slate on which are
inscribed various social 'lessons'. In addition, I will question the role of the
body – understood as the passive mediator of these inscriptions – in these
accounts. These views on mind and body result in a simplistic solution to
female oppression: a programme of re-education which involves the
unlearning of patriarchy's arbitrary and oppressive codes and the relearn-
ing of politically correct and equitable behaviours and traits which will, in
turn, lead to the whole person: the androgyn. It is precisely this alleged
neutrality of the body, the postulated *arbitrary* connection between femininity and the female body, masculinity and the male body, and the
apparent simplicity of the ahistorical and theoretically naive solution of
resocialization that this chapter proposes to challenge.

Before presenting a critique of the sex/gender distinction I should clarify
what I take to be the central issue at stake. It would appear that one of the
most burning issues in the contemporary women's movement is that of
sexual equality versus sexual difference. It is arguable that this debate

brings to a crisis both feminism's association with socialism and feminism's association with (male) homosexual groups. Both associations are often predicated upon an assumed 'essential' or possible equality, in the sense of 'sameness' between the sexes. It is against the backdrop of this question that this essay is situated. I would maintain that the proponents of sexual equality consistently mischaracterize and distort the position of those feminists who favour a politics of sexual difference. The fault may well lie with those feminists who have not made clear what they mean by a 'politics of difference'. This essay is an attempt to amend this situation and, in addition, to quell once and for all the tired (and tiring, if not tiresome) charges of essentialism and biologism so often levelled at theories of sexual difference.[9] Critics of feminists of difference tend to divide the entire theoretical field of social enquiry into an exclusive disjunction: social theory is *either* environmentalist or it is essentialist.[10] Therefore, and it follows quite logically from this premise, if feminist theories of difference are not environmentalist then they must be essentialist. The task remains, then, to reopen the field of social theory from its forced containment in this disjunction and to demonstrate the practical and theoretical viability of a politics of difference. The latter task shall be effected indirectly, by way of a critique of 'degendering' proposals.

The degendering proposal

The problem of the relationship between sex and gender is, of course, not a new one. Freud grappled with the problem of finding a suitable definition of masculinity and femininity and their relation to men and women in the 'Three Essays' published in 1905.[11] However, the authoritative source for the recent prominence of writings which focus on gender is not Freud but Robert J. Stoller, a contemporary psychoanalyst. Stoller published a book titled *Sex and Gender*[12] in 1968, where he reported the findings and theses arising out of his research and involvement with the Gender Identity Research Clinic at the University of California, Los Angeles.

Stoller first studied various *biological* anomalies (for example, neuters and hermaphrodites) in order to ascertain the relationship between sex and gender, and he then considered the biologically normal but *psychologically* disturbed individual (for example, the transsexual). He claimed, on completion of his research, to be able to account for the etiology of both the transvestite and the transsexual – although his account was avowedly more complete in the case of male transvestites and transsexuals than in the (much rarer) cases of female transvestites and transsexuals.[13] Stoller accounted for these psychological anomalies largely in terms of the distinction which he developed and systematized between sex and gender.

The explanation he offered was that the biological sex of a person has a tendency to augment, though not determine, the appropriate gender identity for that sex, (that is, masculinity in the case of the male sex, femininity in the case of the female sex). However, a person's gender identity is primarily a result of postnatal psychological influences. These psychological influences on gender identity, Stoller claimed, can completely override the biological fact of a person's sex and result in, for example, the situation of the transsexual.[14]

Stoller took the genesis of transsexualism to be wholly social, that is, not biologically or physically determined. He posited the cause of male transsexualism to be the mother's attitude to the child from birth. He reported that in all normal infants there is an initial period of symbiosis with the mother but that this symbiosis must be broken, particularly in the case of the boy, if normal masculinity or femininity as a separate (and in the case of the boy, a different) and independent identity is to develop.

In the case of the male transsexual, Stoller claimed to find a marked unwillingness on the part of the mother to allow her infant to separate himself from her and develop as an individual.[15] Stoller stressed that it is not only a matter of how long the child is held close to the mother's body but also in what manner.[16] If the mother sees the child as a part of, or extension to, her own body, then the child will respond by failing to develop an identity separate from the mother's (or developing it at a critically late stage) and so, in the case of a male child, will feel himself to be a woman trapped in a male body.

The details of Stoller's work are not important for the purposes of this essay. What is important is that his work was generally heralded as a breakthrough in the area of sexuality and socialization. As such it was quickly taken up by feminist theorists who saw it as offering theoretical justification for the right to equality for all independently of sex. His work has been used by Greer, Millett, Oakley, and more recently by Chodorow, Dinnerstein and Barrett, to name a few.[17]

Millett, writing in 1971 and acknowledging Stoller as support or 'proof' of her view, speciously reasons that '[p]sychosexually (e.g., in terms of masculine and feminine, and in contradistinction to male and female) there is no differentiation between the sexes at birth. Psychosexual personality is *therefore* postnatal and learned.'[18] Millett's contention that 'patriarchal ascriptions of temperament and role' to the sexes are arbitrary[19] leads to the inevitable and naive feminist tactic of the resocialization of society. She argued that

> [s]ince patriarchy's biological foundations appear to be so very insecure, one has some cause to admire the strength of 'socialization' which can continue a universal condition '*on faith alone*', as it were, or through an acquired value system *exclusively*. What does seem decisive in assuring the maintenance of the temperamental differences between the sexes is the conditioning of early childhood.[20]

Greer and Oakley pursued a similar line of reasoning.

The initial appeal of the implications of Stoller's research, in the late

1960s and early 1970s, is consistent with the social context of liberal humanism. Education or re-education, at that time, seemed a particularly viable programme for radical social change. Ten years later, however, both the context and the sentiment has altered considerably. Previous demands and strategies of the women's movement have backfired or proved to be co-optable.[21] It is in this context that we need to examine both the 'politics of equality' and sentiments originating with the liberal humanists of the eighteenth and nineteenth centuries.[22] The adoption of Stoller's research by writers such as Chodorow and Barrett warrants careful scrutiny.

In order for a programme of 'degendering' to be successful or even theoretically tenable, one would have to allow the validity of at least two unargued assumptions central to the thesis put forward by Stoller and assumed by the 'degendering feminists'. These are:

1 the body is neutral and passive with regard to the formation of con-sciousness, which is implicitly a rationalist view; and
2 one can definitively alter the important effects of the historical and cultural specificity of one's 'lived experience' by consciously changing the material practices of the culture in question.

If the validity of these assumptions is allowed then one could claim that cultural and historical significances or meanings receive their expression in or are made manifest by an (initially or essentially) neutral consciousness which, in turn, acts upon an (initially) neutral body. One could claim, in addition, that masculine and feminine behaviours are arbitrary forms of behaviour, socially inscribed on an indifferent consciousness that is joined to an indifferent body. However, the above-mentioned assumptions warrant no such validity. To clarify the problem in other words, socialization theory, which posits the social acquisition of a particular gender by a particular sex is implicitly a rationalist account, an ahistorical account and an account which posits a spurious neutrality of both body and consciousness. In order to substantiate this position vis-à-vis the resocia-lization feminists who uncritically adopted Stoller's account, the two assumptions outlined above will be treated in detail. Although they are obviously interrelated, they will be treated separately for the sake of clarity.

Sex/gender and the rationalist conception of the subject

It is in the area of the heredity versus environment debate that the difficulty of avoiding conceptualizing the person as a split body/consciousness is most apparent. The sex/gender distinction is situated in such a debate and is deeply entrenched in the conceptual problematic that characterizes that debate. The sex/gender distinction was understood, by socialization theor-ists, to be a body/consciousness distinction. Of course, this understanding does have an immediate, commonsense appeal. Nevertheless, such an understanding commits its user to a set of assumptions that have proved to be untenable.[23] Theorists who uncritically use the mind/body distinction consistently characterize the human subject as either predominantly (or wholly) determined by biological forces, that is, heredity, or predominantly (or wholly) determined by the influence of social or familial relations, that is, environment. Both these positions posit a naive causal relation between either the body and the mind or the environment and the mind which commits both viewpoints, as two sides of the same coin, to an a priori, neutral and passive conception of the subject. If we conceive the body to be neutral and passive and consciousness to be socially determined, then we are at least halfway to a behavioural conception of subjectivity. It is unclear if the behaviourist conception of conditioning has any valid application in the sphere of human behaviour. The stimulus–response model of conditioned behaviour assumes a passive and non-signifying subject who can be trained to respond appropriately and who can be relied upon to *consistently* respond appropriately. Psychoanalysis, understood as a *descriptive* theory of the constitution of subjectivity in Western patriarchal societies, seriously undermines the behaviourist conception of 'conditioning' and the assumed passivity of the subject.

The problem of the interrelation and interaction of the body and the mind is by no means an archaic theoretical preoccupation. It is out of this problem that psychoanalysis arose. The Freud of 1889, that is, Freud the neurophysiologist, was perplexed by the phenomenon of hysteria, a disorder he once described as representing a 'mysterious leap from the mind to the body'.[24] Since Freud's early work on hysterics with Charcot and Breuer both physiological and psychoanalytic understandings of the so-called mind–body problem have drastically altered.[25] A cogent and theoretically useful account posits that there is one unitary reality underlying two (or more) distinct levels of theoretical abstraction and that the 'mysterious leap' is actually a leap from one kind of discourse, say the psychological, to another, the physiological.[26] It remains to integrate this insight into everyday and theoretical conceptions of the person – a task not always achieved even by those who offer acknowledgement of the necessity of such integration.

Freud stressed, from his earliest papers, that even perception cannot be regarded as passive, but is rather an active process.[27] He argued further that consciousness cannot be equated with the perceptual system and that, in fact, much of what is perceived never even enters consciousness but remains preconscious or unconscious.[28] This implies an activity, and not necessarily a conscious activity, on the part of the subject that cannot be accounted for by the behaviourist. Perception can be reduced to neither the body nor consciousness but must be seen as an activity of the subject.[29]

Concerning the neutrality of the body, let me be explicit, there is no neutral body, there are at least two kinds of bodies: the male body and the female body.[30] If we locate social practices and behaviours as embedded in the subject, as we have with perception, rather than 'in consciousness' or 'in the body' then this has the important repercussion that the subject is always a *sexed* subject. If one accepts the notion of the sexually specific subject, that is, the male or female subject, then one must dismiss the notion that patriarchy can be characterized as a system of social organization that valorizes the masculine *gender* over the feminine gender. Gender is not the issue; sexual difference is. The very same behaviours (whether they be masculine or feminine) have quite different personal and social significances when acted out by the male subject on the one hand and the female subject on the other. Identical social 'training', attitudes or, if you will, conditioning acquire different significances when applied to male or female subjects.

This is largely a result of the activity of the subject and its drive to master social relations and meanings.[31] Each gesture, attitude, perception that enters human consciousness does so charged with significances that relate to all that has gone before. That the male body and the female body have quite different social value and significance cannot help but have a marked effect on male and female consciousness.[32]

The orthodox account of the gender/sex distinction claims that the social determination of personal identity operates at the level of ideas, the level of 'the mind'. What this account fails to note is the obvious divergence between feminine behaviour or experience that is lived out by a female subject and feminine behaviour or experience that is lived out by a male subject (and vice versa with masculine behaviour). To claim this does not imply any commitment to a fixity or essence of the social significance of bodily functions, events or experience. The importance of signification, and its constitutive role in the construction of subjectivity, is curiously absent from the writings of the proponents of degendering. This is likely to be an effect of their implicit commitment to a behaviourist conception of the person and the resultant stress on passive conditioning and socialization rather than the active processes involved in becoming a signifying subject.[33]

While explicitly wishing to distance this essay from ahistorical and a priori accounts of the social significance of the sexed body and its behaviour, I would suggest that some bodily experiences and events, though lacking any *fixed* significance, are likely, in all social structures, to be privileged sites of significance. Various anthropological, ethnological and historical evidence would seem to support this claim. For example, menstruation is likely to be one of these privileged sites. The fact that menstruation occurs only in (normal) female bodies is of considerable import for this essay. Given that in this society there is a network of relations obtaining between femininity and femaleness, that is, between the female *body* and femininity, then there must be a qualitative difference between the kind of femininity 'lived' by women and that 'lived' by men.[34] To take again the example of menstruation, in our culture it is associated with shame and modesty – both characteristically feminine attributes. An interesting speculation would be whether this shame could be connected to the more general shame involved in the failure to control one's bodily fluids, excretions, wastes, given the great store put on this control in our culture. Freud's neglect of the effect of the menses on the pubertal girl's psyche is significant. That the flow of blood would have profound psychical significance for her is clear and that this significance would centre around ideas of castration, sexual attack and socially reinforced shame is highly probable. The female's first act of coitus would probably also bear on this.

The point is that the body can and does intervene to confirm or to deny various social significances in a way that lends an air of inevitability to patriarchal social relations. A thorough analysis of the construction of the specificity of female experience, which takes account of the female *body*, is essential to dispelling this 'air'. To slide from 'male' and 'female' experience to 'masculine' and 'feminine' experience further confuses the issue. The 'feminine male' may have experiences that are socially coded as 'feminine' but these experiences must be *qualitatively* different from female experience of the feminine. His experiences are parasitically dependent on the female body, more particularly on the maternal body, by a process of identification.[35] This point shall be further elaborated below.

It has been the purpose of this section to argue against the tenability of the view that consciousness is socially constituted through the socialization of a neutral body. I have argued that the conception of a passive subject (supported by various behaviourist-oriented assertions), central to the programme of degendering, is demonstrably inadequate to account for human behaviour and, in particular, for the activity of signification.[36]

Contextual specificity

A most common claim made against feminists of sexual difference is that their theories are essentialist and a priori, in short, ahistorical. This claim operates like the infamous blade that cuts both ways. The irony of the accusation is that feminists who propose degendering propose it outside history and often fail to consider the resilience of expressions of sexual difference along with the network of linguistic and other systems of signification that both constitute and perpetuate this difference. Again, Chodorow provides us with the stereotype of this claim. She states: 'To see men and women as qualitatively different kinds of people, rather than seeing gender as processual, reflexive, and constructed, is to reify and deny relations of gender, to see gender differences as permanent rather than as created and situated.'[37] It is significant that Chodorow slides from notions of sex to notions of gender in this passage, that is, from biological terminology (men, women) to psychological terminology (feminine, masculine). What is quite remarkable is that she does not have anything to say about the body, except in a footnote where she does little more than acknowledge this 'oversight'. She writes there:

> We cannot know what children would make of their bodies in a non-gender or nonsexually organized world, what kind of sexual structuration or gender identities would develop. But it is not obvious that there would be *major* significance to biological sex differences, to gender difference, or to different sexualities.[38]

This passage misses the point, that is, that we *are* historically and culturally situated in a society that is divided and organized in terms of sex. This is a historical fact. The charges of essentialism and ahistoricism can be made both ways. The recognition of the historicity of the significance of sex and gender can be shown to be of prime importance to theorists of sexual difference. It is this historicity upon which their analyses are based. Theorists of sexual difference do not take as their object of study the physical body, the anatomical body, the neutral, dead body, but the body as lived, the animate body – the *situated* body.

It is striking that the body figures in socialization theory only as the biological, anatomical or physiological body. There is little analysis of the body as lived: of the body's morphology or of the imaginary body. If one wants to understand sex and gender or, put another way, a person's biology and the social and personal significance of that biology as lived, then one needs an analysis of the imaginary body. It is here that the feminist rereadings of Freud's work in terms of a theoretical description of how it is that male and female biologies are lived as masculine and feminine subjectivities in patriarchal culture become important.

As was mentioned above, it was largely due to Freud's early work with hysterics that the discipline of psychoanalysis arose. What Freud posited as crucial in order to understand the hysteric's symptom was an understanding of the emotional and libidinal investment obtaining between the subject and her (or his) body.[39] This insight opened the way for future advances in the still prevalent mechanism of dualist conceptions of the subject. Recent French psychoanalytic research, in particular the work of Laplanche[40] and Lacan, can be seen as such an advance. In Lacan's formulation of the 'mirror stage' he claims to have shown 'an essential libidinal relationship with the body image'.[41]

In both his papers dealing with the genesis of the ego, Lacan stressed the importance of the mirror phase in relation to both hysteria and the imaginary body. He writes:

> To call these (hysterical) symptoms functional is but to confess our ignorance, for they follow the pattern of a certain imaginary anatomy which has typical forms of its own. In other words, the astonishing somatic compliance which is the outward sign of the imaginary

anatomy is only shown within certain definite limits. I would emphasize that *the imaginary anatomy referred to here varies with the ideas (clear or confused) about bodily functions which are prevalent in a given culture.*[42]

The existence and operations of the imaginary body are most clearly demonstrated by the etiologically related phenomena of 'phantom limb' and hysteria.[43] What these phenomena illustrate is a libidinal or narcissistic relation of the subject with its body. This relation defies mechanistic or purely empirical explanation along either rationalist or behaviourist lines. The dispute concerning the experience of the unity of the body tends to centre around what this experience is predicated upon, and whether it is an experience given immediately in perception or developed in a milieu of social meaning and value. There is abundant evidence to favour the latter description. Schilder maintains that both 'phantom limb' and hysteria can be understood only if we take into account the fact that all healthy people are, or have, in addition to a material body, a body-phantom or an imaginary body. This psychical image of the body is necessary in order for us to have motility in the world, without which we could not be intentional subjects. The imaginary body is developed, learnt, connected to the body image of others, and is not static.[44]

Hysterical symptoms have a demonstrably clear relation to the (culturally specific) imaginary body. Hysterical paralysis, for example, conforms to the culturally and linguistically delineated imaginary body. Hysterical paralysis of the arm does not correspond to the anatomical or physiological organization of the body but rather to the anatomically naive conception of the body, where the arm ends at the place where the shirtsleeve meets the shoulder seam. Or again, there is an intimate relation of equivalence between the mouth and the vagina,[45] which, in the case of Dora,[46] is used to express her unconscious desire via the symptom of *tussis nervosa*. Knowledge of the particular form of the culturally constructed imaginary body is essential in order to understand the social (rather than individual) character of hysteria. The surprising homogeneity in the expression of the hysterical symptom, such as *anorexia nervosa*, within a given culture signals the social character of the imaginary body. The imaginary body is socially and historically specific in that it is constructed by: a shared language; the shared psychical significance and privileging of various zones of the body (for example, the mouth, the anus, the genitals); and common institutional practices and discourses (for example, medical, juridical and educational) which act on and through the body.

An analysis of the imaginary body will show it to be the site of the historical and cultural specificity of masculinity and femininity. It is to the imaginary body that we must look to find the key or the code to the decipherment of the social and personal significance of male and female biologies as lived in culture, that is, masculinity and femininity.

In this connection it is also clear that there is a contingent, though not arbitrary, relation between the male body and masculinity and the female body and femininity. To claim this is neither biologism nor essentialism but is rather to acknowledge the importance of complex and ubiquitous networks of signification to the historically, psychologically and culturally variable ways of being a man or a woman. To deny these networks and the specificity of historical forms of femininity and masculinity in favour of a conception of the subject as essentially sex-neutral will lead to the reproduction of present relations between the sexes.

When Freud describes femininity and masculinity as end results of a developmental chain, he is quite explicit. The respective tasks of women and men in our culture are, for women, to 'take over' the place of the object, passive, castrated, the feminine and, for the man, to 'combine' the values of subject, active, phallic, masculine.[47] Among the traits that epitomize femininity for Freud (and our culture) are: passivity, masochism, narcissism, envy, shame. I suggest that these feminine behaviours are not merely the result of patriarchal socialization and conditioning but rather are modes of defensive behaviour that utilize culturally shared phantasies about biology. Put differently, these traits are manifestations of and reactions to the (conscious and unconscious) ideas which we share about our biology.

Freud saw the biology of women and men as unproblematic – the ovum is passive, the sperm active – the problem for him was the psychology of masculinity and femininity which 'mirrors' this biology: the man actively penetrates the passive vagina. However, it is not given a priori that the penis is active and the vagina is passive. This understanding of heterosexuality is implicated in an imaginary anatomy, where the vagina is conceived of as a 'hole', a 'lack' and the penis as a 'phallus'. One could just as well, given a different relational mode between men and women, conceive of the penis as being enveloped or 'embraced' by the active vagina. In this context an interesting addendum is provided by recent biological research which maintains that the ovum is not as passive as it appears – it rejects some sperm and only allows entry, or envelops, sperm(s) of its 'choice'.

Masculinity and femininity as forms of sex-appropriate behaviours are manifestations of a historically based, culturally shared phantasy about male and female biologies, and as such sex and gender are not arbitrarily connected. The connection between the female body and femininity is not arbitrary in the same way that the symptom is not arbitrarily related to its etiology. Hence, to treat gender, the 'symptom', as the problem is to misread its genesis. Again, we can here note parallels between behaviourist psychology and 'degendering'. The therapeutic techniques of behaviourism – systematic desensitization, behaviour modification, and so on – treat the symptom only.

In the above analysis of the two assumptions taken to be crucial to the theory of degendering it has been argued that masculine and feminine forms of behaviour are not arbitrary inscriptions on an indifferent consciousness which is joined to an indifferent body. To speak of 'acquiring' a particular gender is to be mistaken about the significance of gender and its intimate relation to biology-as-lived in a social and historical context. The account of 'difference' that has been affected only indirectly, is an ongoing project and as such is both tentative and incomplete. However, even at this stage we can oppose the naive simplicity of degendering and its questionable theoretical basis.

Transsexualism reconsidered

It has been argued throughout this essay that the relation between masculine behaviour acted out by a male subject and masculine behaviour acted out by a female subject (or feminine behaviour acted out by a female subject and feminine behaviour acted out by a male subject) cannot be symmetrical. In other words, it has been argued that masculinity and femininity do not differ with regard to the sexes in terms of quantity only, but also *qualitatively*. If this thesis is correct, then to suggest the degendering of society as political strategy is hopelessly utopian, ahistorical and functions theoretically and practically as a diversionary tactic. Additionally, it has been argued that the programme of degendering is based on a misunderstanding of patriarchal social relations.

This all but concluding section is titled 'Transsexualism reconsidered' because it is the case of the transsexual that most clearly demonstrates the dissymmetry between masculinity/femininity and male/female. An understanding of the determination of male and female transsexualism is not to be found in the sex/gender distinction or in an analysis of the acquisition of gender identity. It was mentioned early in this chapter that Stoller's account of transsexualism is more complete in the case of male transsexuals than female transsexuals. Contrary to Stoller's hopes,[48] it is clear that the same account will not cover both cases. It has been suggested that the male transsexual can be understood only if we first understand the genesis of the primitive ego and the notion of the imaginary body. Due to the nature of his primary relations with his mother, the male transsexual is constituted in such a way that his (primitive) ego conflicts with his imaginary (and biological) body, leading to his subjectivity being conceived by him as 'female-in-a-male-body'. Briefly, this would involve the non-resolution of the misrecognition of the body of the other for one's own, that is, the male transsexual's primitive (bodily) ego is predicated upon a female body (the maternal body)[49] and he does not develop, until comparatively late, a separate identity from his mother. His transsexualism, in fact, is evidence that this separation is never adequately achieved. The desire of the mother[50] is active in this non-resolution or critically *late* resolution.

The case of the female transsexual cannot be symmetrical. The relation of the female infant to the mother's body is not and cannot be problematic *in the same way.*[51] This may partially explain the relative rarity of female transsexualism. (Though the extremely common phenomenon of the 'tomboy' is transsexualism, of a sort.) Female transsexualism is much more likely to be a reaction against oppression, that is, against the socially required forfeit of activity that was once enjoyed and socially tolerated. This situation may be reinforced by a desire on the mother's part to make a husband substitute of the girl and/or by the mother's own resentment of the female role in patriarchy. The transsexual knows, most clearly, that the issue is not one of gender but one of sex. It is not masculinity *per se* that is valorized in our culture but the *masculine male.*

On another level, this dissymmetry between the sexes is reflected in feminist musings on whether women are excluded (or all but excluded) from certain professions *because they are prestigious* or whether those professions are prestigious *because women are excluded.* The implication being that it is not what is done or how it is done but who does it that determines social value. The problem is not the socialization of women to femininity and men to masculinity but the place of these behaviours in the network of social meaning and the valorizing of one (the male) over the other (the female). Such valorization is at the core of the representation of relations of sexual difference as relations of superiority and inferiority.

There is another aspect to the theory of gender that is also important to consider, and that is the political use to which the sex/gender distinction is put.

The effect of the sex/gender distinction in political analysis and action

The commitment to economism or humanism in many Marxist accounts of the social and political status of women each, in their different ways, effect the neutralization of sexual difference. Economism neutralizes sexual difference by privileging the relations of production over psychical and social forms of subjectivity that are prior to, or inadequately captured by, the capitalist mode of production. Humanism neutralizes sexual difference by its adherence to an a priori and universal conception of human nature that fails to take account of sexual difference. Socialist-feminists seek to offer an account of the construction of male and female subjectivity under both patriarchy and capitalism. Some socialist-feminists seek to avoid problems of 'individualism' by shifting the site of the analysis of sexual relations from 'male' and 'female' to 'masculine' and 'feminine'. This strategy merely succeeds in presenting us with another set of problems. For example, masculinity and femininity and their constitutive role in sexual difference are often, on this account, reduced to the status of a *deus ex machina.*[52]

Michèle Barrett in *Women's Oppression Today* uses the category of gender to argue that socialism and feminism are compatible and 'that the ideology of masculinity and femininity has a crucial role in the division of labour as it has developed historically'.[53] Barrett's extensive use of the category gender is problematic in that she does not state, support or defend its theoretical status, but rather assumes a general agreement concerning its explanatory merits. She writes:

> The processes by which gender, and particularly femininity, is socially constructed in capitalist society have been extensively explored. This topic falls within the well-researched area of 'socialization studies' in sociology and has also been a major focus of feminist accounts.[54]

It has been argued that both the explanatory value and theoretical adequacy of 'socialization studies' are extremely tenuous. The question arises, then, why a theorist, familiar with the implications of psychoanalytic theory for socialization theory,[55] should adopt the use of gender, knowing it is based on questionable theoretical grounds. A likely explanation is that prior political investments and allegiances led some feminists to neglect casting their otherwise critical eye in the appropriate direction.

Some gay publications around the early 1980s showed a similar enthusiasm for the notion of gender. Some gay men argued that the diversity of sexual preference and practice is such that a biological distinction, male/female, is inadequate to account for forms of sexuality.[56] There is no quarrel here. However, to introduce gendered forms of sexuality takes us out of one hiatus into another. This move adopts, in keeping with socialization theory, only a quantitative distinction between masculinity and femininity and their relation to the construction of male and female subjectivities. Again, the body is treated as sex-neutral and consciousness as a passive *tabula rasa*.

It is in the above context that I maintain that the programme of degendering put forward initially by feminists such as Millett and Oakley and taken over by Chodorow is based on a misunderstanding (originating with Stoller's mistaken thesis of the genesis of transsexualism) of masculinity and femininity as conditioned forms of behaviour. Rather, I would suggest that 'masculinity' and 'femininity' correspond at the level of the imaginary body to 'male' and 'female' at the level of biology. It bears repetition that this statement does not imply a fixed essence to 'masculine' and 'feminine' but rather a historical specificity.

What brought equality feminists and difference feminists into sharp confrontation was, partly, the so-called 'crisis' in Marxism and the withdrawal of the labour of many feminists from Marxist-oriented research. At another level, the influence of French feminism[57] was instrumental in the formulation and defence of a politics of difference, which was often placed in opposition to the politics of Marxist-feminism.

One could also argue that the gradual demise of the call for sexual equality and the rise of the insistence on sexual difference can be accounted for in purely pragmatic terms. Practically, this has been the case in a number of areas. For example, the demand for equal legal status is now thought by some to be counterproductive. Feminist campaigns for the acquittal of women who have been found guilty of killing their violent husbands argue that the law of provocation does not take account of the usually disproportionate strength of men and women.[58] Likewise, many feminists have pointed out the abuse by men of the recently introduced antidiscrimination legislation.

However, there are also theoretical reasons for the tactical shift from equality to difference. The most important of these is disillusionment with key theoretical concepts in analyses of oppression (whether racial, class or sex). The notion of ideology – a notion that has its base in a rationalist conception of the subject – is a case in point. Overcoming ideology was seen as prerequisite to planned social change or revolution.

Early feminist contributions to this social change included challenging the naturalness of the sexual division of labour. Ideology was thus understood to be in the service of patriarchy as well as capital. Hence, the struggle against capitalism needed to be supplemented by the struggle against patriarchy. The stumbling block to the proposed 'equal society' was (both/either) women's reproductive capacity and/or their almost exclusive responsibility for childrearing. Early feminist responses to this problem included Firestone's 'cybernetic communism',[59] which proposed the literal neutering of bodies by means of the complete technologization, and hence socialization, of the reproductive capacity.

What Firestone overlooked is that the desired neutrality was not a neutrality at all but a 'masculinization' or 'normalization' (in a society where men are seen as the norm, the standard) of women – a making of 'woman' into 'man'.[60] This move has many echoes in discourse and politics, as many feminists have tirelessly pointed out.[61] An assumption implicit in the aim of neutralizing the body, which thereby allots primacy to the ideological, is the total passivity of the body. What this analysis yields, at best, is the predominantly Anglo-American crass empirical equation between patriarchal sex-role socialization and patriarchal consciousness.

In addition to the neutralization of sexual difference, the sex/gender distinction lends itself to those groups or individuals whose analyses reveal a desire to ignore sexual difference and prioritize 'class', 'discourse', 'power' or some other 'hobby-horse'. Their accounts attempt to co-opt or trivialize feminist struggles and feminist theory, reducing sexual politics to gender difference and positing as primary the relations obtaining between gender and power, gender and discourse, or gender and class – as if women's bodies and the representation and control of women's *bodies* were not a crucial stake in these struggles.

Notes

An earlier version of this chapter was published in 'Beyond Marxism? Interventions After Marx', *Intervention*, no. 17 (1983) ed. J. Allen and P. Patton. I would like to thank Judith Allen for encouraging me to submit my paper to *Intervention*.

1 B. Weinbaum, *The Curious Courtship of Socialism and Feminism*, Boston, Mass., South End Press, 1978.
2 For example, local experiences in Camp Inc. and CAMP.
3 See, for example, J. Mitchell's attempt at the tripartite amalgamation in *Psychoanalysis and Feminism*, Harmondsworth, Penguin, 1974.
4 J. Gallop, *Feminism and Psychoanalysis*, London, Macmillan, 1982.
5 See *m/f*, esp. vols. 2, 5–6 and 7; N. Chodorow, *The Reproduction of Mothering*, Berkeley, Calif., University of California Press, 1978; D. Dinnerstein, *The Mermaid and the Minotaur*, New York, Harper & Row, 1977; M. Barrett, *Women's Oppression Today*, London, Verso, 1980.
6 Barrett, *Women's Oppression*, p. 13.
7 See ibid., ch. 1; any editorial of *m/f*; and Chodorow, *The Reproduction of Mothering*, ch. 2, esp. pp. 34–5.
8 See, for example, G. Greer, *The Female Eunuch*, London, Paladin, 1971, pp. 25–30; and K. Millett, *Sexual Politics*, London, Abacus, 1971.
9 The question of difference is almost invariably understood by its critics as being essentialist. For example, see M. Plaza, '"Phallomorphic Power" and the Psychology of "Woman"', *Ideology and Consciousness*, no. 4 (1978) and the editorial of *m/f*, no. 2 (1978), p. 2: 'When feminists explain the present position of women in terms of a point of origin of sexual difference, then they deny specific practices and politics any effectivity since they are thereby expressions of a fixed unchanging essence. Sexual difference is then not instituted within specific practices but functions outside it.'
10 For example, N. Chodorow, 'Gender Relations and Difference in Psychoanalytic Perspective', in H. Eisenstein and A. Jardine, eds., *The Future of Difference*, Boston, G.K. Hall, 1980, p. 3.
11 *The Standard Edition of the Complete Psychological Works of Sigmund Freud* (hereafter S.E.), J. Strachey, ed., London, Hogarth Press, 1978, vol. VII, pp. 219–20: 'It is possible to distinguish at least three uses. "Masculine" and "feminine" are used sometimes in the sense of activity and passivity, sometimes in a biological, and sometimes again, in a sociological sense. The first of these three meanings is the essential one and the most serviceable in psychoanalysis.' See also 'An Outline of Psychoanalysis', S.E. XXIII, p. 188.
12 R.J. Stoller, *Sex and Gender*, London, Hogarth Press, 1968.
13 See the discussion on pp. 14–15 for alternative suggestions concerning female transsexualism and Stoller himself in R.J. Stoller, *The Transsexual Experiment*, London, Hogarth Press, 1975.
14 Stoller writes: 'A transsexual is a person who feels himself consciously and unconsciously to belong to the opposite sex while not denying his sexual anatomy', *Sex and Gender*, p. 187.
15 See the case of Lance, ibid., pp. 118–25, esp. p. 125.
16 Ibid., p. 307f.
17 See Greer, *The Female Eunuch*; Millett, *Sexual Politics*; A. Oakley, *Sex, Gender and Society*, London, Temple Smith, 1972; Chodorow, *The Reproduction of Mothering*; Dinnerstein, *Mermaid and Minotaur*.
18 Millett, *Sexual Politics*, p. 30, my emphasis.
19 Ibid., p. 32.
20 Ibid., p. 31, my emphasis.

21 For example, the number of men who have built their academic reputations on feminism and 'teach' feminism.

22 For example, M. Wollstonecraft, *Vindication of the Rights of Woman* Harmondsworth, Penguin, 1975; and J.S. Mill, 'On the Subjection of Women', in *Essays on Sex Equality*, ed. A. Rossi, Chicago, University of Chicago Press, 1970.

23 First, Cartesian dualism and later reductionist attempts to overcome it – idealism and empiricism. All three positions yield demonstrably inadequate conceptions of the subject.

24 'Notes upon a Case of Obsessional Neurosis', S.E. X, p. 157.

25 For example, see F. Deutsch, ed., *On the Mysterious Leap from the Mind to the Body*, New York, International Universities Press, 1973; P. Schilder, *The Image and Appearance of the Human Body*, New York, International Universities Press, 1979, and J. Lacan, 'The Mirror Stage as Formative of the Function of the I', in *Ecrits*, London, Tavistock, 1977.

26 See Deutsch, *On the Mysterious Leap*, p. 1.

27 See 'Project for a Scientific Psychology', S.E. I and Letter 52 to Fliess, S.E. II.

28 See 'The Interpretation of Dreams', S.E. VI, pp. 537–42.

29 M. Merleau-Ponty has an interesting account of perception as an activity of the body-subject in *The Phenomenology of Perception*, London, Routledge & Kegan Paul, 1970, esp. pp. 203–7.

30 To insist on two bodies is strategically important given that we live in a patriarchal society that organizes itself around pure sexual difference, that is male or female, and will not tolerate sexual ambiguity, for example, hermaphrodites, but forces a definite either/or sex on each person. (See M. Foucault, Herculine Barbin, New York, Pantheon, 1980.) However, even the *biological* determination of sex is not so straightforwardly clear and we must acknowledge sex as a continuum and bodies as multiple.

31 A clear account of this drive for mastery can be found in 'Beyond the Pleasure Principle', S.E. XVIII, where Freud describes the *fort/da* game, a game of mastering the conceptions of presence and absence necessary to the acquisition of both subjectivity and language.

32 It is interesting to remark in this context that Marxism does not object to the notion of class consciousness which develops through the subject's 'awareness' of where its interests lie, but cannot tolerate the notion of a sex(ed) consciousness.

33 See M. Merleau-Ponty, 'The Child's Relations with Others', in *The Primacy of Perception*, Evanston, Ill., Northwestern University Press, 1964, for an account of signification, introjection and projection closely paralleling Lacan's, especially in terms of the centrality of the body image in both accounts.

34 Both Freud and Stoller describe masculinity and femininity and their relation to maleness and femaleness in *quantitative* terms only. See S.E. VII, pp. 219–20, fn. 1; and Stoller, *Sex and Gender*, p. 9. *Qualitative* distinctions are not considered.

35 See Lacan, 'The Mirror Stage' and 'Some Reflections on the Ego', *International Journal of Psychoanalysis*, vol. 34 (1953).

36 See introduction to M. Mannoni, *The Child, his Illness and Others*, Harmondsworth, Penguin, 1970; and J. Lacan, 'The Function and Field of Speech and Language in Psychoanalysis' and 'The Agency of the Letter in the Unconscious or Reason since Freud', in *Ecrits*, London, Tavistock, 1977.

37 Chodorow, 'Gender Relations', p. 16.

38 Ibid., p. 18, my emphasis.

39 See S. Freud, 'On Narcissism: An Introduction', S.E. XIV.

40 J. Laplanche, *Life and Death in Psychoanalysis*, London, Johns Hopkins University Press, 1976, esp. ch. 4.

41 Lacan, 'Some Reflections on the Ego', p. 14.

42 Ibid., p. 13, my emphasis.

43 See Merleau-Ponty, *The Phenomenology of Perception*, esp. pp. 76–88; and Schilder, *Image and Appearance of the Human Body*, pp. 63f, 119f.

44 Ibid., pp. 66f.

45 This unconscious equation is the inverse of Freud's breast = faeces = penis = baby, that is, mouth = anus = vagina. This phantasy is revealed in the pornographic films of Linda Lovelace where she has a clitoris at the back of her throat.

46 'Fragment of an Analysis of a Case of Hysteria', S.E. VII.

47 See 'Infantile Genital Organisation', S.E. XIX, p. 145.

48 Although Stoller himself begins to doubt this view in 1975, in *The Transsexual Experiment* (see esp. pp. 223–46).

49 He is not, of course, peculiar in this respect. However, the point is that the *duration* of this misrecognition is much greater in his case, largely due to the *quality* of the mothering he receives and the desire of his mother.

50 'The desire of the mother' should not, necessarily, be understood as her conscious desire. It is important to note Freud's claim here that '[i]t is a very remarkable thing that the unconscious of one human being can react upon that of another, without passing through the conscious', 'The Unconscious', S.E. XIV, p. 194. See also Lacan, *Ecrits*, pp. 288–9.

51 The 'sense of self' developed in the first two years of the child's life is, in the case of both male and female children predicated upon identification with the mother. For girls this identification is not problematic as it is a sex appropriate identification. However, for boys this identification must be overlaid with male identifications at a later stage if they are to develop an appropriate male identity.

52 See, for example, the editorial discussion with M. Barrett and R. Coward, *m/f*, vol. 7 (1982), pp. 87f.

53 Barrett, *Women's Oppression*, p. 79.

54 Ibid., p. 62. She cites in this context L. Comer and E. Belotti.

55 As Barrett clearly is; see, for example, *Women's Oppression*, pp. 53f.

56 See, for example, T. Carrigan, 'Of Marx and Men', *Gay Information*, no. 11 (1982); and C. Johnston, 'Radical Homosexual Politics', *Gay Information*, nos. 2–3 (1980).

57 See Eisenstein and Jardine, *The Future of Difference*, pt. II.

58 See W. Bacon and R. Landsdown, 'Women who Kill Husbands: The Battered Wife on Trial', in C. O'Donnell, and J. Craney, eds., *Family Violence in Australia*, Melbourne, Longmans-Cheshire, 1982.

59 See S. Firestone, *The Dialectic of Sex*, London, Paladin, 1972, esp. ch. 10.

60 In this context see J. Flax, 'Mother–Daughter Relationships: Psychodynamics, Politics and Philosophy', in H. Eisenstein and A. Jardine, eds., *The Future of Difference*, Boston, G.K. Hall & Co., 1980, esp. pp. 29f, for an account of the phantasy of no women in the state of nature.

61 See, for instance, S. Moller Okin, *Women in Western Political Thought*, Princeton, N.J., Princeton University Press, 1979; C. Miller and K. Swift, *Words and Women*, New York, Anchor Doubleday, 1977, ch. 10; and D. Spender, *Man-Made Language*, London, Routledge & Kegan Paul, 1980.

2 Corporeal representation in/and the body politic

The rather awkward title of this paper is intended to draw attention to an ambiguity in the term 'representation' as it is used in political theory. First I want to focus on the construction of the *image* of the modern body politic. This involves examining the claim that the body politic is constituted by a creative act, by a work of art or artifice, that uses the human body as its image, model or metaphor. The background to this claim is provided by certain seventeenth- and eighteenth-century social contract theorists who argued in favour of the conventionality or artificiality of monarchical political authority.[1] If such authority is neither natural nor God-given but rather based on agreement and convention then it is mutable. The way the metaphor of the body functions here is by analogy. Just as man can be understood as a representation of God's creative power, so the political body can be understood as a representation of man's creative power, that is, as *art(ifice)*.

The second sense of 'representation' surfaces when considering *whose* body it is that is entitled to be represented by this political corporation. This involves understanding 'representation' in the sense where one body or agent is taken to stand for a group of diverse bodies. Here we are considering the metonymical representation of a complex body by a privileged part of that body. The metaphor here *slides* into metonymy. The relevant background literature to this question is provided by various texts, from the seventeenth century on, concerning the natural authority of men over women and the propriety of taking the male head of households as representative of the concerns of the entire household.[2]

The first use of 'representation' – what I have called the metaphorical – concerns the way in which this image affects who is represented by the body politic. To address the first strand – the metaphorical – I will begin with a quotation from a mid-seventeenth century text that posits, in a manner typical of the period, a detailed correspondence between the parts and functions of the human body and the parts and functions of the political body. The text is the Leviathan, the author is Thomas Hobbes:

> by art is created that great *leviathan* called a *commonwealth*, or *state*, in Latin *civitas*, which is but an artificial man; though of greater stature and

strength than the natural, for whose protection and defence it was intended; and in which the *sovereignty* is an artificial *soul*, as giving life and motion to the whole body; the *magistrates*, and other *officers* of judicature and execution, artificial *joints*; *reward* and *punishment*, by which fastened to the seat of the sovereignty every joint and member is moved to perform his duty, are the *nerves* that do the same in the body natural; and *wealth* and *riches* of all the particular members are the *strength*; *salus populi*, the people's safety, its *business*; counsellors, by whom all things needful for it to know are suggested unto it, are the *memory*; *equity* and *laws*, an artificial *reason* and *will*; *concord, health*; *sedition, sickness*; and civil war, death. Lastly the *pacts* and *covenants*, by which the parts of this body politic were at first made, set together, and united, resemble that *fiat*, or the *let us make man*, pronounced by God in the creation.[3]

I want to draw attention to two important aspects of the view Hobbes offers. First, Hobbes claims that the motivation behind the creation of the artificial man is the 'protection' or 'defence' of natural man. We may well wonder from whom or what natural man requires protection. Hobbes' answer is that he requires protection from other men and from nature. Man, in a state of nature, he tells us, is in 'continual fear' and in 'danger of violent death' and the quality of his life is summed up with the words 'solitary, poor, nasty, brutish, and short'.[4] The second thing I want to highlight is the *fiat*, the God-like pronouncement, that breathes life into the political body. For Hobbes this *fiat* refers to the pacts and covenants made by men and between men. These demigods, whose speech has such awesome creative power, do not go on, in God-like fashion, to create an artificial Eve. Perhaps the sons can learn from the father's mistakes, after all.

The artificial man, a creation of 'the word' of men united, thus frees himself from the dangers of the necessary but difficult dealings with both women and nature. This masculine image of unity and independence from women and nature has strong resonances in psychoanalytic accounts of infantile anxieties and the fantasies created to cope with them.[5] The image of artificial man, the body politic, perfectly mirrors the infantile wish for independence from the maternal body. It is a fantasy that can be found in mythology too. Classical Athens, often considered the first true body politic, is named after Athena who was born not 'of woman' but 'of man': she sprang fully formed from the head of Zeus. Athens is named after Athena as a tribute to her for ridding that city of its 'uncivilized' divinities. When she relegates the feminine Furies to the subterranean regions of Athens, she confirms the masculinity of the Athenian political body. Like Hobbes' artificial man, she is the product of man's reason; she has no mother. Or did she? An often neglected part of this myth is that Zeus 'gave birth' to Athena only after he had swallowed whole the body of his pregnant wife.

In the absence of a female leviathan, natural woman is left unprotected, undefended, and so is easy prey for the monstrous leviathan. Like the hapless Jonah, she dwells in the belly of the artificial man, swallowed whole, made part of the corporation not by pact, nor by covenant, but by incorporation. The modern body politic has 'lived off' its consumption of women's bodies. Women have serviced the internal organs and needs of this artificial body, preserving its viability, its unity and integrity, replacing its bodyparts, without ever being seen to do so.

In political theory, the metaphor of the unified body politic has functioned to achieve two important effects. First, the artificial man incorporates and so controls and regulates women's bodies in a manner which does not undermine his claim to autonomy, since her contributions are neither visible nor acknowledged. Second, in so far as he can maintain this apparent unity through incorporation, he is not required to acknowledge difference. The metaphor functions to restrict our political vocabulary to one voice only: a voice that can speak of only *one* body, *one* reason, and *one* ethic.

Perhaps the metaphor of the human body is an obvious way of describing political life; so obvious that the metaphor passes into common usage, no longer mindful of its origins. If this is the case then perhaps it seems far-fetched to argue that the conception of the body politic is anthropomorphic. Yet there is a sense in which the image of the polity is anthropomorphic if we limit this claim to a literal or etymological understanding of 'anthropos', which means 'man'. This leads me to the second strand of the use of 'representation' in modern political theory – the metonymical.

Here we need to consider *who* is represented by this image of bodily unity. Certainly, not any human form, by virtue of its humanity, is entitled to consider itself author of or actor in the body politic. From its classical articulation in Greek philosophy, only a body deemed capable of reason and sacrifice can be admitted into the political body as an active member. Such admission always involves *forfeit*. From the original covenant between God and Abraham – which involved the forfeit of his very flesh, his foreskin – corporeal sacrifice has been a constant feature of the compact. Even the Amazons, the only female body politic that we 'know' of, practised ritual mastectomy.

At different times, different kinds of beings have been excluded from the pact, often simply by virtue of their corporeal specificity. Slaves, foreigners, women, the conquered, children, the working classes have all been excluded from political participation, at one time or another, by their bodily specificity. Could the common denominator of these exclusions be 'those incapable of fulfilling the appropriate forfeit'? That is, those whose corporeal specificity marks them as inappropriate analogues to the political body? Constructing women as incapable of performing military service and so incapable of defending the political body from attack could serve as an example here. This incapacity, constructed or not, is sufficient to exclude them from active citizenship. At this level the metonymical aspects of the metaphor of the body function to exclude. Those who are not capable of the appropriate political forfeit are excluded from political and ethical relations. Rather they are defined by *mere* nature, *mere* corporeality and they have no place in the semi-divine political body except to serve it at its most basic and material level. To explain how metonymical aspects of the image of the body politic function to exclude, it is necessary to examine this image of bodily unity in greater detail.

Discourses which employ this image of the unified body assume that the metaphor of the human body is a coherent one, and of course it's not. At least I have never encountered an image of a human body. Images of human bodies are images of either men's bodies or women's bodies. A glance at any standard anatomical text offers graphic evidence of the problem with this phrase, 'the human body'. Representations of the human body are most often of the male body and, perhaps, around the borders, one will find insets of representations of the female reproductive system: a lactating breast, a vagina, ovaries; bits of bodies, body fragments. They appear there in a way that reminds one of specialized pornographic magazines which show pictures of isolated, fragmented, disjointed bits: breasts, vaginas, buttocks. Female bits, fragments to be consumed, taken in a bit at a time.

This imaging has its correlate in political theory. Recent feminist work has shown that the neutral body assumed by the liberal state is implicitly a masculine body.[6] Our legal and political arrangements have man as the model, the centre-piece, with the occasional surrounding legislative insets concerning abortion, rape, maternity allowance, and so on. None of these insets, however, take female embodiment seriously. It is still the exception, the deviation, confined literally to the margins of man's representations. It is still 'anthropos' who is taken to be capable of representing the universal type, the universal body. Man is the model and it is his body which is taken for the human body; his reason which is taken for Reason; his morality which is formalized into a system of ethics.

In our relatively recent history, the strategies for silencing those who have dared to speak in another voice, of another reason and another ethic, are instructive. Here I will briefly mention two strategies that seem to be dominant in the history of feminist interventions. The first is to 'animalize' the speaker; the second, to reduce her to her 'sex'. Women who step outside their allotted place in the body politic are frequently abused with terms like harpy, virago, vixen, bitch, shrew; terms that make clear that if she attempts to speak from the political body, about the political body, her speech is not recognized as human speech. When Mary Wollstonecraft, for example, had the audacity to address the issue of women's political rights,[7] Walpole called her a 'hyena in petticoats'. The other strategy, of reducing woman to her 'sex', involves treating her speech and her behaviour as hysterical. The root of 'hysteria' is the Greek 'hystera', meaning uterus. Disorder created by women, in the political body, is thus retranslated into a physical disorder thought to be inherent in the female sex.

Both these strategies insist on the difference between the image of the political body and the image of woman's body. However, it is a difference which is interpreted as evidence of woman's inadequacy in the political sphere. But perhaps this difference no longer exists. After all, women are now admitted to the public sphere, they participate in politics, and sometimes they even become prime ministers. However, to say this would be to miss the point. It is true that if women want to escape from the dreary cycles of repetition in the private sphere, then often they can. If they want to escape from the hysteria and mutism of domestic confinement, then often they can. But at what cost? We can be 'cured' of mere animal existence by 'becoming men'; 'cured' of hysteria by 'hysterectomy'.

I am willing to concede that the metaphor of the body politic is quite anachronistic and precariously anchored in present political and social practices. This body has been fragmented and weakened by successive invasions from the excluded: the slaves, the foreigners, the women, the working class; but this does not imply that we presently have a polymorphous body politic. Certainly, the last two to three hundred years have witnessed the removal of many formal barriers and formal methods of exclusion, but there is a lot more to be said about methods of exclusion than formalized principles of equity can address. If woman, for example, speaks from this body, she is limited in what she can say. If she lives by this reason and this ethic, she still lives from the body of another: an actress, still a body bit, a mouthpiece.

It is not clear to me, taking into account the history of the constitution of this body politic, that it can accommodate anything but the same. I have suggested that the modern body politic is based on an image of a *masculine* body which reflects fantasies about the value and capacities of that body. The effects of this image show its contemporary influence in our social and political behaviour which continues to implicitly accord privilege to particular bodies and their concerns as they are reflected in our ways of speaking and in what we speak about. It refuses to admit anyone who is not capable of miming its reason and its ethics, in its voice. Its political language has no vocabulary and no space for the articulation of certain questions. Our political body continues to assume that its active members are free from the tasks of reproduction, free from domestic work, free from any desires other than those 'whispered' to it by one of its Hobbesian 'counsellors' or 'willed' in it by one of its laws. All this body can address is questions of access to 'predefined' positions, and 'pre-constituted' points of power or authority. It cannot address the question of *how* or in what manner one occupies these points or positions. Nor can it address the limiting conditions, dictated by the corporeal specificity of the occupant, on the possible actions open to that occupant. What it cannot address is how different bodies 'fill' the same 'empty' social or political space. I wonder, in this context, whether the withdrawal of Pat Schroeder from the 1987 US Presidential candidacy was related to this problem. She said in her speech that she was withdrawing because she could not 'figure out' how to occupy the political sphere without turning over her desires, behaviour and plans to predetermined meanings which were at odds with her own intentions.

I would suggest that this problem is, at least partly, related to the continuing fascination that we have for the image of the one body. It is an image that belongs to a dream of equity, based on corporeal interchangeability, that was developed to the full in nineteenth-century liberalism. And it is a 'dream of men'. Women, and others, were not co-partners in this dream and to attempt to join it at this late stage is as futile as trying to share someone's psychosis. The socially shared psychosis of egalitarianism was constructed to deal with a specific problem: to diffuse the power structure of seventeenth- and eighteenth-century politics. This fantasy of the modern body politic, constituted by 'the word' of men united, is not appropriate to women, and others, who were specifically excluded from it. For these 'others', who have never experienced the satisfaction of having their image reflected back to themselves 'whole' or 'complete', the fascination with this dream is not so binding. The cultural ego-ideal was never something that they could live up to without a massive act of bad faith. But what are the alternatives?

If what one is fascinated by is the image of one body, one voice, one reason, any deviation takes the form of gibberish. If woman speaks from her body, with her voice, who can hear? Who can decipher the language of a hysteric, the wails of a hyena, the jabbering of a savage – apart from other hysterics, hyenas and savages? Our political vocabulary is so limited that it is not possible, within its parameters, to raise the kinds of questions that would allow the articulation of bodily difference: it will not tolerate an embodied speech.

The impotence of our political vocabulary leads me to suggest that the more appropriate sphere for a consideration of these questions may be the ethical. And here I am using 'ethical' in a sense perhaps long forgotten, where ethics is crucially concerned with the specificity of one's embodiment. It is certainly a pre-Kantian notion.[8] It is prior to the ever-narrowing political organization of ethics and prior to the conceptualization of ethics as reducible to a set of universal principles dictated by reason (whose reason?). It is opposed to any system of ethics which elevates itself from a contingent form of life to the pretension of being the *one* necessary form of life. The most a universal ethic will permit is the *expansion* of the one body. Under pressure from its own insistence on equity, it may be forced to admit women, slaves and others. It will not, however, tolerate the positing of a second, or a third, or a fourth body. Prime Minister Hawke's courting of the Aboriginal land rights movement prior to the Australian Bicentennial celebrations in 1988 could provide an example of my point here. He wanted to take the body politic off to the beauty parlour so it would look its best for its big birthday party. An important component of this beauty treatment involved attending to the blemishes on this body caused by the history of its abuse of Aboriginal bodies. It is instructive that Hawke wanted to make up by calling for a *compact*, a term that is more at home in seventeenth-century political texts. The term carries connotations of an agreement between equals, between like beings, to join as a *single* body. Some Aborigines, on the other hand, called for a *treaty*, a term that carries connotations of an agreement between unlike beings to respect each other's differences. It also implies a demand for the recognition of *two* bodies. Hawke resisted a treaty because this would be to recognize another voice, another body, and this raises the deepest fears. To recognize another body is to leave oneself open to *dialogue*, debate and engagement with the other's law and the other's ethics.

It seems important, if the possibility of dialogue and engagement is to be opened up, that feminist politics recognize the futility of continuing to ask to be fully admitted into this fantasy of unity. This would be to stop asking of that body that it be 'host', since for women this would be to ask how can I live off myself – how can I engage in self-cannibalism? I would rather want to raise the question: whose body is this? How many metamorphoses has it undergone? And what possible forms could it take? And in responding to these questions it seems crucial to resist the temptation, noticeable in some feminist writing, to replace *one* body with *two*, one ethic with two, one reason with two. For this would be merely to repeat, in dual fashion, the same old narcissistic fascination involved in the contemplation of one's own image. The most this will achieve is that we would succeed in throwing off the persona of Echo, who speaks but is not heard, only to join Narcissus at the pool.

Since this paper opened with a quotation that I take to be typical of a certain kind of male fantasy, I will also close with one. It comes from Italo Calvino's book, *Invisible Cities* which is constructed as a dialogue of sorts between Kublai Khan – the demigod state-builder, and Marco Polo – the inquisitive explorer who entertains Kublai Khan with accounts of the many cities he has seen. It is from a section entitled 'Cities and Desire'.

From there, after six days and seven nights, you arrive at Zobeide, the White City, well exposed to the moon, with streets wound about themselves as in a skein. They tell this story of its foundation: men of various nations had an identical dream. They saw a woman running at night through an unknown city; she was seen from behind, with long hair and she was naked. They dreamed of pursuing her. As they twisted and turned, each of them lost her. After the dream they set out in search of that city; they never found it, but they found one another; they decided to build a city like the one in the dream. In laying out the streets, each followed the course of his pursuit; at the place where they had lost the fugitive's trail, they arranged spaces and walls differently from the dream, so she would be unable to escape again.

This was the city of Zobeide, where they settled, waiting for that scene to be repeated one night. None of them, asleep or awake, ever saw the woman again. The City's streets were streets where they went to work every day, with no link any more to the dreamed chase. Which, for that matter, had long been forgotten.

The first to arrive could not understand what drew these people to Zobeide, this ugly City, this trap.[9]

I take this dream to be rather atypical, for it tells of the failure of the desire to 'capture' and to 'contain' difference in a monument to unity. It also speaks of masculine impotence in the face of a loss suffered but not remembered. There is an interesting point of overlap between these dreams and fantasies of cities and states. The women of Zobeide are walled into that city just as surely as the Furies are contained in Athens. The possibility of hearing the speech of women and others, is crucially tied to the remembrance and 'working through' of this initial dream.

Notes

An earlier version of this chapter was presented in 1987 at the 'Performance Space' in Sydney and published in R. Diprose and R. Ferrell, eds., *Cartographies: Post-structuralism and the Mapping of Bodies and Spaces*, Sydney, Allen & Unwin, 1991.

1 For example, J. Locke, *Two Treatises of Government*, London, Cambridge University Press, 1967; J.-J. Rousseau, *The Social Contract*, Harmondsworth, Penguin, 1968.
2 Both Locke and Rousseau held this view. See Locke, *Two Treatises of Government*, bk. II, s. 82; and Rousseau, *Emile*, London, Dent & Sons, 1972, pp. 370, 412, 442.
3 T. Hobbes, *Leviathan*, Harmondsworth, Penguin, 1968, pp. 81–2.
4 Ibid., p. 186.
5 See J. Flax, 'Mother–Daughter Relationships: Psychodynamics, Politics and Philosophy', in H. Eisenstein and A. Jardine, eds., *The Future of Difference*, Boston, G.K. Hall, 1980, esp. pp. 29f.
6 See C. Pateman, *The Sexual Contract*, Cambridge, Polity Press, 1988, esp. ch. 4.
7 M. Wollstonecraft, *A Vindication of the Rights of Woman*, Harmondsworth, Penguin, 1975.
8 The notion of ethics I have in mind is one that takes the body, its pleasures, powers and capacities into account. A good example is B. Spinoza's *Ethics*. For an account of what Spinoza's ethical theory can offer us today, see G. Deleuze, *Spinoza: Practical Philosophy*, San Fransisco, City Lights Books, 1988, esp. chs. 2 and 6.
9 I. Calvino, *Invisible Cities*, London, Picador, 1979, p. 39.

3 Woman and her double(s)

Sex, gender and ethics

The terms sex and gender have had an interesting and increasingly contentious relation in the course of recent feminist theorizing. The connections between being a female and exhibiting feminine qualities, or being a male and being masculine, have been characterized as anything from necessary, natural connections to social, arbitrary connections, or as some mixture between these two extremes. In many circles the term gender has come to displace completely that of sex, this latter term being frequently employed as an abbreviation for sexual intercourse – hence the joke of responding 'Yes' to a question concerning one's sex, rather than ticking 'M' or 'F'. These days a joke of another kind arises, at least for me, when asked to tick M or F for gender. Should a feminine man tick F, a masculine woman M? I think not, simply because that is not the information the form is seeking – the information sought is the biological sex of the person, not her or his gender.

How has this slide from sex to gender come about and what underlies the ubiquity of the use of the term gender? Clearly, there is no simple answer to this question. Any response needs to be complex. Some possible responses may include:

1 to avoid confusion between sex as a biological classification with sex understood as the sexual act
2 to indicate that biological men are not the target or the enemy of feminist criticism. Rather its target is a historically and culturally produced configuration where masculinity is associated with power and dominance
3 to avoid biologistic or essentialist accounts of the social and political relations between the sexes by placing emphasis on the sociological category of gender, thus highlighting the mutability of current social relations and leaving the way open for possibilities of social change
4 to indicate the complexity of human life and behaviour by signalling that neither men nor women spring from culture fully formed like Athena from the head of Zeus; rather, 'one is not born, but rather becomes, a woman'.[1]

No doubt there are other important defences which could be made of the sex/gender distinction. But what exactly is one defending when one argues for the retention of such a distinction? What is gender? Of course, one could list traits associated with masculinity (aggressiveness, strength, independence, activity) and femininity (submissiveness, weakness, dependence, passivity), but these are just lists and tell us little about the meaning or genesis of gender. At most, such lists draw attention to the antithetical yet complementary relation between femininity and masculinity. Passivity stands in both an antithetical and complementary relation to activity, as does strength to weakness, aggressiveness to submissiveness, and independence to dependence. One can note here a *doubling* of terms or behaviours, each of which assumes or implies the other, which combine to form a whole. This notion of 'doubling' and 'the double' will be further dealt with below.[2]

Another problem associated with our conceptions of masculinity and femininity is that there are no 'pure' types: empirical men and women display mixtures of both masculine and feminine traits. Both Robert Stoller and Sigmund Freud insist on this variable composition of both masculine and feminine characteristics in the lives of men and women. Yet both see this mixture of types in terms of a variation in *quantity* only. Both theorists accept the normative standard that women possess a greater *quantity* of femininity than men, and men a greater *quantity* of masculinity than women.[3] *Qualitative* differences in the way in which a woman lives her femininity compared with the way a man may live his femininity are not considered.[4]

This failure to treat the *qualitative* differences in the lived experience of gender difference for men and women is alone reason enough for us to be cautious in our employment of the term gender. This failure should alert us to the fact that the term is being used in an abstract and idealist way, that is, in a way that abstracts from *embodied* beings. For the very same behaviour which makes a man appear well adjusted, 'attractive' and (socially) appropriate may well make a woman appear maladjusted, 'unattractive' and (socially) inappropriate. Although we may be dealing with the same type of behaviour, in the one case it is rewarded, commended, in the other punished, condemned. These social responses cannot help but have a profound effect on the *meaning* of masculinity and femininity for the individuals concerned, which will in turn effect a qualitative difference in the way each lives and experiences his or her own particular (quantitative) combination of masculine and feminine characteristics. I have argued elsewhere that this qualitative difference in the way we live out our particular balances (or imbalances) of masculine and feminine traits is crucially connected to our bodies: the meaning and significance of our own bodies for us and – what cannot be separated from this – the meaning and significance of the sexed body in culture. It is the significance of the sexed body that is obscured by the sex/gender distinction, which typically understands sex as a biological given and gender as a social construction which overlays this biology.

Much of the criticism that has been levelled at the sex/gender distinction has been made from the perspective of feminist interpretations of psycho-analytic theory. This perspective explicitly rejects the socialization theory that underpins most accounts of the sex/gender distinction. Biology itself is taken to be a problematic term for psychoanalysis. The human body is not, on this view, somehow external to culture or part of an unchanging nature. The human body is always lived in culture, understandings of its workings are themselves cultural productions, and the values and assumptions of culture inevitably find their way into our theorizations. In this paper I will use two conceptions taken from psychoanalytic theory – the body image and the body double – in order to explore what I take to be a useful and productive understanding of the term 'gender'.

Clearly, all human beings have an investment (both positive *and* nega-tive) in their own bodies and in the bodies of others. This investment in one's own body is revealed in 'phantom limb', hysteria, anorexia and bulimia. It is not only through the existence of these pathologies that we are made aware of our investments in the body. Ordinary friendships, familial and love relations reveal our investments in the bodies of those we love or admire by the way in which we typically 'acquire' their gestures, movements, habits of speech, and so on. This mimetic, or introjective, tendency is particularly evident in those cases where the love object has been lost. As Freud has shown in 'Mourning and Melanch-olia',[5] we attempt to preserve that which we have lost by incorporating it into our own ego. Importantly, much of this incorporation is at the level of the body ego, body image or postural model of the body, where it takes on the structure of *mimesis*. Not only does this body image have little to do with what we think of as biology, it has little to do with any *single* body since this mimetic activity is ceaseless and, as with much of human development, past investments are not cancelled, but rather augmented.

These identificatory structures are inherent in, and constitutive of the human condition. One important implication of these structures is that all human bodies are part of this system of exchange, identification and mimesis. Moreover, the system is dynamic and plastic. It is beyond the scope of this paper to take up the varied ways in which Freud, Jacques Lacan, Maurice Merleau-Ponty, Paul Schilder, Henri Wallon and others have theorized this intertwining system of bodies. That is a book-length project. What I can do here is offer a sketch of the most important aspects of these theorists' claims and indicate some important ways in which these can be brought to bear on contemporary feminist theorizations of gender and sexual difference.

Perhaps the single most important point of convergence of the views of the theorists listed above is their insistence on the self as a social con-struction rather than as given in nature. In a manner which echoes Hegel's observations on the genesis of self-consciousness, these theorists all main-tain that self-consciousness assumes a duality or doubling of conscious-nesses. The self emerges in *opposition* to (on some views, in *relation with*) an other. Hegel, like most theorists of the modern period, assumes that the emergence of self-consciousness through opposition takes place between two fully fledged consciousnesses, thus lending it the air of an adult and equal confrontation. This reflects a tendency of much modern social and political theory to disavow the developmental aspects of human life and, in particular, to deny the dependence of the human infant on an other (traditionally, the mother) for survival. Jane Flax has convincingly demon-strated this disavowal in relation to seventeenth- and eighteenth-century accounts of the state of nature, which typically exclude women and children.[6] Later theorists were not so remiss. Indeed, many believe that contemporary psychoanalytic theorists have gone too far in the other direction, tending to locate the etiology of every adult idiosyncracy in childhood. This may well be a justifiable criticism. The point remains, however, that many contemporary accounts of the genesis and development of the self take the primary relation between mother and child as crucial to the etiology of everything from schizophrenia (see, for example, R.D. Laing and D. Cooper) to transsexualism (see, for example, R. Stoller).

More recently, feminist theorists such as Jessica Benjamin,[7] Carol Gilligan,[8] Nancy Chodorow[9] and Sandra Harding,[10] have used the devel-opmental theory of the emergence of the self to explain not only the construction of gender difference, but also sadomasochism, the gender-specificity of different forms of morality, and even the character of philosophy and science. Yet these accounts – with the possible exception of Benjamin, who, implicitly at least, signals the part played by the male and female body in her analysis of *The Story of O* – pay little attention to the place of the body in their different accounts of the emergence of the male and female self. This oversight can be partially explained by their reliance on object-relations theory which pays attention to the *parts* of the body, which the child internalizes, rather than to the body as *gestalt*, the body as whole.

Object-relations theory owes much to Kleinian psychoanalysis, which stresses the interrelatedness of the child with his or her environment. This seems to be an important correction to much orthodox psychoanalytic theory which may well suffer from emphasizing separation at the expense of connectedness. Yet this stress on connectedness in the emergence of the self itself suffers from paying insufficient attention to the role which the *body-as-a-whole* plays in the child's development. The child's body may well be made up of 'bits and pieces' but it is also grasped by the child as a total scheme, as gestalt. The body of the other, as a whole, is crucial to the child gaining an identity distinct from the other. In stressing interconnect-edness over separation, feminist theorists should take care not to throw the (whole) baby out with the bath water.

Wallon, Schilder, Lacan and Merleau-Ponty are among those who, following up relatively undeveloped notions in Freud, have stressed the importance of the whole body of the (m)other for the formation of the child's subjectivity. The distinction between subject and object is itself learned, initially, in this relation between the (m)other and child. More-over, this relation is determined, at least in part, by the differential development of the child's motor, visual, aural and tactile skills. Specifically, it is claimed, the child is able to recognize the image of the other's whole-ness, the other's bodily integrity, and to anticipate this integrity as its own 'to be' before its motor competence 'justifies' such integrity, that is, before its kinaesthetic experience is integrated. Hence Lacan's well-known phrase that the mirror-phase child's gestalt or body image 'is certainly more constituent than constituted'.[11] Clearly, this account places considerable emphasis on the scopic. The child *sees* its wholeness before it *feels* its wholeness, and this seeing is actually constituent of its future identity as a distinct and whole being.

This scopophilic tendency of psychoanalytic theory has been criticized by feminists who argue that there is something particularly masculine about this privileging of sight over all the other senses, such as the tactile, which, it has been suggested, is more closely aligned with the feminine.[12] This tendency to privilege the seen is perhaps most in evi-dence in Freud's account of sexual difference. Recall, for example, Freud's comments on the female castration complex: 'she makes her judgement and her decision in a flash [sic]. She has seen it and knows that she is without it and wants to have it.'[13] This bias toward the scopic is even more evident in Lacan's theorization of the 'primordial formation' of the I in the mirror phase: 'sworn champions of the autonomy of female sexuality' will not like it, but nevertheless 'the penis is dominant in the shaping of the body image' and this 'cannot be put down to cultural influences alone'.[14]

Yet in this very insistence on the privileging of the seen and the visible lurks the archaic defence mechanism of disavowal. Freud describes dis-avowal as a process which allows both denial and acknowledgement to operate simultaneously. The subject entertains two conflicting or contra-dictory ideas at once: one idea acknowledging 'reality'; the other denying it. The mechanism of disavowal, like the unconscious, happily contravenes the law of non-contradiction. Freud maintained that disavowal is 'a process which in the mental life of children seems neither uncommon nor very dangerous but which in an adult would mean the beginning of a psychosis'.[15]

Significantly, in his later work he allows one, and only one, exception to this rule: the mechanism of disavowal, when employed in the realm of the sexual life of the adult *male*, does *not* lead to psychosis but merely to *fetishism*. It is only the fetish of the adult male that allows him to approach the castrated female, as a *sexual* object, without fear. Women can be treated as sexual objects by the fetishist only because he has displaced the value of the missing phallus onto some other part of the female body or female clothing.[16] The fetish, in fact, protects the fetishist from 'seeing', specifically, from seeing that 'there is nothing to see'. So, for Freud, male heterosexuality may not be psychotic, but it is certainly, to a greater or lesser degree, fetishistic.

All this of course begs the question of what distinguishes a psychotic construction of reality from a social construction of reality. Does the distinction turn on individual 'madness' versus a socially shared and constructed 'reality'? Freud himself states that *it is only at a certain stage* of the (male) child's development that the sight of female genitals gives rise to 'horror, contempt, or pity'[17] – earlier sightings do not elicit these responses and, indeed, one wonders just what the (pre-oedipal male) child *does* see. What is clear, from Lacan's formulation of the symbolic and the law of the Father, is that *difference* must intrude into the mirror-phase child's narcissistic identification with its counterpart. On Lacan's view, if sociality is to be achieved at all then the Law, the third element, must intervene to break the captured gaze of the child. It is by the intervention of the Symbolic Father – who brings the law, difference and language – that the child is inserted into culture. It is only after *this* stage that the male child 'sees' female castration. Difference is exhausted by (phallic) presence and (phallic) absence. The other is henceforth either 'the Same' (phallic) or 'lacking' (castrated). Positive difference is repressed, quite literally *banished from sight*.

Yet the subject must 'know' what it is that needs to be banished from sight at the same time as he denies what he 'knows'. A feminist reading of masculine fetishism may argue, against Freud, that what the fetishist 'knows' is the positive difference between the sexes and his denial consists in assenting to the construction of difference as (phallic) presence or absence.

One of the most neglected insights of psychoanalysis is that the perceptual system is not simply the province of consciousness but may be 'censored' and/or structured by the unconscious system. In other words, 'seeing' is itself an active and constructive process rather than a passive experience.[18] The importance of this idea, in this context, is that it cannot be a passive visual experience which accounts for the perception of the male body image as 'complete' or phallic, any more than it can account for the female body image as 'incomplete' or castrated. These images are themselves social and it is only the social that can be haunted by 'lack'. Such 'lack' is constructed and learned, not discovered. Even in Lacanian terms, lack can only ever appear at the level of the Symbolic – the Real lacks nothing.

Perhaps, from this perspective, one could reassess why it is the scopic that has particular privilege in psychoanalytic theory; why it is that vision is particularly amenable to the constructive work of the social/Symbolic. Aestheticians from Plato onwards seem well aware of the propensity of the eye to accept, without a qualm, that which is otherwise in-credible. Art theory and practice are well aware of the techniques employed to seduce the sight to accept the *trompe-l'œil*. It is widely recognized that cultural objects, such as art objects, require an analysis of the conditions under which they function. But the body is a cultural product too, and we need to enquire into the conditions of possibility for its social functioning. One important aspect of the human body's ability to function as an apparently independent entity is the body image. Writers on the body image argue that such an image or gestalt is the basis of our intentional and of our social lives. Later in this chapter I will suggest that it is also crucial to our ethical lives.

This body image is a double of sorts which allows us to imagine and reflect upon ourselves in our present situations – to be in a sense our own 'other' – but it is also involved in what allows us to project ourselves into future situations and back to past situations. We can be objects, for ourselves and to ourselves: recipients of our own sadism/masochism; esteem/disdain; punishment/reward; love/hate. Our body image is a body double that can be as 'other' to us as any genuine 'other' can be. This point is particularly clearly illustrated in persecutory paranoia.[19] Part of the point in highlighting the 'otherness' of ourselves, to ourselves, is to draw out the implication that my experience of my body, for me, is just as socially constructed as my experience of the body of the other. The privileged relation which each individual has to her or his own body does *not* include a privilege over its construction. We may think of our own bodies as the most private of all our 'possessions', but in fact the body – and the way we each 'live' the body – has about it an eerie anonymity and otherness that is especially strongly felt at times of illness (both mental and physical), times at which we feel alienated from our social surroundings and times at which we are vulnerable to objectification by others.

Some theorists and philosophers would claim that for some of us this condition of otherness is a permanent structure of existence. To be socio-politically defined in terms of otherness, that is, to be defined as the permanent other of the culture in which one finds oneself, is to live the structure of alienation as a way of being. Much of the oppression and liberation literature of the 1960s and 70s – including women's liberation theory – sought to address this structure of alienation.[20] Alienation was understood to arise from the unreflective internalization of social norms and attitudes: in short, to be the result of internalized oppressive ideologies. The liberatory power of this sort of social theory was thought to lie in its ability to bring critical reflection to bear on these internalized ideologies, which were previously accepted and lived unreflectively. The internalization of those qualities which the dominant culture projects onto its others is understood as constitutive of the oppressed condition of various social groups, for example Jews and blacks. In anti-Semitic and racist cultures it is the Jewish or the black person who is taken to exemplify the unattractive traits which the anti-Semite and the racist would rather not recognize in themselves. As well as functioning as repositories of undesirable traits, stereotyped groups can become the scapegoats for social and political malaise. These structures have been well documented.[21] However, little attention has been paid to the part that doubling plays in these dynamics.

This mechanism of doubling is obvious enough in film and literature dealing with (often identical) twins – each twin being the antithesis and complement of the other. In recent times, the film *Dead Ringers* has shown this with an especially sharp clarity. Each twin mirrors, and so is the inversion of, the other and each assumes the existence of the other as complement to his own identity. And there is always a dominant, 'evil', or sadistic twin who (more or less) controls the other one. This asymmetric power relation is apparent in stereotypes, too. It is, of course, possible for the Jewish or the black person to project onto the anti-Semite and the racist qualities which she or he takes to be undesirable, but in so far as these groups lack the social and political power necessary to transform personal prejudice into social reality, these views remain socially 'unconfirmed'. Consequently, it will be highly unlikely that the anti-Semite or racist will internalize these qualities or recognize themselves in them. The racist may well be dependent on the black person in order to maintain his or her racism, but – leaving aside filmic characterizations of racists – there is usually a lot more to the racist's identity than his or her racism. There is a crucial *lack of reciprocity* in the situation of the black person and the racist: the power of definition is not mutual. The dynamic does not, then, involve a mutual or interdefining component and so will not display (unconscious or involuntary) *mutual* complicity. The absence of such complicity short-circuits the closure of the self-authenticating circle, a closure so neatly demonstrated in the case of identical twins.

I suggest that a dynamic very similar to that at work in the phenomenon of doubling can be discerned in the gendered relations between the sexes. Each gender is at once the antithesis of, and the complement to, the other. Each projects (and so, predictably, finds) those qualities antithetical to itself, to its 'ideal image', onto its double. Each therefore becomes the indispensable complement to the other. Each is deeply complicit in maintaining not only her or his *own* body image, but also that which it assumes: the body image *of the other*. Aggression requires submission, independence requires dependence, and sadism requires its masochistic counterpart. Each only 'sees' what is antithetical to it, that which complements it, and this 'seeing' is itself socially constructed. This is not to say that the system does not generate some anomalies; rather, that in so far as it does reproduce sexual difference as an antithetical yet complementary relation, it assumes deep complicity from both sexes. It involves a *reciprocity* and a necessary interdefinition that is absent from the other cases of social stereotyping considered above. This reciprocal interdefinition makes the relations between the sexes seem natural, necessary and immutable. Jessica Benjamin[22] has shown the presence of this complicity, in the context of sadomasochistic relations between the sexes, with great clarity. However, sadomasochism aside, we are still left with a puzzle concerning why it is that women seem to be complicit in an interdefining process which actually constructs important aspects of their own subordinate position.

The case of gender relations is not *reducible* either to personal power relations (as in the case of identical twins) or to sociopolitical relations (as in the case of racist and other stereotypes). Relations between the sexes appear to be a strange mix of these two. As de Beauvoir and many others since have remarked, the situation between men and women is a particularly complex one. It is complicated by love relations, by an apparently necessary species tie of each to the other, by eroticism *and* by political, social and economic oppression. It seems necessary to add that at least some of these relations between the sexes hold quite independently of sexual preference. Every woman is normatively defined, in our culture, as the opposite and complement of man. Deviation can only be defined, as such, by reference to some normative standard. For this reason, I will use the term '*inter*sexual' rather than heterosexual to signal the irrelevance of sexual preference to the functioning of certain aspects of the reproduction of sexual difference.[23] The how and why of women's *complicity* – to resurrect the term which earned de Beauvoir the scorn of feminists in the 1970s – in their own oppression is a riddle worthy of the Theban sphinx. And de Beauvoir herself, in *The Second Sex*, did not feel tempted to play the role of Oedipus. The riddle remains (and, if the fate of Oedipus is anything to go by, perhaps should remain) unanswered.

I am inclined to share de Beauvoir's scepticism concerning the notion that history, economics, psychology or politics might be able to provide a definitive answer to this question. More pertinently, answers are not what is required. We are not dealing with an 'exact science' but with living, dynamic and highly malleable human beings. Nor, as de Beauvoir pointed out, can we claim an unbiased perspective from which to assess this question. On the issue of sexual difference there are no neutral parties. The mechanism of doubling in the social construction of sexual difference ensures that each sex has an investment in the other sex. The investment that each has in her or his own body image necessarily involves a corresponding investment in an antithetical and complementary body image. This reflexive relation of each sex to the other requires, in turn, a reflexive understanding of the construction of sexual difference, which then can be brought to bear on creative and experimental attempts to transform ways of being male or female in the present and the future. We need to imagine and create new conditions of possibility for intersexual relations with the full awareness that our 'imaginings' and 'creations' will probably turn out to be no less limited than de Beauvoir's now appear to us.[24]

It is in this experimental and imaginative spirit that the three issues presented below should be considered. I do not take this to mean, however, that these proposals should be understood as mere theoretical or abstract possibilities. To treat the conceptual dismantling of the construction of self, sex and gender as activities that are limited to the (strictly) textual or the (strictly) discursive misses the inter(con)textuality of these texts and discourses with our lives, our bodies and our gendered – or sexed – selves. Put another way, many women who read Irigaray's 'This Sex which is Not One' become aware of the phenomenology of their own labial contiguity. (Presumably, many men would not 'read' this text in an analogous way, but this is precisely the point. Perhaps their reading(s) may throw into question the phallic image of the male body?) The body's own text is 'written upon' by other bodies, other texts, and it in turn 'writes upon' other bodies and other texts. It is in this context that the work of theorists on the body image or the gestalt becomes salient.

There is a deep complicity between self and other which is based on the *necessary* interconnectedness of our (social) images of ourselves. This complicity, as I indicated above, is particularly strong in relations between the sexes. The full, phallic, masculine body *necessarily assumes* its antithesis: the lacking, castrated feminine body, which is its complement, its body double. Put crudely, there is no lack without the phallus, and there is no phallus without lack. The feminist project of articulating, constructing or 'inventing' a full female form cannot amount to a 'separatist strategy'. Those who understand the positing of this full female morphology as working toward an *autonomous* feminine sexuality or feminine subjectivity are clearly mistaken. This would involve a regression to the mirror-phase child's fantasy of autonomy, which can only be maintained by the disavowal of one's counterpart. What is required is the acknowledgement of interconnectedness, not a repetition of the (typically masculine) insistence on autonomy. The self only exists in the complex web of its varied relations – there is no 'above or beyond' of these relations, no a priori or transcendent 'I'. To posit a full female morphology inevitably involves *addressing* the phallic morphology of the male form. No change can take place in any part of this web of intersexuality without reverberations being felt throughout the whole web. Paul Schilder has made this point in the following way:

> Our own body image gets its possibilities and existence only because our body is not isolated. A body is necessarily a body among other bodies. We must have others about us. There is no sense in the word 'ego' when there is not a 'thou'.[25]

Recasting the points made above concerning the complicity of both men and women in the maintenance of a certain kind of 'gendered' body image in which each takes its opposite and complement as its double, the import of the necessary connections between self and other, the 'ego' and the 'thou', begins to emerge. The 'writing of the feminine body',[26] far from being an exercise in feminist separatism, involves – and *necessarily* involves – addressing the other, the 'thou' of our social relations. This abandonment of the solipsism of autonomy involves the acknowledgement of the other both in intrasexual and intersexual relations. This interconnectedness of each with every other follows from the view that:

> A body image is in some way always the sum of the body images of the community according to the various relations in the community . . . Erotic changes in the body image are always social phenomena and are accompanied by corresponding phenomena in the body image of others.[27]

It is against this sketchy backdrop that I will raise three issues for consideration which bear on the body image, gender and sexual difference. First, how does the body image function in the field of ethical relations? Here I am interested to explore the ways in which our (cultural) understandings of bodies affect the way those bodies are treated ethically.[28] Second, how does gender, as an extremely prominent element of the body image, function in relation to intrasexual and intersexual ethical relations? Put another way, how do our ideas about male and female embodiment affect the way women treat other women, women treat men, men treat other men, and men treat women? Finally, I will raise the question of how, or if, the notion of corporeal multiplicity might be exploited in order to open up the current dualistic conceptualization of two bodies – which, as I have tried to show, are in fact one body and its lack or complement – to other possibilities. This, in turn, may provide a space for critical reflection on the dualistic conceptualization of so-called sex-appropriate behaviour or gender identity.[29] This last issue bears on the other two, since to disrupt and unsettle a binary understanding of bodily difference would be to disrupt what we take to be the appropriate ethical treatment of such bodies.

On the first issue, we should note that, in their discussions of ethics, morality and concern for others, philosophers rarely consider the *genesis* of our concern for others. They rarely consider the developmental or primitive basis of ethical life. At a fundamental level ethical judgements amount to judgements concerning how this or that body *ought* to be treated. At a fundamental level ethical relations depend upon the recognition of another body that we take to be sufficiently similar to our own for us to have concern for it. (This is not to say that one cannot also have concern for the environment, non-human animals, and so on; rather, it is to say that one cannot have an ethical *relation of reciprocity* with them.) Of course, not *all* ethical relations can be reduced to this level of identification on the basis of corporeal similarity, but that is not the claim being made here. My claim is that it is this kind of concern for others that forms the *primitive core* of ethical concerns and judgements. It is this identification that makes ethics (and of course *cruelty*) a specifically human possibility. For example, this primitive form of concern for the other can be discerned in the common phenomenon of *infantile transitivism.*

In psychoanalytic theory, in particular in the work of Lacan, this phenomenon is explained by way of the genesis of the ego, or the primitive self. This primitive sense of self is predicated on a specular image. The primitive ego, as Freud claimed, is 'first and foremost a *bodily* ego' or, more explicitly, the projection of an *image* of a unified body.[30] It is that stage of the infant's life when she or he is fascinated by, even ensnared in, images, identifications and doubles. The importance of this stage for later relations with others is often overlooked in philosophical theories of ethical and moral life. I suggest that this theory of the genesis of the self is promising in relation to developing a theory of ethical relations between different *kinds* of bodies. For this relation, between my body and the body of the other, is one based on both the *recognition* of similarity and a *misrecognition* of the other as the self. It is from the tension in this contrariety that both love/masochism and hate/sadism toward the other stem. This is why Merleau-Ponty, among others, insists that the child assumes this unified image of him- or herself 'in both jubilation and suffering'. He writes that the mirror phase represents

> the acquisition not only of a new content but of a new function as well: the narcissistic function . . . At the same time that the image of oneself makes possible the knowledge of oneself, it makes possible a sort of alienation . . . The general function of the specular image would be to tear us away from our immediate reality; it would be a 'de-realizing' function . . . inevitably there is conflict between the *me* as I feel myself and the *me* as I see myself or as others see me. The specular image will be, among other things, the first occasion for aggressiveness towards others to manifest itself. That is why it will be assumed by the child in both jubilation and suffering. The acquisition of a specular image, therefore, bears not only on our *relations of understanding* but also on our *relations of being*, with the world and with others.[31]

From this point on the child will, for the first time, be capable of displaying both kindness and cruelty towards others. It should be obvious from what has been said above that this image of the self and of the other is the basis for all future identifications. The contrariety of self and other, love and hate, sadism and masochism is, arguably, split post-oedipally into 'masculine' and 'feminine' components. Reconsider, in this light, the antithetical and complementary lists of masculine and feminine traits which appear at the beginning of this paper. Various stages of the child's development will reveal the *specific* cultural value of his or her own body along with the value of the gendered body. And *this* body, and its image, have only a tentative relation to what we understand as the *biological* body. To speak of a body as somehow being outside culture and its influences is nonsensical – even to speak or write about the body (even the biological body) is already to subject it to language, itself a cultural product.

Introducing the body image into our considerations of ethics, then, involves no commitment to sociobiological theories of our ethical lives. Rather, it is to strike at the very foundations of ethical life in an attempt to question what can be changed, what can be posited, what can be disrupted. In short, what are the possibilities for creating alternative ethical relations that include working from an understanding of the genesis, the richness and the plasticity of the body image? For the body image is never static or closed; rather it is a component of a dynamic circuit of exchanges.

The second issue concerns the centrality of gender to the body image of both sexes and how these gendered body images function in both intrasexual and intersexual ethics. Here the psychoanalytic theory of the genesis of the self can offer a critique of the body as a neutral surface for social inscriptions. The theory of the body image shows that our bodies are lived and constituted as part of a *network of bodies*; and these bodies have *depth* and are *dynamic*. The dynamism of this network is crucial to actualizing potentials and possibilities for changing our understandings of bodies and the way we 'live' our bodies. The female body, in our culture, is seen and no doubt often 'lived' as an *envelope, vessel* or *receptacle*. The post-oedipal female body, to paraphrase Freud, is first a home for the penis and later for a baby. It is important to recall, however, that this is the *post-oedipal* female body only – we would be justified in saying that it is a particular body image – that of the *feminine* body, the *gendered* female body. And this body 'takes over' the passive, devalued side of the dualisms which were initially conflicts *within* the primitive self. For Freud, the post-oedipal male body image is that of a whole, active *subject* – a phallic body. The masculine type then 'combines' the active, valued side of the dualism.[32] The post-oedipal female body image is that of a partial, passive *object* – a castrated body that requires first a man and then a baby to 'complete' it. Put bluntly, women's bodies are not seen to have integrity, they are socially constructed as partial and lacking. And here we should note the etymological links between *integrity* and *morality*. The root of integrity (Latin 'integritas') involves not only the notion of wholeness but also notions of moral soundness, honour and honesty.

Without confessing to Dalyism, I maintain that this etymological link is not incidental. Women are not thought to be 'morally sound' or to possess 'honour' – that is, to have integrity – precisely because they are not thought of as *whole* beings. It should be noted here, though I am unable to develop it any further in this chapter, that this account of the relation between morality and wholeness would bear further investigation in the context of rape, culturally enforced heterosexuality and enforced pregnancy. Is it not a common view that the fetus, *in utero*, represents the 'completion' of the female body rather than an 'addition' to it? Is the social complacence concerning the rape of women and girls (in contrast to the seriousness with which our society views the rape of men and boys) connected to the idea that women's bodies 'beg the question' of their 'completion' by the sexual act? Certainly, pornographic representations of women's bodies reveal an obsessive investment in presenting those bodies as 'full of holes' that require 'filling'. (Recall Sartre's views on 'the feminine sex', that obscenity which 'gapes open' and is an 'appeal to being' – that is, an appeal to *male* being, which contrasts with female nothingness.)[33] The sexual abuse of women is not considered to be an *ethical* outrage committed against women so much as a *legal* problem upon which 'men among men' arbitrate.

What ethical obligations do men have toward women *qua* women? Why is it that ethical relations between the sexes are exclusively limited to the sphere of *familial* and *conjugal* ethics? It is significant that we do not, in the history of philosophy or jurisprudence, have an account of women's political or moral being that does not reduce women to the role of wife/ mother. This is because women are quite simply not thought to be *whole* beings. Ethical relations take place only between whole persons and consequently they are the preserve of men. It is only men who emerge from culturization as whole and independent subjects, that is, as *human beings*. Women (and children) can expect ethical treatment only in so far as they are appendages to men: that is, as wives/mothers (and sons/daughters).

Ethical relations among women fare even worse than ethical relations between women and men: these relations are in the realm of the unthinkable. How can two 'partial' beings have an ethical relation?[34] The blanket notion of sisterhood has done little to alleviate this situation. It is clear that a (so-called) biological commonality is insufficient to constitute an ethical community even exclusively among women. De Beauvoir has written about the difficulty of socially devalued groups achieving an ethical community amongst themselves in an unjustly neglected book: *The Ethics of Ambiguity*.[35] She stresses there that it is crucial, *for the sake of that community*, to engage with the other who defines it as being of low value.

This ethical view tallies with what has been argued above concerning the interwoven nature of gendered and sexual difference. To ignore the other and assume an autonomous power of definition results in the repetition of oppressive relations *within* the very group that is attempting an ethical definition. The concentration on *hetero*sexuality rather than *inter*sexuality, in much feminist theorizing, falls into the traditional trap of reducing relations between women and men to the conjugal model. Luce Irigaray has begun the difficult task of considering ethical relations between the sexes in *An Ethics of Sexual Difference*.[36] To understand this work as committed to a *hetero*sexual relation is to miss the (ethical) point entirely. Moreover, it is to miss the biconditional relation between intersexual ethics and intrasexual ethics.

The final point to raise for consideration is that of corporeal multiplicity. To raise this issue is not to deny that sexual difference is a dominant organizing principle in our culture. It is rather to question why this is the case and what is invested in maintaining it as *the* difference. Recent developments in the abortion debate, in Australia, Britain and the United States, may encourage us to stress, more than ever, a dualistically sexed body. The abortion issue is most often understood as one which is crucial to every woman's existence. But even here we must note that this issue is more important to certain sorts of women (especially women in industrialized countries) than others. For some women the problems of involuntary sterilization and coerced abortion are more pertinent.[37] There is not a single issue on which we could say that the interests of *all* women overlap. Even the demand for women's autonomy would not receive universal agreement. To consider the multiplicity of body types and their specific pleasures and powers would assist in freeing up the normative dualism of two bodies, two sexes and two genders. Indeed, this multiplicity already exists: the homosexual body, the heterosexual body, the celibate body, the narcissistic body, the perverse body, the maternal body, the athletic body.

Each of these bodies has its own specific powers, pleasures and capacities. The pre-oedipal body is, in some sense, the ambiguous source of all these bodies. The pre-oedipal body is the polymorphous body whose pleasures and capacities do not, *contra* Freud and Lacan, *have to be* subjected to oedipality for culture to be possible. This subjection is necessary for a particular kind of culture to come into being: *phallocentric* culture, which depends for its functioning on the disavowal of positive difference. The polymorphous body need not be divided strictly into two kinds: male and female. Indeed, it is this strict division that is the insignia of patriarchy. If different kinds of (non-oedipalized) bodies were acknowledged – for they are subjected not vanquished – then our ethical relations might also develop towards a polyvalence. This would put an end to Enlightenment-inspired notions of a universal ethic which always amounts to the subjection of women, the colonized, the 'barbarian', the 'primitive', and so on, to the one Law, whose author wrongly sees himself as 'the universal man'. This is to claim that traditional Western accounts of (racial, sexual, class) differences, typically reduce difference to *one* valued term and its antithesis, complement or lack. Irigaray has spoken of this 'power [of the philosophic logos] to *reduce all others to the economy of the Same*'.[38] It is this reduction of difference to 'the Same' that underpins the construction of masculine and feminine subjects.

The gendered body images of male and female – that which allows them to 'live' as sexed men and women – are body doubles. To insist on this difference, in *all* contexts, as *the* difference, is to confess to one's fascination with the double. The peculiar complicity of women (and men) in maintaining phallocentric culture is crucially tied to the complex investments of both in their double(s).

Notes

This chapter was originally published in *Australian Feminist Studies*, no. 10 (Summer 1989).

1 S. de Beauvoir, *The Second Sex*, Harmondsworth, Penguin, 1975, p. 295.
2 A good general introduction to the notion of 'the double' is D.L. Eder, 'The Idea of the Double', *Psychoanalytic Review*, vol. 65, no. 4 (1978), pp. 579–614.
3 See *The Standard Edition of the Complete Psychological Works of Sigmund Freud* (hereafter S.E.), J. Strachey, ed., London, Hogarth Press, 1978, vol. VII, pp. 219–20; and R. Stoller, *Sex and Gender*, London, Hogarth Press, 1968, p. 9.
4 This point, and many others which I merely mention in this paper, are treated in more detail in Chapter 1 of this collection.
5 S. Freud, S.E. XIV, pp. 239f.
6 J. Flax, 'Mother/Daughter Relationships: Psychodynamics, Politics and Philosophy', in H. Eisenstein and A. Jardine, eds., *The Future of Difference*, Boston, G.K. Hall, 1980.
7 J. Benjamin, 'The Bonds of Love: Rational Violence and Erotic Domination", in H. Eisenstein and A. Jardine, eds., *The Future of Difference*, Boston, G.K. Hall, 1980.
8 C. Gilligan, 'In a Different Voice: Women's Conceptions of Self and Morality', in H. Eisenstein and A. Jardine, eds., *The Future of Difference*, Boston, G.K. Hall, 1980.
9 N. Chodorow, *The Reproduction of Mothering*, Berkeley, University of California Press, 1978.
10 S. Harding, *The Science Question in Feminism*, Milton Keynes, Open University Press, 1986.
11 J. Lacan, *Ecrits*, London, Tavistock, 1977, p. 2.
12 See, for example, L. Irigaray, 'This Sex Which is Not One', in E. Marks and I. Courtivron, eds., *New French Feminisms*, Amherst, University of Massachusetts Press, 1980, p. 101; and H. Cixous, 'Sorties', ibid., p. 92.
13 'Some Psychological Consequences of the Anatomical Distinction between the Sexes', S.E. XIX, p. 252.
14 J. Lacan, 'Some Reflections on the Ego', *International Journal of Psychoanalysis*, vol. 34 (1953), p. 13.
15 'Some Psychological Consequences', p. 253.
16 See 'Fetishism', S.E. XXI and 'Splitting of the Ego in the Process of Defence', S.E. XXIII.
17 'Some Psychological Consequences', p. 252.
18 See 'Project for a Scientific Psychology', S.E. I.
19 See the case of Schreber, S.E. XII, pp. 1f.
20 See, for example, R.D. Laing, *The Divided Self*, Harmondsworth, Penguin, 1965.
21 See, for example, J.-P. Sartre, *Portrait of the Anti-Semite*, London, Secker & Warburg, 1948.
22 Benjamin, 'The Bonds of Love'.
23 The term '*intra*sexual' will be used to define relations among women or relations among men, that is, the relations *within* one sex, as distinct from the relations *between* two sexes.
24 For an appraisal of the importance of *The Second Sex* in our contemporary context see C. Mackenzie, 'Simone de Beauvoir: Philosophy and/or the Female Body', in C. Pateman and E. Gross, eds., *Feminist Challenges*, Sydney, Allen & Unwin, 1987.

25 P. Schilder, *The Image and Appearance of the Human Body*, New York, International University Press, 1978, p. 281.
26 See E. Gross, 'Philosophy, Subjectivity and the Body: Kristeva and Irigaray', in C. Pateman and E. Gross, eds., *Feminist Challenges*, Sydney, Allen & Unwin, 1987, for an account of writing and the feminine body. Also, by same author, *Sexual Subversions*, Sydney, Allen & Unwin, 1989.
27 Schilder, *Image and Appearance of the Human Body*, p. 302.
28 R. Braidotti has raised the issue of how sexual difference bears on ethics in 'The Ethics of Sexual Difference: The Case of Foucault and Irigaray', *Australian Feminist Studies*, no. 3 (1986).
29 I have explored Spinoza's rejection of dualism and the relevance of his work to feminist theorizations of embodiment and ethics in Chapter 4 of this collection.
30 S. Freud, 'The Ego and the Id', S.E. XIX, p. 26.
31 'The Child's Relations with Others', in *The Primacy of Perception*, J.M. Edie, ed., Evanston, Ill., Northwestern University Press, 1964, pp. 136–7.
32 I have deliberately echoed Freud's use of the words 'takes over' and 'combines' in the context of femininity and masculinity. See 'Infantile Genital Organization', S.E. XIX, p. 145.
33 J.-P. Sartre, *Being and Nothingness*, London, Methuen, 1977, pp. 613–14.
34 See A. Rich, 'Women and Honour: Some Notes on Lying', in *On Lies, Secrets and Silence*, London, Virago, 1980.
35 S. de Beauvoir, *The Ethics of Ambiguity*, Secaucus, N.J., Citadel, 1975.
36 L. Irigaray, *An Ethics of Sexual Difference*, trans. C. Burke and G.C. Gill, Ithaca, Cornell University Press, 1993.
37 See A. Rich, 'Motherhood: The Contemporary Emergency and the Quantum Leap', in *On Lies, Secrets and Silence*, London, Virago, 1980.
38 L. Irigaray, 'The Power of Discourse and the Subordination of the Feminine', in *This Sex Which Is Not One*, Ithaca, Cornell University Press, 1985, p. 74.

Part II

4 Towards a feminist philosophy of the body

Feminists have made women's bodies a focal point around which many campaigns have been fought. The right to the autonomy of the female body has been argued in relation to abortion, contraception and birthing methods. The right to knowledge about the female body, the right to the health of the female body and the insistence on the autonomous pleasure of the female body have all been stressed by feminists in various contexts. Attempts to claim or assert these 'rights' have often involved direct defiance of both church and state. The meaning of the early women's liberation slogan, 'The personal is political', took on an added and unwelcome dimension when acts that women saw as *personal* choices were forbidden or penalized by the state. This raises the question of the relation between woman's body and the state. In spite of this social and political concentration on the female body, I would still argue that feminists have offered little by way of a coherent theory of the body. In particular, there has been little critical work done on the *conceptual* dimension of the relations between women's bodies and the state: between the body of woman and the body politic. In the absence of such theory, it is culturally dominant conceptions of the body that, unconsciously, many feminists work with.

What I propose to do in this chapter is, first, to critically examine some of the features of these dominant conceptions. Second, I will argue that traditional philosophical conceptions of corporeality are counterproductive to the aim of constructing an autonomous conception of women's bodies along with the possibility of women's active participation in the politico-ethical realm. Finally, I will suggest that the onto-ethical writings of Spinoza can provide a rich resource in working towards a feminist theorization of corporeality.

Whatever else we say about conceptions of the body, it is clear that *how* we conceptualize the body forms and limits the meaning of the body in culture in various ways. The historical and philosophical associations between women and corporeality are multiple and complex.[1] Significantly, cultural attitudes to both women and corporeality are often negative and function conceptually as the underside to culturally valued terms such as reason, civilization and progress. Many philosophers have tended to treat the soul or mind as, in essence, sexually neutral. Apparent differences between minds are generally seen to be due to the influence of the passions of the body. This element of sensuous and passionate corporeality allows philosophers to maintain the essential neutrality of the mind while allowing for individual and sexual differences. The most superior minds suffer least from the intrusions of the body. Women are most often understood to be less able to control the passions of the body and this failure is often located in the a priori disorder or anarchy of the female body itself. Some feminists have argued that this dualist notion of the body involves an implicit alignment between women and irrationality. The ideal conception of the rational is, in other words, articulated in direct opposition to qualities typical of the feminine.[2]

This notion of the female body as intrinsically anarchic or disordered has repercussions for women's suitability to political participation. Some feminists – especially the egalitarians of the eighteenth and nineteenth centuries – argued that women are not essentially irrational but are *trained* to be so (for example, Wollstonecraft, Taylor, J.S. Mill). Given proper training, they argued, women would be capable of rational political participation. This does not seem, in our present time, the most productive way of approaching the relation between women and their access to the political realm. As Genevieve Lloyd has shown, it is not so much that women are explicitly conceptualized as irrational but rather that rationality itself is defined against the 'womanly'. In this context it may be profitable to explore the idea that it is not so much that women are biologically unsuited to political participation, as that political participation has been structured and defined in such a way that it excludes women's bodies. If this is so then fighting to have women included in the present body politic will be counterproductive unless it is accompanied by some analysis of the exclusions of women's corporeality that still define that body politic and a working framework from which to think and live other ways of being, of being political and of being ethical.

Motherless births: the miracle of masculine auto-reproduction

The seventeenth century was witness to at least two births of interest to us here. First, the birth of the human *subject* who is both the subject *of* governance, that is, subject to an internal relation of domination, where mind or reason should dominate the body and passion, and one subject *to* governance. Second, the birth of the modern body politic which is represented as a product of reason, designed to govern, manage and administer the needs and desires of its subjects. A twin birth? Clearly, each being presupposes the other. This contiguity between the modern body politic and the modern subject suggests that, in order to understand modern conceptions of the human subject, including its corporeality, one needs to understand its reflexive relation to the modern body politic.

Modern political theory typically conceives of political life as a state created by a contract, entered into by rational decision and designed to ensure the protection and safety of the body and its needs. As it is a contract entered into by men only, one must surmise that it is a contract designed to secure the needs of male bodies and desires. This contract is also thought to create an *artificial* body: Hobbes' leviathan, for example, is an 'artificial man'. What a feminist theorist must consider is woman's relation to this 'artificial man'. Here, I will simply signal the importance of traditional conceptions of the female body and the way these conceptions function in political discourses to justify women's historical (and present) social role.

Woman in fact never makes the transition from the mythical 'state of nature' to the body politic. She *becomes* nature. She is necessary to the functioning of cultural life, she is the very ground which makes cultural life possible, yet she is not part of it. This division between nature and culture, between the reproduction of mere biological life as against the production and regulation of social life, is reflected in the distinction between the private and the public spheres, the family and the state. These divisions are conceptually and historically sexualized, with woman remaining mere nature, mere body, reproducing in the private familial sphere. These associations are viewed as having their ground in woman's ontology. The distinction between the sexes is taken to be a fundamental feature of nature that could only be represented in culture in this dichotomous way. The notion that culture constructs nature or that cultural practices construct bodies as dichotomously sexed is theoretically *inadmissible* in the modern account.

In the modern view the body is understood as part of 'raw' nature, which is progressively integrated or surpassed by the development of culture. Here I will merely signpost the resonances of this view in early feminist theory. Both Firestone and de Beauvoir, for example, entertained a clear nature/culture, body/social split, where both nature and the body were conceived as outside culture and outside history. Yet the effects or the power of both nature and the body can be progressively eroded in history by the advances of culture. The sex/gender distinction, so crucial to early 1970s feminist theory, also displays this acceptance of the division between bodies on one hand and culture on the other.[3] Sex is understood to be a fact of bodies, gender a socialized addition to sex. It is important to note the extent to which these early feminist critiques share the modern conception of the body as a non-cultural, ahistorical phenomenon. All history and culture can do, on this model, is intervene as a mechanic intervenes into the functioning of an already constituted machine.

The antihumanist stance marks a definitive break with this tradition. This stance questions the idea that the body has a priori needs, desires or functions which determine the form of culture and politics. Foucault, for example, rejects the idea that the body has a fixed character which sets the limits to possible sociopolitical structures in which that body could 'live'. He inverts the modern problematic and suggests the exploration of how sociopolitical structures construct particular kinds of bodies with particular kinds of needs and desires. One could argue, for example, that the sexed body is not a product of nature but is rather constituted as dichotomously sexed through elaborate and pervasive practices that act on and through the body.[4] Rather than viewing the forms and functions of bodies as determinant in the organization of culture, we can view them as products of the way that culture organizes, regulates and remakes itself. This approach allows us to shift the conceptual ground from the question 'How is the body taken up in culture?' to the more profitable question 'How does culture construct the body so that it is understood as a biological given?'

The most conspicuous contribution of feminists to the antihumanist critique of modernism is the exposure of the masculine bias of the supposedly 'neutral' humanist subject. Recent feminist research has shown that attending to the specificity of female embodiment disrupts and belies the supposed liberal principles of equal treatment and the right to bodily integrity. However, this research has paid insufficient attention to the congruence between the (implicitly masculine) subject of these rights and principles on the one hand and representations of the body politic on the other. Many theorists seem to assume that this relation of congruence merely reflects a historical fact about the privilege accorded to masculine experience in the construction of both political life and representations of political life. It is necessary to go beyond this 'man-as-author' understanding of political life. In particular, it is necessary to consider the isomorphism between philosophical representations of the 'neutral' human body and the body politic.

The work of Luce Irigaray is an excellent example of recent feminist criticism which seeks to reveal the masculine bias of Western culture. She has argued that an examination of philosophy reveals a certain isomorphism, or mirroring of form, between philosophy and the male body, a mirroring which implicitly privileges the masculine form in Western constructions of logic, language and metaphysics.[5] Her main target is metaphysics, which she seeks to undermine by an internal disruption that creates a space to re-present femininity.[6] Using aspects of her approach, we can present a challenge to the masculine nature of representations of the human body, the body politic and the links between these two. This may open a space where different political and ethical relations can begin to be thought, a 'space' that will be opened by questioning what is repressed in current representations of politico-ethical life.

In this context Freud offers an interesting observation on the mother–son relation, which is for him the primal 'hinge-relation' between the presocial and the social. It is this relation, after all, that for Freud lies at the heart of the riddle of culture; it is the riddle the Theban Sphinx poses to Oedipus. Freud writes: 'All his [the son's] instincts, those of tenderness, gratitude, lustfulness, defiance and independence, find satisfaction in the single wish *to be his own father*.'[7] This primal wish, to take the place of the father, is expressed in political terms by the fantasy of the generation of a man-made social body: a body that is motherless and so immortal. Our cultural unconscious is littered with examples that suggest that those *not* born of woman have awesome powers. Macbeth, who smiles with scorn at 'swords brandish'd by man that's of woman born', can be slain only by the 'unbirthed' Macduff. The motherless Athena can fearlessly confront the Furies, rebuking them for their vengeful pursuit of the matricide Orestes. Asserting her authority by sending them (literally) underground she establishes the priority of (male) citizenship over blood ties and thus institutes the classic patriarchal state, which even bears her name: Athens. Unmothered, such beings are autonomous, immortal and quintessentially masculine. The motherless body politic, product of the fecundity of man's reason, is also a body untouched by death. This fantasy of masculine auto-reproduction is not uncommon in Western political theory. It appears in Greek, medieval and modern writings, and it is a fantasy that feminists need to address.

Discourses on the body and discourses on the body politic each borrow terms from the other. This mutual cross-referencing appears in their shared vocabularies, for example, 'constitution', 'regime' and 'diet'. A philosophically common metaphor for the appropriate relation between the mind and the body is to posit it as a *political* relation, where one (the mind) should dominate, subjugate or govern the other (the body).[8] These conceptual interconnections are historically unstable. They take their present form, in whatever definitive sense can be given to them, largely in response to a series of dichotomies that emerged in the seventeenth century.

Descartes, Hobbes and later La Mettrie are names commonly associated with the mechanization of the body. Each posited a faculty of reason able to dominate the body-machine. Seventeenth-century discourses are obsessed with the question of the legitimate exercise of power in at least two contexts: first, how to enforce the legitimate power of reason over the unruly body (see, for example, Descartes' *The Passions of the Soul*); second, how to establish (or discredit) the legitimacy of the power of the king (the head) over the social (body). These debates concerning the legitimacy of social and political authority had considerable effects not only on conceptions of the appropriate governing relation between minds and bodies, kings and subjects, but also on the relations between men and women.

Carole Pateman[9] has argued against understanding the patriarchal body politic as the 'rule of the father'. She argues that the sons (represented by the writings of Locke) may well have defeated the fathers (represented by the writings of Filmer) but what they introduced was not a democracy but a fraternity. It is also crucial to stress, in this context, that the triumph of the sons required a strict separation between natural and conventional authority. Although the authority of father over son was questioned, the authority of man over woman was not. In order for men to 'legitimately' dominate women it was necessary to exclude women from the political sphere, that is, women were not entitled to be represented by the 'artificial man'. This meant reducing women to roles that have meaning only in relation to men: wife/mother/daughter. It is worth mentioning that considerable physical coercion was employed in late seventeenth and eighteenth-century politics to ensure that women were confined to the private/familial sphere. Attempts by women to take advantage of the considerable social unrest were often quashed. The justification for the often harsh measures used to keep women out of the body politic were commonly put in terms of protecting the health of the social body from invasion, corruption or infection.[10]

One of the main petitions put before the revolutionary government in Paris between 1792 and 1794 demanded that women be given 'a voice' in the newly formed body politic. The terms in which this petition was rejected confirm many of the points I have made here:

> If we take into account the fact that the political education of men is still at its very beginnings, that all the principles are not yet developed, and that we still stammer over the word 'liberty', then how much less enlightened are women, whose moral education has been practically non-existent. Their presence in the *sociétés populaires*, then, would give an active part in government to persons exposed to error and seduction even more than are men. And, let us add that women, by their constitution, are open to an exaltation which could be ominous in public life. The interests of the state would soon be sacrificed to all kinds of disruption and disorder that hysteria can produce.[11]

If women are admitted to the social body and given a 'voice', the feminine disease of hysteria may be transposed to the social body which would result in *political* hysteria. We can see in the above passage the shift that Foucault notes from concern over the well-being of the king's body to concern for the health and asepsis of the social body.[12] Amar, the speaker quoted above, was representing the newly formed 'Committee for General Security', a committee whose task it was to police the health and safety of the nascent social body. That part of this task involved the quarantine of women is instructive. As Cixous,[13] Lyotard[14] and others have commented, in so far as woman is socially 'initiated', she is initiated by decapitation, either metaphorically (mutism) or literally (recall the guillotining of Mme Roland and Olympe de Gouges). She has nothing to forfeit but her 'voice', her head, her reason. Her relation to the body politic will be limited to the corporeal and to her use as a natural resource. She will continue to function as the repressed term 'body', thus allowing the fantasy of the masculine body politic to 'live'.

Recent feminist writing has responded to the self-representation of philosophers by pointing out that the body politic that men give birth to assumes both the appropriation and the disavowal of woman's ability to reproduce life.[15] This response allows us to read the modern political writers in a new light. Clearly, many of the writers of this period share the fantasy of political man's autonomy from both women and the corporeal, specifically, autonomy from the maternal body. It is tempting to argue that the modern body politic has yet to be *embodied*. Any attempt to begin conceptualizing the embodiment of the body politic runs up against immediate problems: the 'neutrality' of the modern subject; women's exclusion from the rational and hence from the political and the ethical also. This situation, then, requires a radical rethinking of the connections between reason, the body and politico-ethical relations. What is required is a theoretical space that is not dominated by the isomorphism between male bodies and political bodies.

However, the construction of alternative perspectives presents us with both practical and theoretical difficulties. The conceptual difficulty of trying to construct other ways to live human corporeality using dominant categories of thought arises partly because these categories are tied in complex ways to present forms of social, political and ethical life. Descartes' dualistic conception of subjectivity, for example, can be viewed as an essential development in Western societies. Mind/body dualism serves to validate the notion that the mind, by an act of will, can alienate the labouring capacities of its body-machine in return for a wage. Offering a coherent account of woman's relation to wage labour has long been problematic for political theorists. It seems fair to suggest that there are conceptual exclusions operating against developing such an account. Of course, theories of being or politics cannot be created *ex nihilo*. We are constrained by our theoretical as well as our practical histories. However, the history of philosophy has a much richer store of conceptions of the body than appears in dominant accounts. For the remainder of this chapter I propose the use of a tradition of conceptualizing the body that derives from the writings of Spinoza and has been largely neglected in Anglo-American philosophy. This tradition offers a multivalent ontology that may provide a basis from which to develop a multiple and *embodied* politico-ethics.

Spinozistic bodies

It may seem a little odd to return to a seventeenth-century conception of the body, given the advances in the biological and natural sciences since then. However, there are good reasons to prefer such a remote account as Spinoza's. His theory may offer another perspective from which to assess the claims and findings of a science and a biology that have been articulated in the shadow of dualism.

If women are going to play an active part in contemporary politics then it is important to begin the task of thinking through how one participates in a context where female embodiment is denied any autonomous political or ethical representation. It is important to begin the exploration of other ontologies which would be developed hand in hand with a politico-ethical stance that accommodates *multiple*, not simply dichotomously *sexed* bodies.

It seems important, in this context, to argue that feminists who are in a position of (relative) social power do not use this power to further entrench polarities that function negatively in relation to other social groups as well. Given the history, and the discourses surrounding the history, of the modern body politic it is necessary for feminists to exert a strong counter-force to the explicit and implicit masculinity of that body. This counter-force will necessarily involve the assertion of a certain homogeneity in the specific situations of women. This seems to be a necessary initial response to a substantive historical fact about political society. But this response must be viewed as based in tactical *nous* rather than in an ontological truth about women that is closed to history. It is necessary for feminist theory to develop an open-ended ontology capable of resisting entrenchment in the romanticism which so often accompanies the 'underdog' position.

The kind of political practice that I am suggesting could be developed from Spinozist metaphysics would require the reconsideration of several dominant feminist principles. The polarization between men and women is a part of our sociopolitical histories which cannot be ignored. But to accept this dualism uncritically is merely to perpetuate relations whose construction is not fully understood. The kind of political practice envisaged here is one where difference could not be decided a priori but rather recognized in the unfolding of shared (or conflicting) aims and objectives of groups of bodies. To seek to create a politico-ethical organization where all, in their own manner, seek to maximize the possibilities of their activity must take into account different beings and their desires, and their understandings of their being and their desires. It is an unavoidable (and welcome) consequence of constructing an *embodied* ethics that ethics would no longer pretend to be universal.

Spinozist philosophy is capable of suggesting an account of the body and its relation to social life, politics and ethics that does not depend on the dualisms that have dominated traditional modern philosophy. Yet neither is it a philosophy which neutralizes difference. Rather it allows a conceptualization of difference which is neither dichotomized nor polarized. Spinoza's writings offer the possibility of resolving some of the current difficulties in the much-debated relation between feminist theory and dominant theory.[16] This 'resolution' is not so much concerned with 'answers' to these difficulties as with providing a framework in which it is possible to pose problems in quite different theoretical terms.

The division between the (bodily, natural, feminine) private sphere and the (rational, cultural, masculine) public sphere is a division that has proved particularly resilient to feminist intervention. To address the tension between the political and the familial spheres is to address the tension between the conceptions 'men' and 'women', and so ultimately to address the tension *within* the present politico-ethical structuring of the 'universal' human subject. Spinozist conceptions of reason, power, activity and *conatus* (that is, the tendency of all things to strive to persist in their own being) offer a provisional terminology in which to begin working towards dissolving these tensions. By abandoning the dualist ontology of mind versus body, nature versus culture, we can circumvent the either/or impasse of contemporary feminist theory between affirming an essential mental equality, which the progress of civilization can be entrusted to expose, and affirming an essential bodily difference. The Spinozist view does not lend itself to an understanding of sexual difference in terms of a consciousness/body or sex/gender distinction. For Spinoza the body is not part of passive nature ruled over by an active mind but rather the body is the ground of human action. The mind is constituted by the affirmation of the actual existence of the body, and reason is active and embodied precisely because it is the affirmation of a *particular* bodily existence. Activity itself cannot be related especially to body, mind, nature or culture, but rather to an understanding of the possibilities of one's participation in one's situation as opposed to the passive 'living' of one's social, political or even brute existence. This active understanding does not, and could not, amount to the mental domination of a body-machine, since thought is dependent for its activity on the character of the body and the manner in which, and the context in which, it recreates itself.

The Spinozist account of the body is of a productive and creative body which cannot be definitively 'known' since it is not identical with itself across time. The body does not have a 'truth' or a 'true' nature since it is a process and its meaning and capacities will vary according to its context. We do not know the limits of this body or the powers that it is capable of attaining. These limits and capacities can only be revealed by the ongoing interactions of the body and its environment.

Traditional political theory takes the body, its passions, its form and function as virtually given. This form is then understood to be taken up in culture in the way that it is because of this a priori or biological nature. Entertaining a non-mechanical view of nature and a non-dichotomized view of nature and culture would involve acknowledging the cultural and historical specificity of bodies. The particular form, structure, character and capabilities of a body confined to the domestic sphere and to the role of wife/mother may then be seen as a historically specific body whose capacities are reduced by its sphere of activity and the conditions under which it recreates itself. This perspective makes essentialist accounts of the female form and its capacities problematic. It allows one to question the traditional alignments between the female body and the private sphere and the male body and the public sphere without disavowing the *historical* facts that support these alignments. One could rather note the ways in which the respective activities of these distinct spheres construct and recreate particular kinds of bodies to perform particular kinds of tasks.

For feminists working in philosophy – or any academic discipline – the most pressing difficulty in relation to affirming the presence of woman is the theoretical exclusions implicit in the discourses with which we have to deal. Creating other modes of conceptualizing human culture that do not involve the passivity or invisibility of women is obviously of the greatest importance. A philosophy of the body that addresses the connections between representations of sexed bodies on the one hand and representations of the politico-ethical on the other is an essential component of any alternative view. Recent work on the body by French feminists,[17] which stresses *morphology* over biology, cultural constructions of embodiment over the 'natural' body, breaks with traditional boundaries between desire and instinct, between consciousness and bodies. Morphological descriptions of the body construct the body as an active, desiring body since the form of the body *is* its being, its form *is* its desiring. I take this conception of morphology to be a useful bridging device – a device that is necessary to get beyond the dilemmas of dualism. Many feminists are working on the creation of an alternative *topos* from which to reject or work through these dominant dualisms of the mind and the body, nature and culture, biology and psychology, and sex and gender. What I have tried to show in this chapter is that the theorization or clarification of this *topos* could benefit from the Spinozist framework. I have suggested that his work offers exciting possibilities in terms of conceptualizing the body as productive and dynamic: a conception which defies traditional divisions between knowing and being, between ontology and epistemology, and between politics and ethics.

No doubt there are other non-dualist conceptions of subjectivity that should be explored. I am not presenting Spinoza as a unique exception in the history of philosophy. Some aspects of the work of Nietzsche, or more recently the work of Foucault and Deleuze, may also prove useful to feminists. My personal preference for the remote figure of Spinoza stems from a worry that more contemporary figures may entrap feminism in the transferential position, to which it is so very vulnerable.[18] Establishing an autonomous relation to one's discipline, and to its history, is a step towards at least *theoretical* independence.

Notes

This chapter was originally presented to the Women's Studies' Centennary Conference, Sydney University, 1985, and published in B. Caine, E. Grosz, and M. de Lepervanche, eds., *Crossing Boundaries*, Sydney, Allen & Unwin, 1988.

1 See E. Spelman, 'Woman as Body: Ancient and Contemporary Views', *Feminist Studies*, vol. 8, no. 1 (1982).
2 M. Le Dœuff, *The Philosophical Imaginary*, trans. C. Gordon, London, Athlone Press, 1989 and G. Lloyd, *The Man of Reason*, London, Methuen, 1984.
3 See Chapter 1, 'A Critique of the Sex/Gender Distinction'.
4 See M. Foucault, *The History of Sexuality*, vol. I, New York, Pantheon, 1978 and M. Foucault, *Herculine Barbin*, New York, Random House, 1980.
5 L. Irigaray, 'Women's Exile', *Ideology and Consciousness*, no. 1 (1977).
6 L. Irigaray, *Speculum of the Other Woman*, Ithaca, Cornell University Press, 1985.
7 S. Freud, 'A Special Type of Object-Choice Made by Men', *The Standard Edition of the Complete Psychological Works of Sigmund Freud*, J. Strachey, ed., London, Hogarth, 1978, vol. XI p. 173.
8 See E. Spelman, 'The Politicization of the Soul', in S. Harding and M.B. Hintikka, eds., *Discovering Reality*, Dordrecht, Reidel, 1983.
9 C. Pateman, 'The Fraternal Social Contract', paper delivered to the Annual American Political Science Association, Washington, D.C., 1984.
10 See J. Abray, 'Feminism in the French Revolution', *American Historical Review*, no. 80 (1975).
11 Ibid., p. 56.
12 See M. Foucault, *Discipline and Punish*, London, Allen Lane, 1977, and *History of Sexuality*, vol. I.
13 H. Cixous, 'The Laugh of the Medusa', in E. Marks and I. Courtivron, eds., *New French Feminisms*, Amherst, University of Massachusetts Press, 1980; H. Cixous, 'Castration or Decapitation?', *Signs*, vol. 7, no. 1 (1981).
14 J.F. Lyotard, 'One of the Things at Stake in Women's Struggles', *Substance*, no. 20 (1978).
15 C. Pateman, 'The Fraternal Social Contract'; Irigaray, *Speculum of the Other Woman*; L. Irigaray, *This Sex Which is Not One*, Ithaca, Cornell University Press, 1985.
16 See M. Gatens, 'Feminism, Philosophy and Riddles Without Answers', in C. Pateman and E. Gross, eds., *Feminist Challenges: Social and Political Theory*, Sydney, Allen & Unwin, 1986.
17 See E. Marks and I. Courtivron, eds., *New French Feminisms*, Amherst, University of Massachusetts Press, 1980; H. Eisentein and A. Jardine, eds., *The Future of Difference*, Boston, G.K. Hall, 1980; Irigaray, 'Women's Exile', *Speculum of the Other Woman* and *This Sex Which is Not One*.
18 See M. Le Dœuff, 'Women and Philosophy', *Radical Philosophy*, no. 17 (Summer 1977).

5 Power, bodies and difference

Over the last two decades the diversification of feminist theories has rendered the rather convenient tripartite division into Marxist feminism, liberal feminism and radical feminism virtually useless. These divisions no longer capture the salient features of the multiple ways which current feminist theories interact with dominant sociopolitical theories.[1] Most noticeably, feminist theories today no longer feel compelled to carry their allegiances 'on their sleeves' (*Marxist* feminism, *liberal* feminism) in order to signal their authority to speak. In this sense, both Marxism and liberalism provided, and sometimes still provide, a legitimizing or patronymic function. Radical feminism distinguished itself from other forms of feminist theory by avowing its independence from so-called patriarchal theories. It alone claimed to be 'unmarked' by the name of the father.

The reluctance of contemporary feminisms to identify themselves with a theory-patronym may be seen as an indication of the profound suspicion and distrust which many feminists display towards dominant sociopolitical theories. Many contemporary feminist theorists no longer have faith in the utility of existing sociopolitical theories to explain or clarify the sociopolitical status of women. This 'loss of faith' in what has variously been named malestream, phallocentric or simply masculinist theory signals that many feminists no longer believe that those theories are marred by only a superficial sex blindness or sexism. The problem is now located at a much more fundamental level. It cannot be simply a matter of removing superficial biases from sociopolitical theories, since the bias is now understood as intrinsic to the structure of the theories in question.[2] For example, feminist philosophers have argued convincingly that reason is not something from which women have been simply excluded. Rather, rationality itself has been defined against the feminine and traditional female roles.[3] Likewise, it has been demonstrated that women's exclusion from the political body is not a contingent feature of their history but a consequence of the dominant conception of political society. Women have been constructed as 'naturally deficient in a specifically *political* capacity, the capacity to create and maintain political right'.[4] These studies have shown that the application of dominant theories of social and political life to the situation of women inevitably involves the devaluation of women and all that women have been associated with historically. The reason is that these theories harbour fundamental, not superficial, biases against women.

This analysis may be seen to imply that many contemporary feminist approaches to theory are themselves forms or varieties of radical feminism. This would be a rather simplistic description, since many recent developments in contemporary feminist theory explicitly stress the necessity to engage with dominant or 'malestream' theories of social and political life – an attitude not easily identified with radical feminism. Such engagement is active and critical. These feminist theorists do not go to Marxism or liberalism hoping for 'the answer' or 'the solution' to 'the woman question' but, more probably, will approach dominant theories, and their implicit biases, as themselves part of the problem. For this reason it seems appropriate to name these contemporary feminist approaches to dominant sociopolitical theories 'deconstructive'.

For the purposes of this essay the term 'deconstructive' will not be used in the strict Derridean sense. Rather, it will be used to identify feminist approaches which eschew viewing theories such as Marxism, liberalism, existentialism, psychoanalysis, and so on as essentially sex-neutral discourses through which women's situation may be 'truly' grasped. Deconstructive feminism is concerned to investigate the elemental make-up of these theories and to expose their latent discursive commitments. For example, much political theory typically treats the family as a natural rather than social phenomenon. A deconstructive approach highlights what is at stake in opposing the family, understood as natural, to the public sphere, understood as a social construct. It is this assumption which allows political theorists to mask the specifically political features of the relations between the sexes by treating these relations as natural.[5]

A feature common to most, if not all, dominant sociopolitical theories is a commitment to the dualisms central to Western thought: nature and culture, body and mind, passion and reason. In the realm of social and political theory, these dualisms often translate as distinctions between reproduction and production, the family and the state, the individual and the social. As many feminists have argued, the left-hand side of these dualisms is more intimately connected with women and femininity and the right-hand side with men and masculinity. It is also important to note that it is only the right-hand side of these distinctions which is deemed to fall within the realm of history. Only culture, the mind and reason, social production, the state and society are understood as having a dynamic and developmental character. The body and its passions, reproduction, the family and the individual are often conceived as timeless and unvarying aspects of nature. This way of conceptualizing human existence is deeply complicit in claims such as 'women have no history'[6] and 'reproduction involves the mere repetition of life'.[7]

It is this thorough interrogation of the discursive commitments of socio-political theories that marks off current forms of feminist theory from their predecessors. It distinguishes deconstructive feminist theory from any feminist theory which theorizes women's existence by attempting to extend the terms of 'malestream' theories; for example, Marxist feminism, liberal feminism, existentialist feminism, and so on. Yet deconstructive feminism is also distinct from radical feminism in that it does not take woman's essence or biology as somehow enabling her to produce, *ex nihilo*, pure or non-patriarchal theory. On the contrary, such claims are viewed with scepticism. Michèle Le Dœuff, for example, claims that,

> [w]hether we like it or not, we are within philosophy, surrounded by masculine–feminine divisions that philosophy has helped to articulate and refine. The problem is to know whether we want to remain there and be dominated by them, or whether we can take up a critical position in relation to them, a position which will necessarily evolve through deciphering the basic philosophical assumptions latent in discourse about women. The worst metaphysical positions are those which one adopts unconsciously whilst believing or claiming that one is speaking from a position outside philosophy.[8]

The last sentence of this passage may serve as a caution to those who believe that it is possible to create feminist theories which owe nothing to the culture from which they emanate. To acknowledge this is not, however, to take up a nihilistic or resigned attitude to the possibility of working towards alternatives to existing sociopolitical theories, where this might involve critically engaging with their 'latent assumptions'. Suppressed or marginalized philosophies – for example, those of Spinoza[9] or Nietzsche – also may be of use to feminist theorists in that they may emphasize features of existence which have been obscured or elided by traditional discourses.

It is obviously impossible to present a fair or extensive treatment of the great variety in contemporary feminist theories in the space of a single essay. Indeed, it is not possible even to present a fair outline of the various deconstructive feminisms. Rather, this chapter will attempt to offer an outline of what I take to be some of the most important conceptual differences between feminist theories of the 1970s on the one hand and contemporary deconstructive feminisms on the other. This contrast will be achieved by concentrating on shifts in the use of three key terms: *power*, *the body* and *difference*. These terms are used by both deconstructive and other feminist theorists; nevertheless it will be argued that they are used in quite different and incompatible ways. Inevitably, in an essay of this sort, there will be many generalizations. The aim is not to belittle feminisms of the 1970s but rather to show that deconstructive feminisms have developed in a historical context, where previous feminist research plays an integral and indispensable role in the articulation of contemporary feminist concerns. This is simply to say that, if previous feminists had not attempted to use dominant theories to explicate women's sociopolitical status, the difficulties inherent in that project would not have come to light. Deconstructive feminisms assume and respond to these difficulties.

Power

Both liberal and Marxist political theories have tended to conceptualize power as something which an individual or a group either does or does not have. Power is conceived as something which is intimately connected with authority, domination or exploitation. In liberal political theory the role of the state is conceived in terms of the exercise of legitimate power over its subjects to ensure the peaceable and equitable opportunity for exchange. Power is thought to reside in, and radiate out from, sovereignty.

Marxist political theory, of course, takes a quite different view of the matter. Power is not thought to be the exercise of the legitimate authority of the sovereign. Rather, the state is conceived as being in the service of the ruling class and the exercise of power in society is the exercise of the power of one class over another. In this sense, power is held by one group which uses this power in order to dominate and exploit another group which lacks power. However, both philosophies assume that power is principally manifested in the regulation and control of politico-economic relations. It is in relation to these that power assumes material forms, although Marxists would also claim that power is exercised by ideological means. Louis Althusser formulated the difference between these two distinct forms of state power in terms of repressive state apparatuses, which include the police, judiciary, army, and so on, and ideological state apparatuses, which include schools, religion, the family, and so forth.[10]

When feminist theorists seek to make use of these sociopolitical theories, the kinds of problem that they address tend to centre on the manner in which the power of the state operates in relation to women. Liberal feminists conceive the problem of women's confinement to the private sphere as central to their low sociopolitical status. Equality, wealth and opportunity are located in the public sphere. Hence the issue of providing women with access to power becomes the issue of providing them with equal access to the public sphere. The state is obliged to provide women with the same opportunities it provides for men. Thus, the struggle for liberal feminists tends to involve equality of opportunity in education and the workplace, equality under the law, and so on. These demands inevitably spill over into related demands for child care or maternity leave. However, since these demands must be put in terms that are sex-neutral, maternity leave must be matched by paternity leave and equal opportunity must be phrased in terms which include men.

The fundamental premise of liberal philosophy to provide equal access to power can be articulated only in terms that are sexually neutral. What this involves, for women, is the difficulty, if not impossibility, of occupying the public sphere on genuinely equal terms with men. Put simply, given that the public sphere has historically been an almost exclusively male sphere, it has developed in a manner which assumes that its occupants have a male body. Specifically, it is a sphere that does not concern itself with reproduction but with production. It does not concern itself with (private) domestic labour but with (social) wage labour. This is to say that liberal society assumes that its citizens continue to be what they were historically, namely male heads of households who have at their disposal the services of an unpaid domestic worker/mother/wife.

In this sense, the (traditionally male) public sphere of liberal society can be understood as one which defines itself in opposition to the (traditionally female) private sphere. The status of women in liberal theory and society presents feminists with a series of a paradoxes.[11] Equality in this context can involve only the abstract opportunity to become equal to men. It is the male body, and its historically and culturally determined powers and capacities, that is taken as the norm or the standard of the liberal 'individual'. Women can achieve this standard provided that they either elide their own corporeal specificity or are able to juggle both their traditional role in the private sphere and their newfound 'equality'. This situation fails to take account of the specific powers and capacities that women have developed in their historical and cultural context, a point which will be treated in the following section.

Marxism also tends to concentrate on a rather narrow use of power, one in which economic relations are taken to be the origin of all power relations. The effect of this, in the context of studying women's sociopolitical status, is that those forms of power that are specific to women's existence can only be perceived in their relation to the economic structure of society. It is tempting to suggest that women would first have to become genuine members of liberal society in order to lend credence to the relevance of the Marxist critique to their situation. This is particularly pertinent to those varieties of Marxism that take the structure of society to be determined by its economic base. It was the economism of much Marxist theory that placed the so-called domestic labour debate high on the agenda for Marxist feminists in the 1970s. This highlights the way in which theories can determine which questions are 'central', irrespective of the specificity of the object being studied. It provides an example of how the deep biases in sociopolitical theories can obscure features of women's existence that may be crucial to an understanding of their situation, while emphasizing instead issues that appear prominent not because of women's situation but because of the underlying commitments of the theory in question.[12]

The difficulties involved in offering a Marxist analysis of women under patriarchal capitalism are obviously tied to the fact that, in Marxist terms, women cannot be seen to constitute a class. Consequently, Marxist feminist theory found it difficult to offer an account of the operations of power in the lives of women. The theory, like the culture, could conceive women, *qua women*, only on the model of appendages to men. Capital extracts surplus value from wage labour, the price of which assumes the subsistence of not only the wage labourer but also his household. Those women who do perform wage labour are conceived as unsexed labour, while those women who do not perform wage labour have only an indirect connection to capital and social relations. Power, as it operates in the lives of women, was largely conceived on the model of the power of ideology. Hence it is not surprising that many Marxist feminists welcomed the addition of psychoanalytic theory in order to explain the way in which the ideology of masculinity and femininity constructs men and women as appropriate patriarchal subjects in capitalist society. Moreover, in that many Marxist feminists took (traditional) women's work to involve the reproduction of labour power, psychoanalysis offered a theoretical perspective from which to examine the way in which *appropriate* kinds of labourer are produced.

The most prominent exponent of the utility of psychoanalytic theory to Marxist feminism was Juliet Mitchell, with her extremely influential book *Psychoanalysis and Feminism*.[13] Mitchell claimed that Marxism offered an account of class and capital whereas psychoanalysis offered an account of sex and patriarchy. Significantly, these two theories were understood as concerned respectively with the economic infrastructure and the ideological superstructure. Men's exploitation centred on the state and class society whereas women's specific oppression centred on ideology and patriarchal society. Mitchell, following Althusser, thus managed to achieve the reduction of psychic life to the domain of ideology. This is an important consequence, primarily because it was often used to 'justify' the postponement of women's struggles or, more benignly, to tie the outcome of women's struggles to that of the class struggle.

This view of the operation of power and oppression in women's lives involved an unconvincing analysis of how gender operates in society, as well as the way in which sexual difference intersects with power and domination. Kate Millett, for example, argued that

> [s]ince patriarchy's biological foundations appear to be so very insecure, one has some cause to admire the strength of a 'socialization' which can continue a universal condition 'on faith alone', as it were, or through an acquired value system exclusively.[14]

This passage reveals the way in which Millett understood biology as referring to the sexed body (male and female) and ideology as referring to the masculine or feminine subject. Such an understanding fails to note the ways in which values are embedded in social practices that take the body as their target. The biology/ideology distinction treats 'value system[s]' in an idealist manner and so obscures the ways in which social values are embedded in bodies, not simply 'minds' – a point to which I will return. Both liberal and Marxist analyses of society suffer from similar problems in relation to the study of women's sociopolitical status. The implicit theory of power held by both approaches is narrowly economic, which is inadequate in the context of women's historically tentative relation to the public sphere and wage labour. This view of power is arguably suitable to an analysis of some aspects of men's sociopolitical lives, but inadequate when applied to women, or indeed in relation to other issues such as racial oppression.

The problem, in part, is the inability of both liberal and Marxist theory to address the issue of corporeal specificity in any terms other than those of biological 'facts' or ideology. Neither theory is able to think difference outside the body/mind, fact/value or science/ideology distinctions. For example, these are precisely the terms in which the sex/gender distinction is couched. Sex concerns the body, facts and science (biology), whereas gender concerns the mind, values and ideology (conditioning).[15] Both theories are committed to a form of humanism which assumes a fundamental universality across history and across cultures in relation to the needs, capacities and 'nature' of the human being or the human body. This is in part an effect of assuming that bodies and their needs are a timeless part of nature. This puts the emphasis on the way in which the biologically given human being becomes a socially produced masculine or feminine subject. Since masculinity and femininity are conceived as psychological traits, their genesis and reproduction must be located at the level of the mind, values or ideology.

This approach to the issues of sexual difference, power and domination is unable to consider the ways in which power differentially *constitutes* particular kinds of body and empowers them to perform particular kinds of task, thus constructing specific kinds of subject. Put differently, one could argue that gender is a material effect of the way in which power takes hold of the body rather than an ideological effect of the way power 'conditions' the mind. To make this kind of claim would involve using a notion of power and the body quite different from that used in dominant sociopolitical theories.

Perhaps the most prominent exponent of this alternative account of power is Michel Foucault. He stresses that dominant accounts of power tend to conceive power on the model of repression, where power is reduced to that which says 'No'.[16] Foucault's work has concentrated on the body–power relation and on the discourses and practices which he takes to involve productive operations of power. This is not to say that he disavows the existence, or indeed the importance, of state power or repressive state practices. Rather, it is to say that his work seeks to emphasize the less spectacular but more insidious forms of power. Moreover, these non-repressive forms of power cannot be adequately captured by the notion of ideology. He summarizes his reservations concerning the utility of the term ideology in three points:

[First,] like it or not, it always stands in virtual opposition to something else which is supposed to count as truth. Now, I believe that the problem does not consist in drawing the line between that in a discourse which falls under the category of scientificity or truth, and that which comes under some other category, but in seeing historically how effects of truth are produced within discourses which in themselves are neither true nor false. The second drawback is that the concept of ideology refers, I think necessarily, to something of the order of a subject. Thirdly, ideology stands in a secondary position relative to something which functions as its infrastructure, as its material, economic determinant.[17]

Foucault's reservations about the concept of ideology overlap in an interesting way with the reservations which have been expressed here concerning the utility of Marxist and liberal sociopolitical theories to the situation of women. First, the science/ideology distinction has been relied upon in understanding women's oppression as linked to a patriarchal value system which constructs gendered subjects, while the 'truth' of the sex of woman is to be determined by the scientific discourse of biology. Second, the notion that gender is a social addition to the human subject is coherent only on the condition that human subjects pre-exist their social contexts. Finally, the limitation in viewing patriarchy as operating primarily by ideological means is that it assumes that the determinant infrastructure of society is economic. For these reasons, the Foucauldian approach to the micropolitics of power is particularly appropriate to an investigation of the ways in which power and domination operate in relation to sexual difference.

One of the main benefits of Foucault's approach is that its emphasis on the body allows one to consider not simply how discourses and practices create ideologically appropriate subjects but also how these practices construct certain sorts of body with particular kinds of power and capacity; that is, how bodies are turned into individuals of various kinds.[18] In short, it allows an analysis of the productiveness of power as well as its repressive functions. From this perspective one might also begin to appreciate how it may well make sense to speak of the body as having a history.

The body

There is probably no simple explanation for the recent proliferation of writings concerning the body. Clearly, Foucault's work has been influential in making the body a favoured subject for analysis in contemporary philosophy, sociology and anthropology. However, the impact of feminist theory in the social sciences has no less a claim to credit for bringing the body into the limelight. The difficulties encountered by primarily middle-class women, who have had the greatest access to 'equality' in the public sphere, may well have served as a catalyst for feminist reflections on the body.

One response to the differential powers and capacities of women and men in the context of public life is to claim that women just are biologically disadvantaged relative to men. From this perspective it seems crucial to call for the further erosion of the reproductive differences between the sexes by way of advances in medical science. On this view, social reform can only achieve so much, leaving the rectification of the remaining determinations of women's situation to the increase in control over nature, that is, biology. Simone de Beauvoir retains the doubtful privilege of being the clearest exponent of this view. In the 1970s, Shulamith Firestone's *The Dialectic of Sex* was influential in perpetuating the view that science could fulfil a liberating role for women.[19] Both theorists assumed that the specificity of the reproductive body must be overcome if sexual equality is to be realized.

An alternative response to questions of corporeal specificity is to claim that women should not aspire to be 'like men'. Interestingly, this response comes from both feminists and anti-feminists alike.[20] Recent feminist research suggests that the history of Western thought shows a deep hatred and fear of the body.[21] This somatophobia is understood by some feminists to be specifically masculine and intimately related to gynophobia and misogyny.[22] In response to this negative attitude towards the body and women, some feminists advocate the affirmation and celebration of women's bodies and their capacity to recreate and nurture. In its strongest form this view argues that the specific capacities and powers of women's bodies imply an essential difference between men and women, where women may be presented as essentially peace-loving, 'biophilic' or caring, and men as essentially aggressive, 'necrophilic' or selfish.[23] These theorists argue that there is an essential sexual difference which should be retained, not eroded by scientific intervention.

These two responses to women's corporeal specificity are often taken to exhaust what has been termed the 'sexual equality versus sexual difference debate'. Yet both responses are caught up within the same paradigm. Both understand the body as a given biological entity which either has or does not have certain ahistorical characteristics and capacities. To this extent, the sexual difference versus sexual equality debate is located within a framework which assumes a body/mind, nature/culture dualism. The different responses are both in answer to the question of which should be given priority: the mind or the body, nature or culture.

An alternative view of the body and power might refuse this dualistic manner of articulating the issue of sexual difference. Specifically, to claim a history for the body involves taking seriously the ways in which diet, environment and the typical activities of a body may vary historically and create its capacities, its desires and its actual material form.[24] The body of a woman confined to the role of wife/mother/domestic worker, for example, is invested with particular desires, capacities and forms that have little in common with the body of a female Olympic athlete. In this case biological commonality fails to account for the specificity of these two bodies. Indeed, the female Olympic athlete may have more in common with a male Olympic athlete than with one confined to the role of wife/ mother. (This is not to deny that some women are both wives/mothers and Olympic athletes.) This commonality is not simply at the level of interests or desires but at the level of the actual form and capacities of the body. By drawing attention to the context in which bodies move and recreate themselves, we also draw attention to the complex dialectic between bodies and their environments. If the body is granted a history then traditional associations between the female body and the domestic sphere and the male body and the public sphere can be acknowledged as historical realities, which have historical effects, without resorting to biological essentialism. The present capacities of female bodies are, by and large, very different from the present capacities of male bodies. It is important to create the means of articulating the historical realities of sexual difference without thereby reifying these differences. Rather, what is required is an account of the ways in which the typical spheres of movement of men and women and their respective activities construct and recreate particular kinds of body to perform particular kinds of task. This sort of analysis is necessary if the historical effects of the ways in which power constructs bodies are to be understood and challenged.[25]

local construct of body

This would involve not simply a study of how men and women become masculine and feminine subjects but how bodies become marked as male and female. Again, Foucault made this point well, arguing that what is needed is

> an analysis in which the biological and the historical are not consecutive to one another, as in the evolutionism of the first sociologists, but are bound together in an increasingly complex fashion in accordance with the development of the modern technologies of power that take life as their objective. Hence, I do not envisage a 'history of mentalities' that would take account of bodies only through the manner in which they have been perceived and given meaning and value; but a 'history of bodies' and the manner in which what is most material and most vital in them has been invested.[26]

Foucault's studies tend to concentrate on the history of the construction of male bodies and are not forthcoming on the question of sexual difference.[27] However, a critical use of psychoanalytic theory, in particular the theory of the body image, in conjunction with Foucault's analysis of power can provide some very useful insights in this context.

The works of Jacques Lacan, Maurice Merleau-Ponty and Paul Schilder offer an account of the body image which posits that a body is not properly a human body, that is, a human subject or individual, unless it has an image of itself as a discrete entity, or as a gestalt.[28] It is this orientation of one's body in space, and in relation to other bodies, that provides a perspective on the world that is assumed in the constitution of the signifying subject. Lacan, in particular, presents the emergence of this gestalt as in some sense genetic. His famous 'Mirror Stage' paper, for example, offers ethological evidence for the identificatory effect produced by images and movements of others of the same species and even images and movements which merely simulate those of the species in question.[29] Lacan takes this 'homeomorphic identification' to be at the origin of an organism's orientation towards its own species. It would seem that it is this genetic basis of his account of the mirror stage that allows him, even while stressing the cultural specificity of body images, to assert the 'natural' dominance of the penis in the shaping of the gestalt.[30]

Foucault's historically dynamic account of the manner in which the micropolitical operations of power produce socially appropriate bodies offers an alternative to Lacan's ethological account. Using Foucault's approach, the imaginary body can be posited as an effect of socially and historically specific practices: an effect, that is, not of genetics but of relations of power. It would be beside the point to insist that, none the less, this imaginary body is in fact the anatomical body overlaid by culture, since the anatomical body is itself a theoretical object for the discourse of anatomy which is produced by human beings in culture. There is a regress involved in positing the anatomical body as the touchstone for cultural bodies since it is a particular culture which chooses to represent bodies anatomically. Another culture might take the clan totem as the essence or truth of particular bodies. The human body is always a signified body and as such cannot be understood as a 'neutral object' upon which science may construct 'true' discourses. The *human* body and its history presuppose each other.

This conception of the imaginary body may provide the framework in which we can give an account of how power, domination and sexual difference intersect in the lived experience of men and women. Gender itself may be understood on this model not as the effect of ideology or cultural values but as the way in which power takes hold of and constructs bodies in particular ways. Significantly, the sexed body can no longer be conceived as the unproblematic biological and factual base upon which gender is inscribed, but must itself be recognized as constructed by discourses and practices that take the body both as their target and as their vehicle of expression. Power is not then reducible to what is imposed, from above, on naturally differentiated male and female bodies, but is also constitutive of those bodies, in so far as they are constituted as male and female.

Shifting the analysis of the operations of power to this microlevel of bodies and their powers and capacities has an interesting effect when one turns to a consideration of the political body. If we understand the masculinity or maleness of the political body and the public sphere as an *arbitrary* historical fact about the genesis of states, then sexual equality should be achievable provided we ensure that women have equal access to the political body and the public sphere. However, the relation between the public sphere and male bodies is not an arbitrary one. The political body was conceived historically as the organization of many bodies into one body which would itself enhance and intensify the powers and capacities of specifically male bodies.[31]

Female embodiment as it is currently lived is itself a barrier to women's 'equal' participation in sociopolitical life. Suppose our body politic were one which was created for the enhancement and intensification of women's historical and present capacities. The primary aim of such a body politic might be to foster conditions for the healthy reproduction of its members. If this were the case, then presumably some men would now be demanding that medical science provide ways for them to overcome their 'natural' or biological disadvantages, by inventing, for example, means by which they could lactate. This may seem a far-fetched suggestion, but it nevertheless makes the point that a biological disadvantage can be posited as such only in a cultural context.

Difference

The crux of the issue of difference as it is understood here is that difference does not have to do with biological 'facts' so much as with the manner in which culture marks bodies and creates specific conditions in which they live and recreate themselves. It is beside the point to 'grant' equal access to women and others excluded from the traditional body politic, since this amounts to 'granting' access to the body politic and the public sphere in terms of an individual's ability to emulate those powers and capacities that have, in a context of male/masculine privilege, been deemed valuable by that sphere. The present and future enhancement of the powers and capacities of women must take account of the ways in which their bodies are presently constituted.

Clearly, the sketch of power and bodies that has been offered here is not one which would lend itself to an understanding of sexual difference in terms of essentialism or biologism. The female body cannot provide the ontological foundation required by those who assert an essential sexual difference. On the contrary, it is the construction of biological discourse as being able to provide this status that is in need of analysis. The cluster of terms 'the female body', 'femininity' and 'woman' needs to be analysed in terms of its historical and discursive associations. If discourses cannot be deemed 'outside', or apart from, power relations then their analysis becomes crucial to an analysis of power. This is why language, signifying practices and discourses have become central stakes in feminist struggles.

Writing itself is a political issue and a political practice for many contemporary feminists. For this reason it is inappropriate to reduce the project of *écriture féminine* to an essentialist strategy. The 'difference' which this form of writing seeks to promote is a difference rooted not in biology but rather in discourse – including biological discourses. It is unhelpful to quibble over whether this writing is an attempt to 'write the female body' or to 'write femininity', since it is no longer clear what this distinction amounts to.[32] What is clear is that discourses, such as Lacanian psychoanalysis, and social practices, such as marriage, construct female and male bodies in ways that constitute and validate the power relations between men and women.

The account of female sexuality offered by Lacanian psychoanalysis constructs female bodies as lacking or castrated and male bodies as full or phallic. This construction tells of a power relation where the actual understanding of sexual difference implies a passive/active relation. Writing of a sexuality that is not simply the inverse or the complement of male sexuality presents a discursive challenge to the traditional psychoanalytic understanding of sexual difference, where difference is exhausted by phallic presence or absence. Irigaray's writing of the 'two lips' of feminine morphology is an active engagement with the construction of what here has been called the imaginary body. It is not an attempt to construct a 'true' theory of sexual difference, starting from the foundation of female biology. Rather, it is a challenge to the traditional construction of feminine morphology where the bodies of women are seen as receptacles for masculine completeness. At the same time as Irigaray's writing offers a challenge to traditional conceptions of women, it introduces the possibility of *dialogue* between men and women in place of the monological pronouncements made by men over the mute body of the (female) hysteric.[33]

Legal practices and discourses surrounding marriage also assume this conception of sexual difference by allotting conjugal rights to the (active) male over the body of the (passive) female. Significantly, the act which is taken to consummate marriage is legally defined as an act performed by a man on a woman. Needless to say, these legal, psychoanalytic and social understandings of the female body have been articulated from the perspective of male writers, who take it upon themselves to represent women, femaleness and femininity. From this perspective, it is not surprising that women are represented as pale shadows and incomplete complements to the more excellent type: 'man'. The project of *écriture féminine* involves challenging the masculine monopoly on the construction of femininity, the female body and woman. It also involves a rejection of the notion that there can be a theory of woman, for this would be to accept that woman *is* some (*one*) thing.

The works of Luce Irigaray, Hélène Cixous and Adrienne Rich are each in their own ways involved in investigating the manner in which women's bodies are constructed and lived in culture.[34] Each could be seen to be writing from an embodied perspective about the female body, femininity and women. Yet none of these writers claim to *represent* (all) women or the multiplicity of women's experiences. This would be for them to take up a masculine attitude in relation to women. Significantly, all three writers critically address the dualisms which have dominated Western thought. Addressing constructions of the feminine in history necessarily involves addressing those terms which have been associated with femininity: the body, emotion, and so on. When Irigaray, for example, writes of the 'repression of the feminine', she is also alluding to the repression of the body and passion in Western thought. To attempt to 'write' the repressed side of these dualisms is not, necessarily, to be working for the reversal of the traditional values associated with each but rather to unbalance or disarrange the discourses in which these dualisms operate. It is to create new conditions for the articulation of difference.

To continue to understand 'difference feminism' as the obverse of 'equality feminism' would be to miss entirely the point of this essay. Difference, as it has been presented here, is not concerned with privileging an essentially biological difference between the sexes. Rather, it is concerned with the mechanisms by which bodies are recognized as different only in so far as they are constructed as possessing or lacking some socially privileged quality or qualities. What is crucial in our current context is the thorough interrogation of the means by which bodies become invested with differences which are then taken to be fundamental ontological differences. Differences as well as commonality must be respected among those who have historically been excluded from speech/writing and are now struggling for expression. If bodies and their powers and capacities are invested in multiple ways, then accordingly their struggles will be multiple.

The conception of difference offered here is not one which seeks to construct a dualistic theory of an essential sexual difference. Rather, it entertains a multiplicity of differences. To insist on sexual difference as the fundamental and eternally immutable difference would be to take for granted the intricate and pervasive ways in which patriarchal culture has made that difference its insignia.

Notes

This chapter was originally published in *Destabilizing Theory: Contemporary Feminist Debates*, ed. M. Barrett and A. Phillips, Cambridge, Polity Press, 1992.

1 An excellent collection of essays which offers an overview of feminist perspectives on political theory from Plato to Habermas is M.L. Shanley and C. Pateman, eds., *Feminist Interpretations and Political Theory*, Cambridge, Polity Press, 1991.
2 See M. Gatens, *Feminism and Philosophy: Perspectives on Difference and Equality*, Cambridge, Polity Press, 1991, for a detailed defence of this view.
3 See G. Lloyd, *The Man of Reason: 'Male' and 'Female' in Western Philosophy*, London, Methuen, 1984; J. Grimshaw, *Feminist Philosophers: Women's*

Perspectives on Philosophical Traditions, Brighton, Harvester, 1986, esp. ch. 2; M. Le Dœuff, *The Philosophical Imaginary*, London, Athlone, 1989.

4 C. Pateman, *The Sexual Contract*, Cambridge, Polity Press, 1988, p. 96.

5 S. Moller Okin's critique of John Rawls's influential *A Theory of Justice* provides a good example of this approach. See her 'John Rawls: Justice as Fairness – For Whom?', in M.L. Shanley and C. Pateman, eds., *Feminist Interpretations and Political Theory*, Cambridge, Polity Press, 1991, pp. 181–98.

6 For example, Andrea Dworkin has stated 'I think that the situation of women is basically ahistorical.' Quoted in Pateman, *The Sexual Contract*, p. 236, n. 24.

7 S. de Beauvoir, *The Second Sex*, Harmondsworth, Penguin, 1975, p. 96.

8 M. Le Dœuff, 'Women and Philosophy', *Radical Philosophy*, no. 17 (1977), pp. 2–11.

9 I have used a Spinozistic approach in Chapter 4, 'Towards a Feminist Philosophy of the Body'. G. Lloyd has also used Spinoza's monist theory of existence to appraise the sex/gender distinction critically in 'Woman as Other: Sex, Gender and Subjectivity', *Australian Feminist Studies*, no. 10 (1989), pp. 13–22.

10 See L. Althusser, 'Ideology and Ideological State Apparatuses', in *Lenin and Philosophy, and Other Essays*, London, New Left Books, 1977, pp. 121–73.

11 I have argued against the possibility of including women in liberal society, *on an equal footing with men*, in *Feminism and Philosophy*, esp. ch. 2.

12 See C. di Stefano, 'Masculine Marx', in M.L. Shanley and C. Pateman, eds., *Feminist Interpretations and Political Theory*, Cambridge, Polity, 1991, pp. 146–63.

13 J. Mitchell, *Psychoanalysis and Feminism*, Harmondsworth, Penguin, 1974.

14 K. Millett, *Sexual Politics*, London, Granada, 1972, p. 31.

15 For a discussion of the difficulties involved in the sex/gender distinction see Chapter 1, 'A Critique of the Sex/Gender Distinction'.

16 See, for example, M. Foucault, *The History of Sexuality*, vol. I, London, Allen Lane, 1978, pt. 2, chs. 1, 2 and pt. 4, ch. 2.

17 M. Foucault, *Power/Knowledge*, C. Gordon, ed., Brighton, Harvester Press, 1980, p. 118.

18 Ibid., p. 98.

19 S. Firestone, *The Dialectic of Sex*, New York, Bantam Books, 1970.

20 For an example of the former, see M. Daly, *Gyn/Ecology: The Metaethics of Radical Feminism*, Boston, Mass., Beacon Press, 1978; and for one of the latter, see C. McMillan, *Women, Reason and Nature*, Oxford, Basil Blackwell, 1982.

21 See E. Spelman, 'Woman as Body: Ancient and Contemporary Views', *Feminist Studies*, vol. 8, no. 1 (1982), pp. 109–31.

22 See Daly, *Gyn/Ecology*, pp. 109–12.

23 Ibid., pp. 61–2.

24 See M. Foucault, 'Nietzsche, Genealogy, History', in *Language, Counter-Memory, Practice*, ed. D. Bouchard, Ithaca, Cornell University Press, 1977, pp. 139–64.

25 See C. Gallagher and T. Laqueur, eds., *The Making of the Modern Body*, Berkeley, University of California Press, 1987.

26 Foucault, *History of Sexuality*, vol. I, p. 152.

27 For a sympathetic feminist reading of Foucault's work, see J. Sawicki, 'Foucault and Feminism: Toward a Politics of Difference', in M.L. Shanley and C. Pateman, eds., *Feminist Interpretations and Political Theory*, Cambridge, Polity, 1991, pp. 217–31.

28 See J. Lacan, 'Some Reflections on the Ego', *International Journal of Psycho-analysis*, vol. 34 (1953), pp. 11–17; J. Lacan, 'The Mirror Stage', in *Ecrits*, London, Tavistock, 1977, pp. 1–7; M. Merleau-Ponty, 'The Child's Relations with Others', in *The Primacy of Perception*, ed. J.M. Edie, Evanston, Ill., Northwestern University Press, 1964, pp. 96–155; P. Schilder, *The Image and Appearance of the Human Body*, New York, International Universities Press, 1978.

29 Lacan writes: 'it is a necessary condition for the maturation of the gonad of the female pigeon that it should see another member of its species, of either sex; so sufficient in itself is this condition that the desired effect may be obtained merely by placing the individual within reach of the field of reflection of a mirror. Similarly, in the case of the migratory locust, the transition within a generation from the solitary to the gregarious form can be obtained by exposing the individual, at a certain stage, to the exclusively visual action of a similar image, provided it is animated by movements of a style sufficiently close to that characteristic of the species' ('Mirror Stage', p. 3).

30 Lacan, 'Some Reflections', p. 13.

31 For a feminist account of the aims of the masculine political body, see Pateman, *Sexual Contract*, ch. 4; and this volume, Chapter 2, 'Corporeal Representation in/and the Body Politic'.

32 See, for example, T. Moi's arguments in *Sexual/Textual Politics*, London, Methuen, 1985, pp. 102–26, which misunderstands the conception of difference employed by Cixous.

33 See, for example, the writings of Freud and Breuer on hysteria and femininity in volume II of *The Standard Edition of the Complete Psychological Works of Sigmund Freud*, ed. J. Strachey, London, Hogarth Press, 1978.

34 See L. Irigaray, *This Sex Which is Not One*, Ithaca, Cornell University Press, 1985; H. Cixous, 'Castration or Decapitation?', *Signs*, vol. 7, no. 1 (1981), pp. 41–55; A. Rich, *Blood, Bread and Poetry*, London, Virago, 1987.

6 Contracting sex

Essence, genealogy, desire

It is not surprising that feminist scholars have been concerned with history, narratives and stories about our past: contesting descriptions of what we have been and done is a crucial aspect of taking an active role in the production of culture. This has involved both criticism of traditional or orthodox histories – which, at best, have given marginal status to the place of women in history – and the construction of an alternative women's history. Some feminist historians, dissatisfied with the idea that one may unproblematically present 'women's history' are engaged in a project of charting a genealogy of the category 'woman' or 'women'.[1] On this approach 'women' itself is understood to have a history, a genealogy, a 'line of descent'. Clearly, this is a very different sort of project from that practised by orthodox historians. The latter assume that 'women' and 'woman' have a stable referent across the centuries, and so women have a traceable linear history that is uniquely their own. By contrast, a genealogical approach asks: how has 'woman'/'women' functioned as a discursive category throughout history? This approach to our past has much in common with what Nietzsche called 'critical history'.

Critical history can be described as a 'diagnostic history of the present', that is, critical history is genealogy which 'traces the history of the present in order to undermine its self-evidences and to open possibilities for the enhancement of life'.[2] It takes nothing for granted – especially not that which appears most 'obvious' to common sense. Rather than enquiring: what is the 'origin' or 'cause' of any particular state of affairs or way of life, genealogy as critical history asks what form of life has been supported or made possible by this conception of a people, a culture, a body politic.

Genealogy investigates:

> not the chronological process of what happened in time, but the historical record, the narrative account of what happened in time. Therefore, Nietzsche is concerned with *the way people record, narrate, and explain their own past and with evaluating the effects of various types of historical narration upon life.*[3]

According to Nietzsche, what underlies such narratives is desire, a (non-personal) will to power or to life. The effects on life, on our present, of these narratives will, in large part, be a function of the nature of that will. Is it a creative and active will or one which is resentful and revengeful? In this sense, all history and all narrative is necessarily 'invested'.

Alasdair MacIntyre, for one, has criticized this notion of genealogy, claiming that it is at this juncture of Nietzsche's thought that he is most open to the accusation of complicity with fascistic politics and practices.[4] Whilst forgetting (in some form) is necessary for life,[5] it is in other forms morally repugnant (MacIntyre mentions both Heidegger and Paul de Man in this context).[6]

Remembering and forgetting are emotionally very loaded terms in the context of groups that have been oppressed or persecuted. Jews, blacks, women have been (and often still are) treated very badly merely by virtue of their membership of the group or 'type' 'Jew', 'Black', 'Woman'. These groups have been subject to various pogroms: the Holocaust, mass lynchings and witch-hunts. Remembering such things involves great pain which could be alleviated by acts of forgetting. Yet there are some things that cannot and should not be forgotten. But *how* they are remembered is important for the present and the future. We need to understand and remember how we became what we are, not in order to live what we have become as our 'truth' but rather as our conditions of possibility for that which we may become. This notion of becoming something other than what we presently are is after all the *sine qua non* of movements for social change. Such movements come to history or philosophy with questions and desires arising from present and past social practices. In this sense their orientation is a self-consciously political or practical one. According to Rajchman, a 'modern practical philosophy' is one 'which, instead of attempting to determine what we should do on the basis of what we essentially are, attempts, by analyzing who we have been constituted to be, to ask what we might become.'[7] This is precisely not to understand one's identity as a given, an a priori, in short an *essence*.

Essentialism: whose risk?

Much contemporary feminist theory is concerned with this question of essentialism, which is typically run together in a confused fashion with biologism and a host of other '-isms'.[8] Some argue that the 'risk' of essentialism must be taken; others that it be adopted 'strategically'.[9] Rosi Braidotti goes so far as to state, in the imperative mode, that 'a feminist woman theoretician who is interested in thinking about sexual difference and the feminine today cannot afford not to be essentialist.'[10] Most theorists who endorse this claim do not pursue the economic, legal, political and ethical implications of such a strategic deployment. Joan Scott has forcefully demonstrated the disastrous consequences for women of exclusively adopting either the equality (constructivist) or the difference (essentialist) stance. Scott analyses the well-known *North American Sears v. Equal Employment Opportunities Commission* case.[11] Not only was essentialism shown to be *bad strategy*, in that it had dire economic consequences for a particular group of women, it also set a dangerous legal precedent. As Scott notes:

> According to the judge, because difference was real and fundamental, it could explain statistical variations in Sears' hiring. Discrimination was redefined as simply recognition of 'natural' difference (however culturally or historically produced), fitting in nicely with the logic of Reagan conservatism. Difference was substituted for inequality, the appropriate antithesis of equality, becoming inequality's explanation and legitimation. The judge's decision illustrates a process literary scholar Naomi Schor has described in another context: it 'essentializes difference and naturalizes social inequity'.[12]

There are other contexts in which the promotion of an essentialized view of women and men has had equally undesirable effects. Both Catharine MacKinnon and Andrea Dworkin propose essentialized conceptions of female and male sexualities that, if encoded in the law, will entrench conservative and destructive active/passive notions of male and female embodiment. As Michel Foucault has convincingly shown, the legal and medical regulation of human behaviour tends to produce subjects who 'recognize' themselves in these regulative discourses.[13] The strategy of essentialism is a strategy that has unwelcome effects because of the manner in which institutionally encoded essentialisms in turn play an active part in the construction of subjects.

Both MacKinnon and Dworkin appear oblivious to the effects that their own discourses on sexuality have on the ongoing construction of masculine and feminine identities.[14] On the Dworkin/MacKinnon view of heterosexuality, sexual ethics is always already foredoomed. MacKinnon, in an article published in the influential journal *Ethics*, tells us that 'forcible violation of women is the essence of sex'.[15] Her collaborator Dworkin offers a description of heterosexual intercourse that perhaps makes it clearer why sex can only ever be 'violation' for women:

> He has to *push in past boundaries*. There is the outline of a body, distinct, separate, *its integrity an illusion*, a tragic deception, because unseen there is a slit between the legs, and he has to push into it. There is never a real privacy of the body that can coexist with intercourse: with being entered. The vagina itself is muscled and the muscles have to be pushed apart. The thrusting is *persistent invasion*. She is opened up, split down the centre. She is *occupied* – physically, internally, in her privacy.[16]

Stories about sexuality are themselves histories of the body and its construction. The stories told by MacKinnon and Dworkin are striking for the frequency with which they employ metaphors of war and invasion: the male body is depicted as a weapon-bearing invader and the female body as invaded or occupied territory. These are the same body morphologies which have played a distinctive part in the construction of notions of the 'ideal' citizen, which in turn have justified the exclusion of certain bodies from citizenship. Women's bodies historically have been seen as unfit for citizenship. Women's bodies are often likened to territories whose borders cannot be defended.[17]

Political bodies

It is this notion of the 'ideal' citizen and the political significance of conceptions of male and female embodiment that will concern me for the remainder of this paper. My concern is the political and ethical consequences of adopting essentialist conceptions of men and women in the context of political theory. My focus will be on Carole Pateman's *The Sexual Contract*. Pateman's concern there is with what she takes to be the contractual underpinnings of '[t]he major institutional bonds of civil society – citizenship, employment and marriage'[18] – which structure Western capitalist democracies. Pateman argues that modern social contract theory 'tells a story of masculine political birth', in which the

> natural paternal body of Filmer's patriarchy is metaphorically put to death by the contract theorists, but the artificial body that replaces it is a construct of the mind, not the creation of a political community by real people. The birth of a human child can produce a new male or female, whereas the creation of civil society produces a social body fashioned after the image of only one of the two bodies of humankind, or, more exactly, after the image of the civil individual who is constituted through the original contract.[19]

Pateman presents a challenge to the notion that the social contract institutes liberty and equality for all. Drawing attention to the third element in the Enlightenment catchcry, she argues that the new order is a *fraternal* order. That it is Locke who emerges from this history as triumphant, rather than the patriarchalist Filmer, should not lead us to assume that patriarchy is thereby defeated. On the contrary, the victory of the sons over the father introduces a new form of patriarchy. According to Pateman, 'modern patriarchy is fraternal in form and the original contract is a fraternal pact.'[20] Using a variety of historical sources (including Hobbes, Rousseau, Hegel, Kant and Freud), Pateman argues that in the story of the brothers' defeat of the father, a crucial element is missing from the narrative. In addition to the fraternal pact made between the brothers, there is another pact, one which ensures that each brother has access to a woman. In this way patriarchal sex-right, which had been wrested away from the father 'is extended to all the brothers through the law of exogamy (kinship). That is, the brothers *make a sexual contract*.'[21] What Pateman variously calls 'patriarchal right', 'sex-right' or 'conjugal right' is prerequisite to membership in the fraternity as 'only men who stand to each other as free and equal masters of "families" can take part in the social contract.'[22]

In spite of Chantal Mouffe's claims, I do not think that Pateman's text can consistently be characterized as essentialist.[23] Rather, her text instantiates the very impasses that are the concern of this chapter: those of essentialism vs. constructionism or difference vs. equality. In *The Sexual Contract* these binary oppositions are organized by a further binary, that of contracts versus institutions. Some political theorists suppose that contracts actually create, constitute or give rise to institutions; others claim that specific institutional arrangements give rise to specific sorts of contract. Still others present the view that contract theory, at least in the political realm, is merely a hypothetical device used to justify political authority. This troubled relation between contracts and institutions repeats the very impasses mentioned above. Do contracts determine the sorts of institution with which we live or, alternatively, do such institutions determine which sorts of contract are formulated? The question is one which presents a quandary to the political theorist, namely, whether to analyse contemporary institutions as constitutive or as reflective of contractual arrangements.

In the context of Pateman's *The Sexual Contract*, this confusion takes on a certain urgency. Does the sexual contract create institutions that are gendered, or is *institutionalized* gender necessarily assumed by the very notion of a sexual contract? This problem then loops back to reveal its complicity with those other troublesome binaries. The theorization of women's place in political society returns us to the same issues, although we approach them from a different path. What does it mean to claim that the sexual contract is the 'true origin' of political right?[24] Or, what are the conditions of possibility for this claim? One of its conditions must be the assumption of an immutable notion of 'woman' and 'man', along with an eternal natural antagonism in their relations. Something like this assumption must be in place for it to appear plausible that the sexual contract is the origin of contemporary sociopolitical life.[25] In the remainder of this chapter, I will propose that such an immutable notion of 'woman' is untenable. Futhermore, I will argue that as 'strategy' or as purported 'truth' it shuts down possible avenues of social and political experimentation. If we accept the untenability of such a notion then it follows that the positing of the sexual contract as an originary contract assumes precisely that which it purports to be attempting to explain. In other words, such arguments, or perhaps more appropriately, narratives, can be shown to transpose to the *beginning* of the story that which properly belongs at *the end*. This, in turn, is to treat historical effects (aspects of present relations between the sexes) as if they were historical causes.

However, Pateman's reading of the social contract story as one which tells the origin of contemporary fraternal patriarchy stands in an uneasy relation with her analysis of actually existing contemporary societies based on free contract. It is by no means clear that Pateman's retelling of the sexual/social contract story can consistently be characterized in essentialist terms. There are points in her text where she seems to be describing the views of others in these terms rather than putting forward a view of natural and immutable sexual difference herself. However, there are other points in her text where she does appear to ground her claims concerning the very different civil and private status of women and men in their different biologies. Much hangs on which view one adopts, since very different strategies and policies for social change would follow in each case. Our views on whether present differences between the sexes are largely constructed or largely natural, would (or at least should) make an enormous difference to the manner in which we formulate policies which seek to promote women's fair treatment in the major social institutions of citizenship, employment and marriage. Indeed, this is surely one of the main thrusts of Pateman's argument: that contractarianism operates (always and everywhere) to the disadvantage of women because they are 'not incorporated [into the civil order] as "individuals" but as women'.[26] This quotation nicely captures the multivalent status of 'women' in the text. To use the term 'incorporated' implies that a stable entity, 'women', preexists any given civil order.

An alternative view might claim that part of what it means to be a woman in contemporary society is to stand in some particular relation to the civil order. That is, it is arguable that what it means to be a 'woman' is constituted or constructed, at least in part, by her economic, social and political placement relative to men. Pateman has arguably already responded to this point: '[t]o draw out the way in which the meaning of "men" and "women" has *helped structure* major social institutions is not to fall back on purely natural categories'.[27] Perhaps – but it is to neglect to question the category of sexual difference itself (men/women). This, in turn, assumes a linear chain of causality, where sexual difference, sexual relations and the sexual contract are the successive links which together enchain us all in the tyranny of our current social and political institutions. However, if 'women' and 'men' are themselves historical and unstable,[28] rather than natural categories then this throws into question the force of 'helped structure' in the above quotation. Our culturally and historically variable understandings of what it is to be a man or a woman, what the terms 'men' and 'women' mean, are also affected by the 'major social institutions' through which and in which we live our lives. Moreover, not only are our institutions plastic but our past is open to constant revision and retelling as our understandings of how we became what we are change. In this sense, one is confronted not so much with a 'chain of necessity', relentlessly linking the past with the present, as with competing 'sets of narratives' which are open to contestation.

The primal scene

Reading the 'primal scene' of patriarchal civil society as a primordial rape (of a woman by a man) obviously has effects on how one then theorizes the political. Pateman's reading of the mythical transition from the state of nature to civil society is a case in point. When referring to the equal capacity of men and women in the Hobbesian state of nature, Pateman argues that it follows from Hobbes' account

> that sexual relations can take place *only under two* circumstances; either a man and woman mutually agree (contract) to have sexual intercourse, or a man, through some strategem, is able to overpower a woman and take her by force, though she also has the capacity to retaliate and kill him.[29]

Perhaps women in the state of nature possess only a reactive form of sexual desire? This seems implausible. Moreover, such assumptions import into the hypothetical origins of sexual relations much that belongs properly in patriarchal society. Again, I think this shows that the causal relation from nature to society and from biology to the lived significance of sexual difference is one that is retrospectively constructed from the present standpoint of gender as constituted through institutions. This present standpoint is already at work in the supposed original contract. Pateman reads the traditional understanding of adult human sexuality, where male = active and female = passive (or at most re-active), back into the state of nature. Implicit in Pateman's reading of Hobbes is the view that if men cannot get sex by consent then rape will do. Women are able to console themselves for this 'fact' only by 'retaliation', which in civil society means through the law courts rather than the more immediate satisfaction that can be had, apparently, in the state of nature. As Sharon Marcus argues:

> To take male violence or female vulnerability as the first and last instances in any explanation of rape is to make the identities of rapist and raped preexist the rape itself.[30]

Marcus further suggests a definition of rape that does not assume that rape has always already happened:

> Rape could best be defined as a sexualized and gendered attack which imposes sexual difference along the lines of violence. Rape engenders a sexualized female body defined as a wound, a body excluded from subject–subject violence, from the ability to engage in a fair fight. Rapists do not beat women at the game of violence, but aim to exclude us from playing it altogether.[31]

In previous chapters I have argued that gender as it is lived in social institutions is more concerned with *imaginary* bodies than with a natural or presocial body. How are men's and women's body morphologies lived and experienced in the present? And how do such morphologies enable the 'naturalizing' of certain sorts of practices, for example, rape? Pateman offers one description in the course of her discussion of the creation of political right:

> [t]he body of the 'individual' is very different from women's bodies. His body is *tightly enclosed within boundaries*, but women's bodies are *permeable, their contours change shape* and they are subject to cyclical processes. All these differences are summed up in the natural bodily process of birth.[32]

These descriptions are, of course, consonant with the representation of men's bodies as impenetrable and inviolable in contrast with the penetrability and violability of women's bodies that was taken to characterize sexual relations in the state of nature. The question 'Are these *natural* differences that are represented and given social and political meanings in civil society or are they meanings of embodiment which are structured by our social and political institutions?' is not helpful in this context. The question that needs to be asked concerns not the referent (the male body or the female body) but the conditions of referentiality for the utterance of meaningful statements about sexual relations (in their broadest sense). Foucault's point that 'there is never an *interpretandum* which is not already an *interpretans*'[33] renders the quest for origins or for the 'pure' referent epistemically bankrupt.

Freud has more in common with Nietzsche and Foucault than is commonly recognized. Freud too shares the view that there is no pure *interpretandum*. Pateman's reading of the psychoanalytic notion of the primal scene is tellingly incomplete. Pateman states that traditional stories concerning the original contract do not take into account that 'the story is about masculinity and femininity and about the *political significance of physical (natural) sexual difference* – or that the structure of civil society *reflects* the division between the sexes'.[34] Again one feels compelled to question the view of causality here. One could claim that sexual difference is *made* politically significant and that civil society does not simply passively reflect, but actively constructs the division between the sexes. Pateman's reconstruction of the polity as sexed stresses a linear determinism from nature to the civil, from the bodies of men and women to their political significance. What this reconstruction does, above all else, is to privilege essence over historical existence and contract over institutions. It does not take institutions seriously except as the *products* of contracts. Thus, time and history are collapsed into a primal and originary moment that itself can exist only in and through time and history.

By contrast, the method of psychoanalysis does not assume a deterministic linear causality in the human psyche. In relation to the primal scene,[35] the task of the analyst is to expose to the analysand the manner in which the primal scene is grasped and interpreted through a *deferred action*;[36] that is, the way in which past experiences or impressions are constantly revised in the light of new experiences. One could take it as an axiom of psychoanalytic theory that 'there is never an *interpretandum* that is not already an *interpretans*'. This constant rearrangement and retranscription of past events lends to human memory and human history a disturbing, necessarily *fictive* status. Personal, social and political meanings are built up bricolage-fashion, and any discernable patterns or overall sense are necessarily tentative and provisional.

From this perspective, the positing of 'true' origins or 'original deeds' lacks any fixed, ontological force. This does not, however, open the floodgates to a radical relativism, nor does it leave history entirely open to rewriting to suit the political climate of the day. Rather, it is to acknowledge that history is a highly contested field. As Joan Scott states:

> What counts as experience is neither self-evident nor straightforward; it is always contested, always therefore political. The study of experience, therefore, must call into question its originary status in historical explanation. This will happen when historians take as their project not the reproduction and transmission of knowledge said to be arrived at through experience, but the analysis of the production of that knowledge itself. Such an analysis would constitute a genuinely non-foundational history, one which retains its explanatory power and its interest in change but does not stand on or reproduce naturalized categories. It also cannot guarantee the historian's neutrality, for the choice of which categories to historicize is inevitably 'political', necessarily tied to the historian's recognition of his/her stake in the production of knowledge. Experience is, in this approach, not the origin of our explanation, but that which we want to explain. This kind of approach does not undercut politics by denying the existence of subjects, it instead interrogates the processes of their creation, and, in so doing, refigures history and the role of the historian, and opens new ways for thinking about change.[37]

To acknowledge this is not to forget, deny, disavow or repress past and present experiences of women but to take seriously the issue of *how* we remember and interpret past social and political arrangements that have made us what we are today.

In places (which will be discussed below), Pateman clearly acknowledges this. However, in others, 'origins' are given the status of ontological truths vis-à-vis the meaning of women's bodies and what it means to be a 'woman'. For example, Pateman asserts that 'the wife's subjection *derives* from the fact that she is a woman'[38] and 'the subjection of wives *derives* from their womanhood'[39] and, '[t]he private and public spheres of civil society are separate, *reflecting* the natural order of sexual difference.'[40] The preceding quotations serve to highlight the priority which Pateman's text accords to contract *over* institution and 'origin' over embodied history. For if one were to reverse her order of priority one could claim that the subjection of wives, through the *institution* of marriage, helps to *construct* what it means to be a woman and that the *institutionalization* of the private/ public split in contemporary civil society, helps *constitute* the meaning of sexual difference.

Pateman's notion of the sexual contract, coupled with the idea that women are always incorporated into civil society *as women* (rather than as individuals), is crucially dependent for its coherence on theories of sexual difference that are essentialist. This allows her to condemn contractarianism *per se*, rather than restrict herself to the historical claim that contractarianism has functioned in specific times and specific places to exclude women from full citizenship (the privilege of the individual) even whilst admitting them to the body politic (as women, that is, wives).

It is in the chapter on prostitution that Pateman takes up the social constructivist position most strongly. She writes there, for example, that 'sexual impulses' are always 'culturally mediated'[41] and that the story of the sexual contract reveals social 'construction[s] of what it means to be a man'.[42] The trouble with these sorts of statement is that we have now come full circle and 'causes' have drifted into 'effects'. What was taken to be a cause in mythical time is now posited as effect in real time. This quandary within the text deepens in the face of statements such as:

> [t]he standard readings of the classic texts . . . fail to show in what kind of enterprise the classic theorists were engaged. Instead of interrogating the texts to see how it came about that a certain conception of free political relations became established, the standard interpretations take their departure from the assumption that sexual difference, relations between the sexes and the private sphere are paradigmatically non-political. *The classics are thus read in the light of the construction of modern civil society in the texts themselves!*[43]

True enough – but is Pateman's version of the *sexual* contract any different? Could any contemporary theorist, who holds to an orthodox view of history and who seeks to critically interpret the classics, avoid the confusion between 'political fictions' and 'political realities'? We are inescapably in the present and even the most committed historical realist must acknowledge that we read the past from a present perspective. An ever present temptation, in face of the past, is to endow it with the inevitability of the present. I believe that this is the temptation at work in the prioritizing of contracts over institutions and the primal scene over deferred action. In short, it is what lies behind the desire to know the origin, the first cause, the 'prime mover' of history. It is, understandably, a particularly powerful desire in much feminist theorizing: what is the origin of the structural power which men as a group exert over women as a group? To argue for the *intrinsic* value of the female body, either as a site and source of male sexual pleasure or as a valued resource in the reproduction of labour, offers little by way of a response to this question of origins. The female body is of no more, nor less, *intrinsic* value than the male body. A presocial, premoral being in the state of nature can not be 'pre-scripted' as (male) master or (female) slave. This is to import social and institutional relations into a mythic and retrospectively constructed past.

The narrative temptation in the telling of the story of the sexual contract is to ground the story in a primal scene, an origin. The price to be paid for succumbing to such a temptation is that the primal scene returns to disrupt the narrative by its undecidable status as recollection/memory, on one hand, and as retrospectively constructed through deferred action, on the other. This undecidability leads to further frustration which may be temporarily alleviated by recourse to the 'ontological' foundation of 'the woman's (or man's) body'. Hence, Pateman argues: 'that the body of a *woman* is precisely what is at issue in the contract'[44] and 'forms of subjection *differ* according to the sex of the body'.[45] But in what sense is the body of a woman at issue? And don't 'forms of subjection' act to differentiate one body from the next? Bodies cannot act as ontological touchstones for the differing social and political treatments of 'men' or 'women', since part of what it means to be a man or woman is to live out, or literally embody, the historically variable social and political significances of sexual difference. So, whether we like it or not, we are led back to narrative and history.

Whose desire?

In the core chapter 4 of her text, the 'strategy' which Pateman deploys to avoid the return to competing narratives is to posit the body of woman as always and preculturally permeable and appropriable.[46] An alternative strategy may recognize that the body of woman is at issue as a conceptual battlefield, that is, as a site of struggle over its signification, its social meaning. This is not to be confused with the issue of the referent. Rather, it concerns the *conditions of referentiality*, that is, what are the prevailing conditions for it to be intelligible to refer to 'woman' or 'women' in these ways? The focus on the original contract obscures the ongoing nature of this struggle by reducing causality to the action of the past on the present. To posit essentialism as strategy in this context involves presenting the battle as already lost (for women). One effect of the focus on the *sexual contract as origin* is to limit the range of possible interpretations of bodies and their relations. The claim that 'nature, biology and sex place limits on contract',[47] closes off possibilities that inverting this claim – specific contracts place limits on nature, biology and sex – opens.

I do not see these problems as peculiar to Pateman's text. On the contrary, I think the problem of origins and the ontological status of female and male embodiment is endemic to contemporary feminist theory. It is a tribute to the force and clarity of Pateman's work that they appear there so starkly. I have argued that Pateman's reading of Freud is incomplete. I would further maintain that Pateman undertakes an incomplete genealogy of the stories which have dominated our understandings of our political contexts. This incompleteness coupled with the mood in much contemporary feminist theory to opt for the 'strategic' adoption of essence leads to a closing off of present possibilities.

Pateman's account of the primal scene is quite plausible in terms of that which is repressed in the social contract story, but this does not, as she occasionally implies, reveal to us the secret origin of our (repressed) *history*. The story of the social contract is a masculine fantasy of our origins and, arguably, Pateman has exposed it. However, once exposed it may all too easily be misunderstood as an originary truth rather than symptomatic of the desire of those who have been the narrators of this history. Pateman concludes her argument with the claim that the stories and fictions of social/sexual contracts must be 'cast aside' if we are to 'create a free society in which women are autonomous citizens', since 'modern patriarchy did not begin with a dramatic act of contract'.[48] The relation between text and world, or myth and reality, is here torn asunder – the text is that which must be cast aside. *The Sexual Contract* is a confusing text because Pateman does not manage to link its two parts: that which concerns social contract stories and history[49] with that which concerns contemporary social institutions.[50] The reader is left to assume that what does link these two parts is the primal scene[51] which dramatizes an *essential* sexual difference. But can we cast aside these stories? Are they simply fictions which can be neatly excised from the world of fact? I think that the two parts of *The Sexual Contract* can be linked by undertaking the second moment of genealogy, that is, by asking the question raised earlier: what forms of life have these stories made possible and maintained?

In an important and influential paper Gayatri Spivak put the following question to the history of Western thought: 'What is man that the itinerary of his desire produces such a text?'[52] As Spivak points out, taken on its own this question can lead to distorted and partial responses. For such a question to have any efficacy in the present, one must put it in the context of economics and politics. I suggest that this is germane to the reading offered here of *The Sexual Contract*. This reading holds that the text is a partial genealogy of the narratives that have formed around our socio-political present – it comprises the *first* moment of genealogy. But it is the *second* moment which is crucial – it is the critical moment which asks: what form of life is made possible by the telling of such stories? What is the nature of the will and the desire which drive such narratives? Given that Pateman does not undertake the second, positive and critical, moment one is entitled to re-pose Spivak's question in the following terms: what is feminism (today) that the itinerary of its desire produces such texts?[53]

At this point I would like to return to MacKinnon and Dworkin and ask this question of their texts: what is the nature of the will or the desire that wills or desires that political origins are to be found in an originary penetrative sexual violence? Is not this precisely the fantasy *par excellence* of patriarchal cultures: the phallus as origin of all value, signifier of signifiers? The 'stylus' that 'writes' the meaning of feminine embodiment as 'lack' by the penetration, the making (w)hole, of its flesh? This is indeed to raise the phallus to the status of fetish. Shouldn't the raising of this flag, on this mast, raise in turn at least a giggle amongst feminists? Why concede to the penis the power to push us around, destroy our integrity, 'scribble on us', invade our borders and boundaries and, as Dworkin says, occupy us in our (always already) conquered 'privacy'? What is the desire at work that asserts that 'victims' reports of rape' and 'women's reports of sex . . . look a lot alike'?[54] What type of will, or desire is operative here? Heterosexual intercourse is taken as the *locus classicus* of an essentially violent relation between the sexes. This view raises a number of difficult questions but ones that must be explored if feminism is not to lapse into a political posture of *ressentiment*.[55]

In spite of itself the political effect, at least in the context of feminist theory, of *The Sexual Contract* is to close the present off from its possibilities – it performs what Nietzsche named a 'genealogy of the English kind',[56] which claims to *discover* origins (the primal deed) rather than create a critical history which is a history in the service of the future. This reading of *The Sexual Contract* raises a number of questions about desire and feminist practices. These questions may be combined into one:

> Our question is whether *feminist* politics can prosper without a moral apparatus, whether feminist theorists and activists will give up substituting Truth and morality for politics. Are we willing to engage in overt struggle for position rather than recrimination, to develop our faculties rather than avenge our weaknesses with moral and epistemological gestures, to fight for a world rather than conduct process on the existing one?[57]

If Wendy Brown is to receive the response that her question deserves then feminists need to continue to theorize power as positive *capacity* as well as acknowledge and fight against power that takes the form of dominance and submission. Alongside this feminist rethinking of power we also need to reconceptualize notions of complicity, responsibility and accountability. We must become strong enough to take responsibility for what we are in order to become something else.

Notes

1 See, for example, D. Riley, *Am I that Name? Feminism and the Category of 'Women' in History*, Macmillan, London, 1988; see also Joan W. Scott, 'Experience', in *Feminists Theorize the Political*, ed. Joan W. Scott and Judith Butler, Routledge, New York, 1992.

2 Michael Mahon, *Foucault's Nietzschean Genealogy: Truth, Power and the Subject*, Albany, SUNY Press, 1992, p. 101

3 Mahon, *Foucault's Nietzschean Genealogy*, p. 95, my emphasis.

4 A. MacIntyre, *Three Rival Versions of Moral Enquiry*, Duckworth, London, 1990, chs. 2 and 9.

5 Nietzsche makes this point in *On the Advantage and Disadvantage of History for Life*, trans. Peter Preuss, Hackett Publishing Co., Indianapolis, 1980, in the following terms: 'without forgetting it is quite impossible to *live* at all. Or, to say it more simply yet: *there is a degree of insomnia, of rumination, of historical sense which injures every living thing and finally destroys it, be it a man, a people or a culture*' (p. 10, emphasis in original).

6 MacIntyre, *Three Rival Versions*, pp. 210–13.

7 J. Rajchman, 'Ethics After Foucault', *Social Text*, 13/14 (1986), p. 166

8 See E. Grosz, 'A Note on Essentialism and Difference', in S. Gunew, ed., *Feminist Knowledge: Critique and Construct*, Routledge, London, 1990.

9 For a representative view of the deployment of 'essentialist strategies' in contemporary feminist theory see *differences*, vol. 1, no. 2 (Summer 1989).

10 R. Braidotti, 'The Politics of Ontological Difference', in T. Brennan, ed., *Between Feminism and Psychoanalysis*, Routledge, London, 1989, p. 93.

11 J. Scott, 'Deconstructing Equality-versus-Difference: Or the Uses of Poststructuralist Theory for Feminism', *Feminist Studies*, vol. 14, no. 1 (Spring 1988), See also R. Milkman, 'Women's History and the Sears Case', *Feminist Studies*, vol. 12, no. 2, (Summer 1986).

12 Scott, 'Deconstructing Equality', p. 43.

13 See M. Foucault, *Discipline and Punish: The Birth of the Prison*, trans. Alan Sheridan, London, Allen Lane, 1977, and *The History of Sexuality I: An Introduction*, trans. Robert Hurley, New York, Pantheon, 1978.

14 For a sharp and perceptive challenge to the Dworkin/MacKinnon line, see S. Marcus, 'Fighting Bodies, Fighting Words: A Theory and Politics of Rape Prevention', in J. Butler and J.W. Scott, eds., *Feminists Theorize the Political*, Routledge, New York, 1992.

15 C. MacKinnon, 'Sexuality, Pornography and Method: "Pleasure Under Patriarchy"', *Ethics*, vol. 99, no. 2 (1989), p. 329.

16 A. Dworkin, *Intercourse*, London, Secker & Warburg, 1987, p. 122, my emphasis. It should be noted here that this is *not* offered as a description of *rape*, but of heterosexual *intercourse*. Apart from the obvious military metaphors employed here, I am struck also by the similarity between this vagina's 'refusal of the "outside"', which is seen to threaten the fragile integrity of the female body, and descriptions offered by anorexics of their relation to food and its 'polluting' and 'invasive' significance for them. Is Dworkin's 'muscled vagina' itself anorexic?

17 This notion is brought out clearly in the obvious tension Queen Elizabeth I felt between her sovereign body and her mortal body. Addressing her subjects in the late 1580s she says:

I know I have the body of a weak and feeble woman, but I have the heart and stomach of a king, and a king of England too; and think foul scorn that Parma or Spain, or any prince of Europe, should dare invade the borders of my realm.

So, in spite of this female body she can defend the borders of the realm since her sovereign body is masculine. (From Queen Elizabeth's speech at Tilbury, quoted in C.R.N. Routh, *Who's Who in History, Vol. II: England 1485 to 1603*, Oxford, Blackwell, 1964, p. 194.)

18 C. Pateman, *The Sexual Contract*, Cambridge, Polity, 1988, p. 180.

19 Ibid., p. 102.
20 Ibid., p. 77.
21 Ibid., p. 109, emphasis in original.
22 Ibid., p. 49.
23 See C. Mouffe, 'Feminism, Citizenship and Radical Democratic Politics', in J. Butler and J.W. Scott, eds., *Feminists Theorize the Political*, Routledge, New York, 1992.
24 Pateman, *Sexual Contract*, p. 3. Further, how does this claim sit with that made on p. 18: '[A]lthough I shall be (re)telling conjectural histories of the origins of political right and repairing some omissions in the stories, I am not advocating the replacement of patriarchal tales with feminist stories of origins'?
25 This point holds for 'women' and 'men' as much as for 'man' and 'woman'. I do not accept Pateman's claim, on p. 17, that the category 'women' is immune from the objections that can be directed at 'Woman'; see Riley, *Am I that Name?*
26 Pateman, *Sexual Contract*, p. 181.
27 Ibid., pp. 17–18.
28 Riley, *Am I that Name?*, ch. 5.
29 Pateman, *Sexual Contract*, p. 44, my emphasis.
30 Marcus, 'Fighting Bodies, Fighting Words', p. 391.
31 Ibid., p. 397
32 Pateman, *Sexual Contract*, p. 96, my emphasis. Note the resonance between Pateman's view here and Dworkin's description of the female body above.
33 M. Foucault, 'Nietzsche, Freud, Marx', *Critical Texts*, vol. 3, no. 2 (Winter 1986), quoted in Mahon, *Foucault's Nietzschean Genealogy*, p. 116.
34 Pateman, *Sexual Contract*, p. 100, my emphasis.
35 J. Laplanche and J.-B. Pontalis, *The Language of Psychoanalysis*, Hogarth Press, London, 1983, p. 335, define the primal scene in the following terms: 'Scene of sexual intercourse between the parents which the child observes or infers on the basis of certain indications, and fantasies. It is generally interpreted by the child as an act of violence on the part of the father.'
36 Laplanche and Pontalis observe that the notion of deferred action 'rule[s] out the summary interpretation which reduces the psychoanalytic view of the subject's history to a linear determinism envisaging nothing but the action of the past upon the present ... Freud had pointed out from the beginning that the subject revises past events at a later date, and that it is this revision which invests them with significance.' Ibid., pp. 111–12.
37 Scott, 'Experience' pp. 37–8.
38 Pateman, *Sexual Contract*, pp. 134–5, my emphasis.
39 Ibid., p. 153, my emphasis.
40 Ibid., p. 131, my emphasis.
41 Ibid., p. 198.
42 Ibid., p. 199.
43 Ibid., p. 221, my emphasis.
44 Ibid., p. 224.
45 Ibid., p. 231, my emphasis.
46 However, as I indicate above, this is not the full story of *The Sexual Contract*. See, for example, Pateman's positive claim that 'if women exercised their freedom to remain single on a large scale, men could not become husbands – and the sexual contract would be shaken' (pp. 132–3).
47 Ibid., p. 228.
48 Ibid., p. 220.
49 Roughly, chs. 3, 5 and 6.

50 Roughly, chs. 7 and 8.
51 See Pateman, *Sexual Contract*, ch. 4.
52 G.C. Spivak, 'Displacement and the Discourse of Woman,' in M. Krupnick, ed., *Displacement: Derrida and After*, Bloomington, Indiana University Press, 1986, p. 186.
53 Of course, feminism produces a multiplicity of texts – including my own here – all of which could have this question posed to them. Here I am concerned with those feminist texts which posit essentialism as truth and/or strategy. However, I do not see *any* text as 'outside' of desire or immune from the very same process of questioning that I undertake here.
54 MacKinnon, 'Sexuality, Pornography and Method', p. 336.
55 For an analysis of *ressentiment* in contemporary feminism see Marion Tapper, '*Ressentiment* and Power: Some Reflections on Feminist Practices', in P. Patton, ed., *Nietzsche, Feminism and Political Theory*, Routledge, New York, 1993; see also A. Yeatman, 'Feminism and Power', *Women's Studies Journal*, vol. 10, no. 1 (1994).
56 See F. Nietzsche, *On the Genealogy of Morals*, New York, Vintage Books, 1989, preface, §4.
57 W. Brown, 'Feminist Hesitations, Postmodern Exposures', *differences*, vol. 3, no. 1 (Spring 1991), p. 78.

Part III

7 Embodiment, ethics and difference

In Chapter 5 I argued that Western thought is governed by the dualisms of nature and culture, body and mind, passion and reason. I also suggested that in the context of political thought these dualisms are transposed onto those of reproduction and production, the family and the state, the individual body and the body politic. Moreover, whereas the left-hand side of these dualisms is seen as timeless and static, the right-hand side allegedly belongs in the realm of history and change. An uncritical acceptance of this conceptualization of human life has led even feminist thinkers such as Andrea Dworkin and Simone de Beauvoir to claim that 'women have no history'[1] and that 'reproduction involves the mere repetition of life'.[2]

Of course, it is not only feminist theorists who have drawn attention to the manner in which political representations of human life have constructed some individuals as social agents or as subjects of history and others as passive objects swept along by the pull of a history which is not of their making. These 'other' voices have thrown into question the *force* of the feminist claim that the dualisms central to Western thought are gendered. Many have claimed that these representations of human life have served to circumscribe and limit not only women's possibilities but also those of many other groups whose differences from one another have been occluded. Feminist theory is thus seen to repeat the tendency of those in the privileged position of the 'theorist', that is, to universalize the particular experience of the theorist to all.[3]

According to some, acknowledging radical differences between women can threaten the legitimacy of feminism as a political movement as well as feminist theory since both depend upon a relatively coherent notion of 'woman'. This is certainly a crucial issue at stake in the essentialist versus social constructionist debate. Some feminists have argued that if the category 'woman' signifies a historically and culturally variable subject then the *raison d'être* of feminist politics is lost.[4] Still others welcome the postmodern challenge to identity, claiming that it offers new ways of envisaging the political realm. Judith Butler, for example, claims that

[i]f identities were no longer fixed as the premises of a political syllogism, and politics no longer understood as a set of practices derived from the alleged interests that belong to a set of ready-made subjects, a new configuration of politics would surely emerge from the ruins of the old.[5]

Just what this 'new configuration' of politics may involve is not easily predicted. Clearly, however, such an approach to the political realm will have a different story to tell from that of the modernists about how we become the subjects that we are.

These different stories or narratives will map, or represent, the social body in quite different ways, resulting in the emergence of different tools of political analysis and disparate political agendas. Of particular interest here is the distinctive ethical stance which may emerge from each approach. I will say more about this shortly.

The aims of this chapter are modest. I will trace some dominant themes in these competing narratives of sociopolitical life, paying particular attention to the place of the body, ethics and difference in each. I see this task as necessary in order to address elements of political discontent in some contemporary theorists' responses to so-called postmodern or post-Enlightenment claims. Some of the disagreements currently canvassed in the literature are based, in my view, on confusion and misunderstanding. I will argue that the critical interrogation of modernist accounts of social and political life does not inevitably engender relativism, individualism, subjectivism or the abandonment of critical theory.

Modernist narratives of the birth of the political body

In this paper, I can do little more than offer a broad-brush outline of modernist accounts of the origin of the polity. Many of these accounts claim that the political body is a product of the fertility of men who have joined in the name of their love for reason, order and justice.[6] Fear of one's fellows as a motivation for forming a collective is not inconsistent with reason since it is rational to desire security of life and goods. Whether prepolitical society was conceived as a primitive social state or as a state of isolated individuals in nature, the passage to political society was consistently represented as a passage undertaken by certain sorts of men only. They were assumed to share certain asocial, apolitical needs and desires which functioned to provide a common ground, sufficient to ensure the cooperation of each with the other. As I argued in Chapter 2, this collective body was explicitly seen as a product of art or convention which removed men from the dangers and inconveniences of the natural state.

Recall Hobbes' comments:

by art is created that great *leviathan* called a *commonwealth*, or *state*, in Latin *civitas*, which is but an artificial man; though of greater stature and strength than the natural, for whose protection and defence it was intended;[7]

and a little further on, he speaks of:

the *pacts* and *covenants*, by which the parts of this body politic were at first made, set together, and united, [which] resemble that *fiat*, or the *let us make man*, pronounced by God in the creation.[8]

An interested reading of this story may take exception to the usurpation, by God, of women's reproductive power to create 'man' and man's imitation of this power in his account of the origin of the political body. Notably, there is no female leviathan in this story, no artificial woman, 'though of greater stature and strength than the natural', who can protect and defend woman. In relation to the body politic she is left unprotected, undefended, virtually in the state of nature where, according to Hobbes, one dwells in 'continual fear' and in 'danger of violent death'.[9]

The precise status of women with respect to this political body and the contracts and covenants which bring it into being, are far from clear, notwithstanding Carole Pateman's interpretation of modernist contractarians in *The Sexual Contract*.[10] The political standing of women during the modern period was not so different from the status of those whom Hobbes described as accepting by word or deed that they had been conquered by war.[11] By submitting to such conquest, that is, by failing to engage in a Hegelian-style life-and-death struggle, these beings are henceforth *bound to obey* the laws of a body that they had no part in forming and which does not 'represent' them.

The metaphor of the 'artificial man' has been important in modern political narratives. It has allowed the sphere of political relations to be constructed as a sphere of relations between certain types of male body. This construction had, and continues to have, political and ethical consequences for those whose bodily specificity bars them from this representation. In so far as the body politic represents only certain sorts of body, those barred from this representation do not infringe upon the artificial man's claim to autonomy, since any contributions that such excluded bodies do make are invisible from the point of view of political and economic discourses. If the narratives surrounding the genesis of the modern political body had included representations of different kinds of body, then, presumably, women's legal status could not have been exhausted by the trichotomy: maiden/wife/widow. Perhaps it is superfluous to add that there was no shortage of women (and men) offering up narratives which could have performed this diversifying function. Given that such narratives were not taken up, women had little choice but to avail themselves of whatever 'protection' they could find, and usually this involved joining themselves to a husband. David Hume came close to acknowledging this state of affairs.

He described these male political corporations as 'confederacies', and observed that:

> though the males, when united, have in all countries bodily force sufficient to maintain [this] severe tyranny, yet such are the insinuation, address and charms of their fair companions, that women are commonly able to break the confederacy, and share with the other sex in all the rights and privileges of society.[12]

This passage warrants reflection in the context of those qualities which are stereotypically associated with femininity and their likely origins. Significantly, these comments are made alongside the judgement that 'we' are not under any obligation to extend to 'barbarous Indians' the rules of justice, nor are 'they' entitled to the possession of rights and property.[13] Again, if these other beings come into contact with the body politic, either by being imported as slaves or by the conquest of their lands, they are incorporated without alteration to the image or the representation of that body. This is important because, in so far as the artificial man can maintain his unity through incorporation, he is not required to acknowledge difference. The metaphor of the artificial body and the narratives concerning its genesis have functioned in the history of Western societies to restrict our political, legal and economic vocabulary. This, in turn, means that some issues, such as the value of women's unpaid labour, are difficult, if not impossible, to represent.

One may want to respond to this by saying that we no longer inhabit the modern period and that, in any case, things are quite different now. It is true that in contemporary times bodies politic more commonly attempt to incorporate 'others' by assimilation. However, I think that the force of the modernist narrative and its embeddedness in our social, political and ethical practices warrants further comment. The problem remains of what these 'others' can say of their 'otherness' within the political body and using the political language that has been developed over the duration of the existence of that body. The admission of women and other groups to citizenship, the civil sphere, public education and economic exchange has not involved a massive restructuring of those spheres as they have developed historically. Therefore, women and others occupy these spheres in a manner which entails considerable suppression of their difference from the normatively conceived abstract individual. This places those who fall outside this norm in contradictory and conflictual situations, with little opportunity to create a language, or a discourse, in which to voice these contradictions, since the failure to match, or live up to, the norm is understood as a failure of the individual concerned. Indeed, such 'failure' may be used by conservatives to argue for the wisdom of past discriminatory practices.[14] This response misses the point. It is a response which does not take seriously the history of social bodies and their practices and the manner in which these practices actually institute and perpetuate differential forms of embodiment. It is a response typical of the modern period and of those in the present who are committed to modernist politics. I will attempt to defend my view by examining salient aspects of modernist sociopolitical and ethical narratives.

If my earlier characterizátion of the numerous exclusions operating on the sort of body that was to be represented by the modern body politic is accepted, and if we accept the self-evident proposition that social as well as individual bodies have a history, then it follows that the notion of the abstract individual is an abstraction in a very specific sense only. Since the political body admitted only very specific types of persons to active membership, to abstract from their specific qualities certain minimal common features is to abstract from an abstraction. In other words, the abstract individual, under these lights, appears as a very specific kind of person. But one needs to go further than this. The laws and ethical systems that are likely to develop in this sociopolitical context are going to amount to the encoding of the values and judgements of very specific kinds of person with very specific kinds of interest. There is nothing neutral or disembodied about the abstract liberal individual when viewed from this perspective. This is a feature of modernist narratives which tends to be repressed – even by those who are its strongest critics. It takes a motivated reader to construct this reading and, of course, it is a reading open to challenge. Nevertheless, it is my reading and I will pursue it further. However, I will do so by entertaining another philosophical tradition, one which is sometimes described as anti-Enlightenment, and which provides an important theoretical underpinning to some postmodernist theories of contemporary life.

Genealogy: embodying sociopolitical narratives

Alasdair MacIntyre, who would not identify himself with the spirit, but would share some of the concerns of theorists of the postmodern condition, has remarked that:

> [m]oral philosophies, however they may aspire to achieve more than this, always do articulate the morality of some particular social and cultural standpoint: Aristotle is the spokesman for one class of fourth century Athenians, Kant . . . provides a rational voice for the emerging social forces of liberal individualism.[15]

MacIntyre acknowledges that ethics has historically been the product of whichever group has monopolized political right: Greek (male) citizens or the liberal (male) individual. Clearly, part of the privilege accorded to members of a political body is that at least some of their needs and desires are dignified with the status of *rationally* grounded principles and are thus converted into rights and virtues. To allow others to share in these rights and to expect them to exhibit these virtues assumes that they share the same

needs and desires and concur with what a specific historical body takes to
be a rational judgement. If, as I believe, most of our needs and desires are
developed in specific social contexts, as are our conceptions of reason,[16]
then individuals who are historically constituted as different will infre-
quently concur in their judgements concerning that which they take to be
rational. Contrary to some, I do not see this claim to involve the twin
spectres of subjectivism and relativism. Quite the opposite. I would argue
that the notions of the social, political and historical construction of
disparate 'ways of life' and different moral claims involve both less freedom than is often assumed, with regard to what it is possible for us to
become, and an implicit accountability for our present values. A fuller
explication of this view requires another broad-brush sketch of a somewhat
different narrative tradition concerning the genesis of sociopolitical bodies
and their practices.

Alongside Hobbes and Locke, Spinoza was theorizing ethics and the
political body in quite different terms.[17] Above all else, Spinoza insisted
that mind and body are not two distinct substances but rather two ways in
which the human understanding grasps that which exists. Among other
things this means that reason, politics and ethics are always embodied; that
is, the ethics or the reason which any particular collective body produces
will bear the marks of that body's genesis, its (adequate or inadequate)
understanding of itself, and will express the power or capacity of that
body's endeavour to sustain its own integrity. It may be worth mentioning
here that a Kantian notion of a universalized ethics, produced by an
autonomous will, is quite simply incoherent in the Spinozist context.
Spinoza's work offers exciting and productive possibilities for rethinking
political and ethical life, which I develop in Chapters 8 and 9. Here, I will
simply indicate that his system is not teleological in the Hegelian sense, so
it disallows the idea that distinct sociopolitical bodies can nevertheless
each be seen as on their way to an inevitable and common completion.
Intrinsic to Spinozist philosophy is a certain irreducible difference between
one (simple or complex) body and the next. Not the least reason for this
irreducibility is the specific location, perspective and historical self-
understanding of each. Now, this kind of narrative concerning the how,
why and when of sociopolitical and ethical life is not going to be one which
can assume a common reason or a common ethic *in the absence of a
common body*. Some form of explicit or implicit mind–body dualism –
where mind provides the principle of universality and the body that of
particularity – was necessary before the notions of the abstract individual
and a universalizable ethic could develop.

The Spinozist viewpoint does not stand alone. Deleuze, among others,
hails Spinoza as the precursor of Nietzsche.[18] Nietzsche claimed to articu-
late a new demand. This was not the demand that we question this or that
moral value, but rather that we provide

a critique of moral values, the value of these values themselves must first be called into question – and for that there is needed a knowledge of *the conditions and circumstances in which they grew*, under which they evolved and changed.[19]

While J.S. Mill was extolling the inevitable progress of reason and culture, Nietzsche was exposing the bloody underside, the genealogy of our virtues and the repressed costs of civilization. Nietzsche shares Spinoza's scepticism concerning the dualisms which have dominated Western thought and proposes that consciousness and conscience should be understood as specific modes of being which arise under specific social and historical conditions. His views concerning the origin of contract, promise-keeping and morality stand in stark contrast to the modernist view.

Nietzsche is critical of 'histories' of morality which purport to explain how it is that we have become ever more moral and humane beings. If we take the moral theories of Rousseau, Kant or J.S. Mill, for example, we see that they consider the history of human moral values to be ever more informed by reason, rational judgement, concern for our fellows, and so on. On this view civilization entails the ever increasing domination and conscious control of those aspects of our nature which are passionate, unreflective and purely egoistic. These aspects of human behaviour are seen as destructive of social advancement, social cohesion and human progress. Those who exhibit these passionate drives (for example, women and 'savages') are seen as brakes on progress and must be either carefully segregated (e.g. Rousseau) or gradually assimilated (e.g. Mill). Nietzsche was extremely critical of the supposed role of reason in these accounts of moral and human progress, stressing instead the cruelty and the horrific practices that underlie 'all good things'.[20] Much of what motivated Nietzsche's work may be seen as the attempt to decipher 'the entire long hieroglyphic record' of the moral past. And his methodology assumes nothing about the features of human nature or its purported a priori tendencies. Rather, the genealogical method is concerned with 'what is documented, what can actually be confirmed and has actually existed'.[21] Genealogy, then, is a way of doing history, and according to a contemporary Nietzsche commentator, Alexander Nehamas,

genealogy has direct practical consequences because by demonstrating the contingent character of the institutions that traditional history exhibits as unchanging, it creates the possibility of altering them. Nietzsche denies both the view that institutions regularly arise in the form in which we now know them and the correlative idea that we can determine what such institutions really aim at, what they really are, and what they always have been by tracing them to their origins. On the contrary, from his earliest writings on, Nietzsche had claimed that such tracings inevitably reveal conditions and purposes totally different from those to which they eventually gave rise, and that the mode in which later stages emerge from earlier ones is anything but logical or rational.[22]

What does a genealogy of the institution of promise-making show? We have seen the traditional modernist account of the genesis of this institution: the rational individual contracts with others who see the benefit of surrendering some of their natural rights in favour of more reliable, if conventional, social and political rights. Nietzsche offers a different account: the origins of contract are steeped in blood, torture and barbarity; a 'mnemonics of pain'. This is the method by which society ensured that the rather stupid and forgetful human animal would acquire a memory:

> five or six 'I will nots', in regard to which one had given one's *promise* so as to participate in the advantages of society – and it was with the aid of this kind of memory that one at last came 'to reason'.[23]

Nietzsche offers a related account of how one develops a conscience, guilt, shame, a sense of responsibility, and so on.

The details of this account are not relevant here. What is relevant is the inversion which Nietzsche effects of the traditional accounts of morality. Where they posit reason as the origin of human social and moral development, Nietzsche posits reason as the effect, the outcome or the product of painful work on the *body* – work which is performed in specific social and political contexts. Reason and ethics are here understood as the outcome of inscribing the body with pain in order that it might develop a memory, an internalized sign system, a code of which behaviours to suppress and which to cultivate. Those features which traditional accounts of society and ethics have assumed as given, that is, the (sexed) 'self', reason, capacity for reflection, are here the results of long and often brutal socially and historically specific processes. These processes, quite obviously, are not going to yield an ethics of universal relevance. As Nietzsche observes in *Zarathustra*, 'a table of values hangs over every people . . . it is the table of its overcomings.'[24]

Specific peoples, specific kinds of body-grouping, are going to produce quite specific 'ways of being'. On this understanding of communities and their 'ways of being', the search for a priori or universal foundations for ethics would be pointless. However, this is not to imply that values, because they are constructed in specific historical and social contexts, are therefore groundless or nonbinding. Clearly, they do not fall from the sky nor are they fabricated by individual subjectivities. On the contrary, such values are thoroughly 'grounded' in the particular needs, desires, struggles, histories and institutions of particular communities.

What the relations could or should be, both within and between various communities, is an issue that is pressing in contemporary times – many contemporary critical theorists are calling for and enacting a 'politics of difference'. But what of an 'ethics of difference'? This call is heard less often and it is a call that inevitably raises the rather awkward question of the connection between *polis* and *ethos*, or politics and ethics. Some mention of the possible connections between these two has been made above, with reference to MacIntyre's comments on Aristotle and Kant.

It seems to me that any notion of morality always assumes a complex body of some sort and, according to Nietzsche, any complex body is always already a political body: a body in which there are obeying parts and commanding parts, that is, a body subject to relations of power and governance. Again, it seems fair to assume that the ethos of such a complex political body would disproportionately reflect the interests and concerns, needs and desires of the dominant components of that body. This follows from Nietzsche's suggestion that moralities are sign systems or encodings of the dominant affects. It seems uncontentious to assume also that any complex body is internally unstable as well as open to change as the result of relations with other external bodies. Hence, not only the political, but also the ethical values and practices of any given body complex are going to be dynamic, open to challenge and revision. Before I say more on this issue of the relation between politics and ethics I will complete the unholy trinity of theorists considered in this section by briefly alluding to the work of Freud.

Freud wrote several long papers on the origins of society, religion and morality, most notably *Totem and Taboo*,[25] *Civilization and its Discontents*,[26] *Moses and Monotheism*[27] and *The Future of an Illusion*.[28] In spite of the evolutionism, linearity and historicism in Freud's account of societies, he makes several points that are of interest here. He sees the main function of religious belief to be that of compensation for the sacrifices and suffering that communal living necessarily brings in its train. Further, he claims that the ultimate domain of religion is morality, that is, the regulation of relations between human beings. As such, the wish to ground morality in anything more certain than our desires and histories is as much an 'illusion' as is the belief in a benevolent and omnipotent Father. Freud prefers an immanent and historical account of how social bodies produce ethical relations. In *Civilization and its Discontents* he maintains that 'communities, as well as individuals, evolve a superego', adding that cultural demands which 'deal with the relations of human beings to one another are comprised under the heading of ethics'.[29]

Just as an individual can reflect upon and be critical of the demands and ideals of her or his superego, so too can cultural historians and critical theorists reflect upon a culture or a community and ask questions about the value and the genealogy of its values. In some ways, communities are more amenable to this critical task, since there are those who, topographically speaking, occupy the place of the 'id'. There are those who have not internalized the dominant values of the society or community of which they are, however tentatively, a part. Freud acknowledges this, often implicitly, throughout his work. For example, he remarks that women are often 'hostile to civilization'.[30] However, in *The Future of an Illusion* he quite explicitly states that 'the internalization of cultural prohibitions by suppressed or exploited people is not to be expected'.[31] One way of reading this statement, in our current context would be to point out that those who have historically been excluded from positions of mastery and domination are now well placed to conduct a genealogical analysis of that history, using perspectives, resources and capacities not previously represented or encoded in the dominant cultural narratives. Carole Pateman's utilization of Freud's work in her articulation of the repressed sexual contract may be read as a case in point. It is significant that Pateman's double reading (of Freud alongside social contract theorists) provides her with one avenue of investigation into what is repressed in the modernist narrative of the social contract: that men's access to women's bodies is prerequisite to political life.

I have attempted to argue that, on a genealogical reading of the traditional modernist narratives of the genesis of political society, difference has been repressed at the level not only of the political but also of the ethical. Much of the character of our contemporary ethical lives has been produced by the encoding of the preferences, desires and interests of a very specific and *embodied* collective and as such is inadequate to the task of addressing pressing contemporary issues concerning those who have been barred from the historical development of the dominant parts of this body. Such disbarment has had material effects on the manner in which those bodies have been constituted in the present as well as on their future possibilities. This calls for not only a *politics* of difference – which seems the obvious register in which to analyse class, race and sex differences – but also for an *ethics* of difference – which would be capable of acknowledging that different forms of embodiment are themselves *historical* and open to change.

Feminist theorists are a particularly interesting group to focus on in this context because their concerns seem to cover the entire field of possible anxieties arising from the postmodern stance. Clearly, this anxiety is not unconnected to the claim that postmodernism spells the end of feminism as a coherent movement, or as able to provide a distinctive theoretical perspective, since it is based on the indefensible essentialist category 'woman'. Moreover, many see postmodernism as presenting a range of threats including the loss of the ability to make truth and falsity claims, relativism, the loss of the right to criticize different 'others', individualism, and subjectivism. I cannot here discuss these anxieties in the detail that I would like. However, I would hope that the sketch that I have offered of a largely repressed philosophical tradition can challenge at least some of the grounds of these fears.

First, to say that 'woman' has no essence, that she is a constructed 'fiction', a product of social narratives and practices is not to say that she does not exist. She exists precisely to the extent that anything else produced or constituted by human history exists. This is not to deny that several inconsistent narratives construct women differently, both across and within different times, histories and cultures. To hanker after an a priori category 'woman', for the convenience of theorizing, is to betray one's allegiance to the pretensions of the modernist narratives criticized above. To acknowledge the social construction of women does not entail the abandonment of critical theory or the spectre of relativism. Rather, it calls for a commitment to a historical, or genealogical, approach to understanding the specificity of social, political and ethical relations *as they are embodied* in this or that community or culture.

In a related manner, to say that our 'natures' are constructed is not to say that we have the freedom to become anything we like. Neither individualism nor subjectivism are going to be able to take root in the soil of theories concerning the social construction of subjectivity. Again, this illusion arises from paying insufficient attention to the embodiedness of this nature. Our embodied history cannot be thrown off as if it were a coat that one has donned only involuntarily in the first place.[32] Whether we like it or not, in so far as our values and our 'ways of being' are embodied they cannot be wished away or dismissed by a pure act of will. Presumably, this is Nietzsche's point in claiming that our 'morals now belong to our "unconquerable flesh and blood" '.[33] Past contingencies become the materials of present necessities. This is why the notion of constructedness involves much less freedom to change our present than some have thought. What our present freedoms are depends very much on our present contexts coupled with the adequacy of our understandings of how we became what we are. To acknowledge this involves a high degree of accountability or responsibility for our values and our 'way of life'. It also entails a responsibility toward differently constituted 'others' whose 'ways of life' intersect, voluntarily or involuntarily, with our own. However, respect for others in their difference does not amount to exempting their values from critical scrutiny – and this is a two-way street.[34] Ethical systems which acknowledge their historical forms of embodiment highlight their own genealogies, their own historical and social production. As such, we are *accountable* for the present in that we are *responsible* for those present possibilities which become actual through our actions. Far from this state of affairs plunging us into a postmodern desert where it is no longer possible to say anything or judge anything, it opens the possibility of engagement with others as genuine others, rather than as inferior, or otherwise subordinated, versions of the same. This engagement should not be limited to the political register – which too easily reduces to the question of who has the sword. It is vital that critical theorists begin to enter difference, and engagement with different others, in the register of the ethical.

Notes

A different version of this paper was published in *Political Theory Newsletter*, vol. 4, no. 1 (1992).

1 A. Dworkin, for example, has stated 'I think that the situation of women is basically ahistorical'; quoted in C. Pateman, *The Sexual Contract*, Cambridge, Polity Press, 1988, p. 236, n. 24.
2 S. de Beauvoir, *The Second Sex*, Harmondsworth, Penguin, 1975, p. 96.
3 This criticism of contemporary feminist theory is discussed in the introduction to *Feminism/Postmodernism*, ed. Linda J. Nicholson, New York, Routledge, 1990, as well as in many of the essays that make up that collection.
4 See, for example, C. Di Stefano, 'Dilemmas of Difference: Feminism, Modernity and Postmodernism', in L.J. Nicholson, ed., *Feminism/Postmodernism*, New York, Routledge, 1990.
5 J. Butler, *Gender Trouble: Feminism and the Subversion of Identity*, New York, Routledge, 1990, p. 149.
6 Pateman's reading of social contract theorists is perhaps the most convincing on this point. See Pateman, *Sexual Contract*.
7 T. Hobbes, *Leviathan*, Harmondsworth, Penguin, 1986, p. 81.
8 Ibid., pp. 81–2.
9 Ibid., p. 186.
10 Pateman, *Sexual Contract*.
11 Hobbes, *Leviathan*, pp. 720–1.
12 D. Hume, *An Enquiry Concerning the Principles of Morals*, ed. L.A. Selby-Bigge, Oxford, Clarendon Press, 1975, p. 191.
13 Ibid., pp. 190–1.
14 See Joan Scott, 'Deconstructing Equality-versus-Difference: Or the Uses of Poststructuralist Theory for Feminism', *Feminist Studies*, vol. 14, no. 1 (Spring 1988), for a compelling account of a contemporary legal case which exhibits this desire to return to the 'wisdom' of past discriminatory practices.
15 A. MacIntyre, *After Virtue: A Study in Moral Theory*, London, Duckworth, 2nd edn., 1985, p. 268.
16 See G. Lloyd, *The Man of Reason: 'Male' and 'Female' in Western Philosophy*, London, Methuen, 1984.
17 See B. Spinoza, *Ethics* and *A Political Treatise*, in *The Chief Works of Benedict de Spinoza*, ed. R.H.M. Elwes, New York, Dover Publications, 1955.
18 See G. Deleuze, *Spinoza: Practical Philosophy*, San Francisco, City Lights Books, 1988.
19 F. Nietzsche, *On The Genealogy of Morals*, New York, Vintage Books, 1989, preface, §6, p. 20.
20 Ibid., essay II, §3, p. 62.
21 Ibid., preface, §7, p. 21.
22 A. Nehamas, *Nietzsche: Life as Literature*, Cambridge, Mass., Harvard University Press, 1985, p. 112. See also M. Foucault, 'Nietzsche, Genealogy, History', in *Language, Counter-Memory, Practice*, ed. D. Bouchard, Ithaca, Cornell University Press, 1977.
23 Nietzsche, *Genealogy*, essay II, §3, p. 62.
24 F. Nietzsche, *Thus Spoke Zarathustra*, Harmondsworth, Penguin, 1976, p. 84.
25 S. Freud, *Totem and Taboo*, The Pelican Freud Library, vol. 12, Harmondsworth, Penguin, 1985
26 S. Freud, *Civilization and its Discontents*, The Pelican Freud Library, vol. 12, Harmondsworth, Penguin, 1985.

27 S. Freud, *Moses and Monotheism*, The Pelican Freud Library, vol. 13, Harmondsworth, Penguin, 1985.
28 Freud, *The Future of an Illusion*, The Pelican Freud Library vol. 12, Harmondsworth, Penguin, 1985.
29 Freud, *Civilization*, pp. 335–6.
30 Ibid., p. 293.
31 Freud, *Future of an Illusion*, p. 191.
32 This is the 'modern' illusion *par excellence*; see R. Descartes, *'Discourse on Method' and the 'Meditations'*, Harmondsworth, Penguin, 1985, esp. meditation I.
33 F. Nietzsche, *Beyond Good and Evil*, New York, Vintage Books, 1989, pt. II, §24, p. 35.
34 See, for example, the interchange between a (white) Australian academic and indigenous Australian women over the issue of rape in an aboriginal community in D. Bell and T. Napurrula Nelson, 'Speaking about Rape is Everyone's Business', *Women's Studies International Forum*, vol. 12, no. 4.

8 Spinoza, law and responsibility

Earlier chapters have shown that traditional accounts of the formation of societies tend to focus on the utility of persons for one another and the capture (of the powers and abilities) of some persons by others. Such accounts have typically conceived of law as a coercive instrument of social control. In this chapter I will be looking to the political and juridical writings of Spinoza in order to address the issue of human sociability. This chapter was prompted by Deleuze's claim that Spinoza's political writings allow us to think about human relations not simply in terms of 'utilizations and captures' but also in terms of 'sociabilities and communities'. This chapter is a response to the questions that Deleuze puts to Spinoza's writings. Deleuze asks

> whether relations (and which ones?) can compound directly to form a new, more 'extensive' relation, or whether capacities can compound directly to constitute a more 'intense' capacity or power . . . How do individuals enter into composition with one another in order to form a higher individual, ad infinitum? How can a being take another being into its world, but while preserving or respecting the other's own relations and world? And in this regard, *what are the different types of sociabilities*, for example? *What is the difference between the society of human beings and the community of rational beings?*[1]

Spinoza contrasts the *sociability* of compatible bodies with other forms of association, for example, those built on *utility* or *capture*. He 'writes' the body and the law on an immanent register which accommodates, without contradiction, multiple forms of sociability: associations built on superstition, tyrannies grounded in fear and hope, communities of rational individuals, societies bound by the ties of friendship. None of these forms of sociability contradict the deceptively simple claim that the right 'of every individual thing [including its right to exist] extends as far as its power'.[2] This seems an unlikely starting point for a philosopher whose major work is titled *Ethics*. It will be necessary to offer some account of his understanding of bodies, rights and powers before considering his thoughts on law and ethics. The first two sections of this chapter will consider

Spinoza's notions of the body and law, respectively. The third and final section will present an understanding of the civil body as a locus of responsibility.

What is a body?

The originality of Spinoza's account of the manner in which bodies are composed and decomposed can be thrown into stark relief by recalling Descartes' explanation of the distinction between death and life:

> the body of a living man differs from that of a dead man just as does a watch or other automaton . . . when it is wound up . . . from the same watch or other machine when it is broken.[3]

This thoroughly mechanistic conception of the body has led to insoluble problems at the level of accounting for that strange hybrid which is human being. According to Descartes, all that exists does so under one of two radically distinct substances, mind and matter. Human being, thus radically divided within itself, is composed of a free soul whose essence is to think and a determined body whose essence is to be extended. The unity of mind and body cannot be rationally demonstrated but is 'experienced'.[4] Such 'experience' involves the soul's suffering the actions of the body and the body suffering the actions of the soul. Action in one equals passion in the other with soul and body incapable of acting or suffering in concert. It is not difficult to see the compatibility of Cartesian dualism with the legal notion of *mens rea*, along with exceptions to this rule. The soul (mind) that freely forms an intention to perform an evil act is deemed responsible for that act. Exceptions to this law include insanity and diminished responsibility. Such conceptualizations of responsibility or guilt rely heavily on a Cartesian view of the subject.

By contrast, Spinoza argues that there is only one substance, which is single and indivisible; body and mind enjoy only a modal existence and may be understood as 'expressions' or modifications of the *attributes* of substance, that is, extension and thought, respectively. Human being is conceived as part of a dynamic and interconnected whole:

> we have conceived an individual which is composed only of bodies which are distinguished from one another only by motion and rest, speed and slowness, i.e., which is composed of the simplest bodies. But if we should now conceive of another, composed of a number of individuals of a different nature, we shall find that it can be affected in a great many other ways, and still preserve its nature. For since each part of it is composed of a number of bodies, each part will therefore (by L7) be able, without any change of its nature, to move now more slowly, now more quickly, and consequently communicate its motion more quickly or more slowly to the others. But if we should further conceive a third

kind of individual composed of this second kind, we shall find that it can
be affected in many other ways, without any change of its form. And if
we proceed in this way to infinity, we shall easily conceive that the
whole of nature is one individual, whose parts, i.e., all bodies, vary in
infinite ways without any change of the whole individual.[5]

The human body is understood by Spinoza to be a relatively complex
individual, made up of a number of other bodies. Its identity can never
be viewed as a final or finished product as in the case of the Cartesian
automaton, since it is a body that is in constant interchange with its
environment. The human body is radically open to its surroundings and
can be composed, recomposed and decomposed by other bodies. Its open-
ness is a condition of both its life, that is, its continuance in nature as the
same individual – '[t]he human body, to be preserved, requires a great
many other bodies, by which it is, as it were, continually regenerated'[6] –
and its death, since it is bound to encounter bodies more powerful than it,
which will eventually destroy its integrity as an individual – though such
destruction always and necessarily implies further compositions, distinct
from the first. Such 'encounters' with other bodies are good or bad
depending on whether they aid or harm our characteristic constitution.

The human body, like every other animate body, does not owe its power
of movement to either an inbuilt automatic mechanism or a mysterious
'soul-substance' which can will movement in the body. Rather, the human
mind expresses under the attribute of thought 'the idea of a singular thing
which actually exists', that is, '[t]he object of the idea constituting the
human mind is the body, or a certain mode of extension which actually
exists, and nothing else.'[7] The complexity of any particular mind – and
Spinoza does not deny that animals have minds – depends on the complexity of the body of which it is the idea.

As Hans Jonas has observed, Spinoza's account of the mind and body
offers, for the first time in modern theory, 'a speculative means . . . for
relating the degree of organization of a body to the degree of awareness
belonging to it'.[8] Reason is thus not seen as a transcendent or disembodied
quality of the soul or mind; rather, reason, desire and knowledge are
embodied and dependent, at least in the first instance, on the quality and
complexity of the corporeal affects. There is no question of mind–body
interaction here since '[t]he body cannot determine the mind to thinking,
and the mind cannot determine the body to motion, to rest or to anything
else'.[9]

Descartes' attempt to account for mind–body interaction through the
'occult hypothesis'[10] of the pineal gland is not the only casualty of this
monistic conception of human being. Spinoza also rejects outright that
which this hypothesis assumes: a soul possessed of free will. He does
not consider the will and the intellect to be separate faculties, rather
'there is no volition, or affirmation and negation, except that which the

idea involves in so far as it is an idea.'[11] Nature in all its aspects is governed by necessary laws, and human being no less than the rest of nature is determined in all its actions and passions, contrary to those who conceive of it as 'a dominion within a dominion'.[12] The fundamental and determined desire of any existing body is its endeavour to persevere in its existence. Such endeavour, or striving, Spinoza names *conatus*. Deleuze indicates the complexity of this notion in the following terms:

> the *conatus* defines the *right* [*droit*] of the existing mode. All that I am determined *to do* in order to continue existing (destroy what doesn't agree with me, what harms me, preserve what is useful to me or suits me) *by means of* given affections (ideas of objects), *under* determinate affects (joy and sadness, love and hate . . .) – all this is my natural right. This right is strictly identical with my power and is independent of any other ends, of any consideration of duties, since the *conatus* is the first foundation, the *primum movens*, the efficient and not the final cause . . . The rational man and the foolish man differ in their affections and their affects but both strive to persevere in existing according to these affections and affects; from this standpoint, their only difference is one of power.[13]

This passage makes clear the gulf which separates Descartes and Spinoza. For Spinoza, body and mind *necessarily* suffer or act in concert. For 'in proportion as a body is more capable of doing many things at once, or being acted on in many ways at once, so its mind is more capable than others of perceiving many things at once.'[14] An increase of power in the body has as its necessary correlate an increase in the power of the mind, and vice versa. And an individual who thrives does not indicate a will that is both free and enlightened, but the determinate power of that particular thing to maintain itself in existence and to combine with those things that agree with and enhance its power. Human freedom, though not free will, amounts to the power that one possesses to assert and extend oneself in the face of other (human and non-human) bodies that strive to do likewise. On this ethical stance, virtue cannot be reduced to the cultivation of 'good habits', but rather concerns the power of any particular individual to continue in its existence. All bodies (including non-human bodies) possess this virtue, though to varying degrees. Human virtue is qualitatively distinct from the virtue of other things in so far as it concerns the endeavour to increase one's power of existing in accordance with reason, which is a specifically human power. For Spinoza, human being is determined to the exercise of such reason in pursuit of that which it understands to increase its power.

Where does this leave legal and moral responsibility? If all our actions are determined then how can we be held responsible for them? It is this issue, more than any other, that earned Spinoza the title of 'immoralist' and 'atheist'. Spinoza maintains that the notions of right and wrong, just and unjust can arise only in a polity. Hence, any notion of responsibility for particular actions can arise only in the context of a complex civil body.

   If one examined Spinoza's view of the human individual in isolation one would be confronted by an individualistic ethical theory of extreme ego-centrism. However, one cannot make sense of Spinoza's philosophy – which is deeply opposed to all forms of anthropocentrism – if one privileges the human body. Since a large component of the striving of any body is made up of its necessary relations with other bodies, human striving, like all striving, seeks to join itself to that which increases its power (hence Spinoza's definition of joy)[15] and to destroy those bodies that decrease its power of acting (hence Spinoza's definition of sadness).[16] This is why Deleuze understands Spinozistic reason, at its most fundamental level, as 'the effort to organize encounters on the basis of perceived agreements and disagreements' between one body and the next.[17] This effort to select or organize our encounters leads to the formation of associations or sociabilities between bodies of similar or compatible powers and capacities: that is, it leads human beings to society. As will be argued at the close of the second section, Spinoza's account of the formation of *types* of sociability implies historically and culturally variable conceptions of reason. This view of reason is another important departure from Descartes, who applied the same method in the ethico-political realm that he elsewhere applied to optics and science – 'there cannot be more than one opinion which is true' – and who, in relation to civil life, further remarked that 'the single fact of diversity among states suffices to assure us that some states are imperfect'.[18] Diversity in legal and moral codes, from this perspective, is inevitably a sign of error. Spinoza, on the contrary, offers a perspective from which to think through difference and embodiment in terms other than error or notions of cultural superiority and inferiority.

   Spinoza does not define human being as essentially *homo socius*. He claims on the contrary that 'men are not born fit for citizenship, but must be made so'.[19] Human beings come to form associations not because of an inherent sociability but rather because in pursuing their own preservation and their own increase in power they come to see that by joining or conquering other human bodies they increase their power and hence their right, since 'each has as much right as he has power'.[20] Such associations, in other words, are formed indirectly (through the pursuit of something else which is perceived as good) rather than directly. It is only within such associations that human beings may develop their power of reason and justice. This is because 'nothing is forbidden by the law of nature, except what is beyond everyone's power'.[21] Hence '[w]rong is conceivable only in an organized community'[22] and 'justice and injustice cannot be conceived of, except under dominion'.[23] It is only in civil society that human being can strive effectively and directly to increase its peculiar power: understanding, or reason, which entails a power of *selecting* encounters with others. And it is in civil society only that human freedom – conceived as an increase in one's power to act rather than be acted upon – is possible.

However, in so far as Spinoza's account of the emergence of civil society is based on hope and fear and threats, it is not markedly different from the better-known accounts of social contract theory, for example, Hobbes'. In order to see what the Spinozistic view contributes to the notion of responsibility and the manner in which that notion is tied to his notion of civil society, attention needs to be paid to both his peculiar conception of law and its relation to bodies and powers.

Law as command versus law as knowledge

In *A Theologico-Political Treatise* Spinoza treats divine (or natural) law, ceremonial law and civil (or human) law.[24] Each of these occupies a special role with reference to his epistemology. The three kinds of knowledge (corresponding to imagination, reason and intuition) outlined in the *Ethics*[25] find their analogues, though not in a one-to-one relation, in his typology of law.

According to Spinoza great confusion and considerable human misery result from the fact that natural law is so frequently understood on the model of law as command or decree. He insists that natural laws, whereby 'all things exist and are determined' are impossible to break, change or disobey, since they 'always involve eternal truth and necessity'.[26] It is the imagination only which sees god as a lawgiver and punisher.[27] As one commentator explains:

> there is no law intrinsic to nature that is not the law of god, since god is taken as coextensive with nature . . . it is impossible to speak of events or behaviour as obeying or not obeying the natural law. Rather this law is the actual nature of the entity itself, the actual order of the occasion, which entity and occasion are manifestations of god's nature.[28]

This adequate understanding of natural law concerns knowledge of the second kind, or reason, and far from such necessity representing a limit on our freedom, it is, according to Spinoza, the very condition of such liberty.[29] It is the illusion of free will, which is then projected onto an anthropomorphized nature, that obscures the freedom that we do possess: that is, the freedom to understand our situation and, on the basis of such understanding, act to maximize our power and our joys.

Civil law concerns 'a plan of life laid down by man for himself or others with a certain object', namely, 'to render life and the state secure'.[30] Such laws will not be universal and will both reflect and contribute to the reproduction of the particular historical, religious or national character of different peoples. Above all, the laws of any given civil body will reveal the historical and continuing basis of such complex associations. In contrast to natural law, human or civil law can be understood as command or decree but in a limited sense only. This sense concerns both the virtue or power of the state and Spinoza's conception of volition as inseparable from particular modes of understanding.

Civil law may be understood as command, though not in the sense often assumed by philosophers of jurisprudence. A sovereign or a state cannot command or decree anything at all, without qualification.[31] There is for Spinoza no absolute right of rule. This has some very interesting consequences for determining whether or not the state is exercising its power responsibly. As Cairns has pointed out, 'Spinoza shows that there is an inescapable connection between power and its proper exercise'.[32] Spinoza conceives of the state as a complex body that must possess a degree of self-knowledge if it is to persevere in its own existence.[33] The sense in which the state can exceed the proper exercise of its power is tied, precisely, to its continuing existence as a state. As Belaief argues:

> [i]f anything lacks the power to function according to its essential nature, it can no longer be said to participate as the SAME thing in reality. This is as true for an individual law as it is for an entire legal system, as true for an individual man as it is for the state.[34]

From this basis, one could argue that a state that exercises its power to enslave, oppress or exploit its population will be inferior in kind to a state that exercises its power in order to expand the capacities of its citizens. In this connection consider the distinction Belaief draws between Hobbes and Spinoza: 'In Hobbes' view there is no distinction between force and power with respect to the sovereign; in Spinoza's view force must be guided by reason if it is to become power.'[35] It is important to recall here that power *is* virtue for Spinoza. He writes, 'civil jurisprudence depends on the mere decree of commonwealth, which is not bound to please any but itself, nor to hold anything to be good or bad, but what it judges to be such for itself.'[36] The ambiguity in the last phrase – 'nor to hold anything to be good or bad, but what it judges to be such *for itself*' – is a telling one. If something is bad for it then the virtue of the state dictates its avoidance, just as every individual strives to seek that which it thinks is good for it and avoid that which is harmful. This understanding of the state entails an inherent, if self-imposed, curb on state power: the avoidance of those decrees, commands or enactments that will certainly lead to its harm or ruin. Thus, Spinoza is entitled to assert that

> he who holds dominion is not bound to observe the terms of the contract by any other cause than that, which bids a man in the state of nature to beware of being his own enemy, lest he should destroy himself.[37]

The second sense in which the power of the state is limited concerns Spinoza's particular understanding of volition, that is, he denies that the intellect and the will are separate faculties. He cannot, then, be a proponent of the command theory of law in the same sense as, say, Hobbes or

Austin.[38] Again, this feature of Spinoza's jurisprudence offers a means of determining the excellence or otherwise of any particular state, since its particular decrees or commands are manifestations of its own self-understanding. The will of the state, for Spinoza, can be no more arbitrary than the will of the individual; in both cases that which the body wills is determined by its relative virtue or ignorance. Again, Belaief makes this point succinctly:

> since [on Spinoza's account] law is held to be a product of will this is tantamount to having it as a product of thinking and judging ... the will of the sovereign, that is, laws, are not consecrations of the sovereign's desires but rather the ideas which he affirms. The goodness or badness of the laws will depend on whether these affirmed ideas are adequate or inadequate, true or false.[39]

These 'checks' on sovereign power are interesting for two reasons. First, the notion that bad governments are responsible for their own ruin, common in political and legal theory, takes on an extra dimension in the context of Spinoza's philosophy. Bad government is also 'responsible' for bad citizens. Spinoza argues that the *raison d'être* for civil society and the laws it institutes concerns the establishment of peace and security *in order that* both the minds and the bodies of citizens may be developed to their highest degree. On this basis Belaief argues that one may distinguish between a 'good' law and a 'bad' law in terms of its tendency either to aid 'an individual in the fullest development of his powers or virtues'[40] or to fail to 'aim towards aiding the development of men's powers'.[41]

Those who would claim Spinoza as an early proponent of liberal political philosophy must turn a blind eye to a crucial difference between him and liberalism. Spinoza does not allow the existence of any special rights to property or the person prior to civil life. The sovereign, on Spinoza's view, does not exist to enforce pre-civil moral, personal or property rights. Consequently, Spinoza's sovereign has a much greater responsibility to, and for, its citizens than on the liberal view. Spinoza's rejection of the existence of a priori rights or justice places responsibilities on the civil body which go much further than its acts of omission, for example, the failure to provide protection for its citizens. Such a rejection places the onus of responsibility on the civil body for acts of commission also, that is, the actual behaviour and values of the citizens, since their morality is largely derived from and dependent on the particular laws of that state.

Second, because of the profound effect that laws have on the character of a people,[42] the ideas which the sovereign affirms become embodied in the population and perpetuated by social institutions. Further, if the social understanding of law as command is promulgated, it will have an inhibiting effect on the development of the capacities of citizens since obedience is not knowledge and can, at best, only imitate knowledge.[43] For Spinoza, it is the distinction between grasping law as arbitrary command and law as knowledge that marks the difference between human freedom and human bondage. If one understands the law as those ideas affirmed by the sovereign body for its preservation, and if one obeys the law, not to avoid punishment but because one understands and pursues the preservation of civil society then one acts *directly*.[44] If, however, one obeys the law from fear of punishment or hope of reward then one is under the external control of another and so in bondage. One acts only *indirectly*, in order to avoid some evil. Nothing follows from the second sort of acting, which is strictly speaking not an action at all but a passive reaction to an outside authority which is recognized as more powerful than oneself. Hence, a state that encourages obedience without understanding will be one whose citizens are incapable of either acting or expanding their powers of acting. By Belaief's reasoning, this would be a bad government with 'bad' laws. Those who act in the first manner, that is, directly, would constitute a community of rational beings; those who (re)act in the second manner, that is, indirectly, can easily become a society of slaves.[45] (This view of the law and civil society obviously begs the question in relation to those who are disadvantaged by civil arrangements, for example, indigenous peoples, women and others. Some consideration will be given to this question in the third section.)[46]

Such an analysis offers grounds for understanding in its strongest possible sense Spinoza's claim that the state has a duty to develop the minds and bodies of its citizens. As he says in the section on freedom of thought and speech in *A Theologico-Political Treatise*:

> the ultimate aim of government is not to rule, or restrain, by fear, nor to exact obedience, but contrariwise, to free every man from fear, that he may live in all possible security; in other words, to strengthen his natural right to exist and work without injury to himself or others ... the object of government is not to change men from rational beings into beasts or puppets, but to enable them to develop their minds and bodies in security, and to employ their reason unshackled ... In fact, the true aim of government is liberty.[47]

This contrast between obedience and knowledge is certainly one way in which we could distinguish between an association of human beings founded upon fear and a community of rational beings. What would be the differences in the civil bodies and laws of each type of sociability? A state whose peace depends entirely on punishment will produce a particular type of sociability – a weak sociability that is built on sad passions, in particular, upon fear. However, a state that conceives and enacts punishment as 'just desert' is arguably even more harmful than one that concerns itself with utility, since such a state validates and gives free reign to the most malignant passions by encouraging the worst excesses of revenge, hatred and cruelty. Such a state is arguably not performing its ultimate function as Spinoza conceived it: the increase of the capacity of its citizens to act, that is, freedom. Here I must disagree with Yovel and others who maintain that Spinoza lacks a dynamic or historical account of reason.[48] Moreover, Spinoza's historical appreciation of the dynamic nature of human capacities must be both extensive and intensive in the sense Deleuze implies in his comments cited at the beginning of this paper. On Spinoza's view, the democratization of sovereignty would inevitably bring about both an extensive and an intensive development of the capacities and powers of its citizens. However, the democratization of sovereignty will inevitably alter the material composition of the sovereign body, along with the ideas which it affirms. Present notions of justice and fairness will sit less and less comfortably with ideas of the past that have become institutionalized in law and other social practices. The civil body becomes ill at ease with itself as institutionally embodied traditions and orthodoxy clash with the desire for change in various domains of social life, for example, relations between women and men, the treatment of minorities, and so on.

What can a philosophy of immanence call upon in the task of evaluating its values? Evidently, one cannot go beyond the present and actual world – including its possibilities, its contradictions and tensions. As Yovel says:

> human life is neither static nor repetitive, the ethical universe, too, assumes various faces and is open to change . . . The vehicle of these changes is human desire, embodied in actual life and practice and structured by social habits and institutions in which tradition and change, orthodoxy and revolt both play their respective parts.[49]

In the following section it will be argued that Spinoza's conception of human and civil bodies offers the rudiments for a new way of evaluating social habits, institutions and ethical responsibility.

Towards a conception of embodied responsibility

There are many senses in which a notion of embodied responsibility could be understood. Two disclaimers may assist to distinguish the Spinozistic position from others. First, Spinoza should be distinguished from contemporary versions of communitarianism. Community attitudes, for all their diversity, tend toward conservatism when it comes to the 'place', status and capacities of women and other so-called minority groups. Recent philosophical attempts to return to traditional notions of community-based virtue ethics are at their weakest on the question of women.[50] Second, Spinoza's position should not be conflated with a 'no-blame' individualistic determinism, such as that practised by the American attorney Clarence Darrow in the early part of this century. Individualistic determinism cannot explain, for example, men's disproportionate representation among the perpetrators of violent crimes and women's disproportionate representation among victims of violent crimes.[51]

How does a deterministic view such as Spinoza's treat the issue of individual responsibility? This is a question which worried several of Spinoza's correspondents, including Blijenbergh, Oldenburg and Tschirnhausen. Oldenburg and Tschirnhausen questioned both Spinoza's notion of necessity and his dismissal of free will, claiming that such notions 'excuse wickedness' and render 'rewards and punishments ineffectual'. Spinoza's responses are brief and to the point: '[h]e who goes mad from the bite of a dog is excusable, yet he is rightly suffocated',[52] and '[w]icked men are not less to be feared, and are not less harmful, when they are wicked from necessity'.[53] What more, then, can this view offer us here? I do not believe that it has very much to offer at the level of the individual. An analysis that limits itself to the individual and her or his affects cannot be any more coherent on Spinoza's view than the notion of just desert. He does not accept the immortality of the 'soul' nor the absolute existence of good and evil, or right and wrong. Civilly sanctioned moralities will be historically and culturally variable. This is simply to say that the meaning of human actions as well as the moralities of individuals are not ahistorical constants but rather are developed in particular historical and political contexts. This, of course, creates great difficulty for those who would wish for a single locus of responsibility. If the reading of Spinoza offered here has any value then it lies in the claim that a community of rational beings would assume some responsibility for its particular constitution. Such an assumption would draw attention away from the punishment of individuals and towards the social and structural causes of such behaviour.

If one accepts the reading of Spinoza offered here then one must also accept the notion that a rational civil body should take some responsibility for the acts committed by its citizens. Criminal acts are wrong or unjust, according to Spinoza, because they break the laws instituted to ensure civil peace. The breaking of such laws also breaks up the coherence, or the integrity, of the civil body. As this chapter was being written, two cases of domestic murder were reported in a local Sydney paper on the same day. In each case a notion of embodied responsibility, incipient in Spinoza's philosophy of law, will be shown to be crucial to an adequate understanding of the actions of the individuals involved.

In the first case, Brian Maxwell killed his former wife, Marilyn Maxwell. He was in 'violation of a restraining order' as he waited outside the childcare centre where she worked, and he forced her into her car where he shot her three times. Outside the court which was hearing Maxwell's case, the dead woman's sister responded to a reporter's question concerning Maxwell's manslaughter plea by saying that if such a plea were accepted then 'it's going to give men . . . like Brian Maxwell a licence to kill their wives. Everybody who commits a crime could say at the time that they were in the wrong state of mind. Everybody could say that, surely.'[54]

In the second case, Steven Helsby killed his stepfather, David Helsby, by stabbing him through the throat with a carving knife while he slept. During

Steven Helsby's trial the jury heard evidence from his mother, Mrs Helsby, that her husband 'had beaten her with brooms and metal rods, chained her up under the house in winter, punched her, sexually abused her, burnt her and choked her until she was unconscious'. Despite a domestic violence restraining order she had obtained several months before the stabbing and despite an attempt to leave her husband and go to a refuge, he had traced her to the refuge and brought her back home where the abuse had continued.[55]

These are particular cases which undoubtedly would have their own peculiar histories; nevertheless they have some features in common with similar cases that one can read about reasonably frequently in the newspapers. The pertinent question here concerns the nature of the civil body from which such acts arise. Historical and present attitudes towards relations between men and women, husbands and wives, parents and children are writ so large in these cases as to be initially indecipherable. The history of women's tentative association with the civil body is, I suggest, germane to these incidents. In Australia it is not yet twenty years since the Family Law Act was amended to allow so-called 'no-fault' divorce and it is overwhelmingly women who are now filing for divorce. The relatively new powers of the Family Law Court are clearly resented in some sectors of the community. In the early 1980s the court was bombed and one Family Law Court judge was murdered. Large sections of the community do not support recent Family Law legislation that recognizes women's civil right to live as they see fit and to be protected from violence and rape in the domestic as well as the public sphere. It is important to note that both husbands in the cases cited above acted in defiance of restraining orders. In each case the existence of restraining orders was completely ineffective in protecting the women involved. Both husbands could be seen as grotesque caricatures straining against the changing civil status of women by attempting to uphold the law of coverture. Like all caricatures they capture a truth in and through their very distortion.

What would it mean to argue that these 'caricatures' capture a truth concerning dominant social habits, practices and beliefs – in short, that they capture something about social attitudes to women and marriage that are embodied in our civil existences? Women have not historically been entitled to protection from the civil body. Rather, the civil body had extended protection to its citizens, who as (male) heads of households were expected to provide protection for their wives in return for service and obedience. Marilyn Maxwell's sister's comment above captures something of the unease many feel in these sorts of cases. Her comment prods at the question I would like to raise here: what do these cases tell about the civil and private structures which underpin these incidents? Why does Marilyn Maxwell's sister think that to accept Maxwell's plea of manslaughter would give 'men . . . like Brian Maxwell a *licence* to kill their wives'? Unlike the judge in Maxwell's case (who appeared to agree with the sister), the court had no hesitation in accepting David Helsby's plea of manslaughter. Presumably this is partly because his act was construed as protecting his mother – something the civil body was patently unable to do – in the only manner that seemed possible: to destroy the cause of her suffering.

Punishing individual offenders in these cases does not address the underlying causes of such behaviour. An understanding of these underlying causes would need to confront the type of sociability in which we presently participate. This would involve, in turn, some recognition of the manner in which the history of our civil body has become embodied in our laws and other institutional practices. With reference to Deleuze's comment at the beginning of this paper, it would mean recognizing that the modern civil body was instituted by and for a particular politico-economic group of men and explicitly excluded women (and others). The historical relation of that body to women's powers and capacities has been one of 'capture' and 'utility' rather than one of 'combining' to form a 'sociability' or 'ethical community' between men and women. Of course, similar points could, and should, be made concerning indigenous peoples, working-class men and others.

What would a civil body have to be like in order to be capable of accepting responsibility for its embodied history and the affects of its citizens? A civil body whose principle of sociability is based in reason should be capable of undertaking an analysis of the history of its traditions and its institutions – an analysis, that is, of how we became what we are. Such an analysis needs to face and acknowledge the brutality of some of our past laws as well as past treatment meted out to women and other non-enfranchised groups.

So long as the law continues to treat the criminal as an 'aberrant individual' or a 'monster' and as the sole locus of responsibility, our civil body will continue to structure human relations in ways which systematically encourage violence. What is required is an analysis of women's historical and present relation to citizenship, that is, a study of the specific conditions of women's civil existence. This would have to include attention to the marriage contract,[56] social arrangements for child-rearing, women's economic status, as well as the connections between these. In short, the structural problem concerns how to bring women *fully* into civil society. Again, Spinoza makes a pertinent point here. If a democratic civil body is to provide all its citizens with safety and security then it must ensure a concordance, or harmony, among its various members.[57] Harmony depends, above all, on an agreement in power, which in this context means civil power (or right).

Spinoza's largely neglected political and juridical theory offers a novel perspective from which to begin to think through these issues. This perspective should be of interest to those concerned to discriminate between different sorts of sociability without appeal to transcendent moral or crypto-theological categories. It offers an ethical stance without reducing ethics to a universal system of moral rules, and so does not have pretensions to universalism. It provides a means by which one may value a sociability that has its basis in a community of rational beings, over one based on 'capture' and 'utility', at the same time as showing the difference in attitude of each type of sociability towards notions of ethical and legal responsibility. A community of rational beings would look to the structural, as well as to the immediate, causes of violent behaviour and assume responsibility for such causes where appropriate – for example, attitudes to women that are embedded in the customs and laws of the civil body. Perhaps then the construction of men as essentially violent or of the criminal offender as a distinct 'species' would be understood as symptomatic of our ignorance concerning the type of body complex of which we are a part. Such an understanding would, in turn, be the harbinger of the death of a 'type': the intrinsically and wilfully evil criminal.

By contrast, societies which are predominantly governed by sad affects are those which expiate 'the sins of the people' by sacrificing the proverbial scapegoat. There is no dearth of examples of scapegoating in the present: Australia, England and the USA have all recently experienced instances of angry mobs gathering outside courthouses and police stations carrying primitive rope nooses and calling for the death penalty. These are affective responses to alarmingly violent incidents of child murder, serial murder, rape, and so on. Presumably the specific causes of the affects of the individuals which make up the crowd are diverse (fear, guilt, shame, horror, envy). It is likely, for example, that men and women would have quite different underlying causes for their angry responses to rapists or sex-specific murderers. However, the focus here is on the affect of the mob. Whatever the particular individuals concerned may feel, the group affect is hatred towards that which they perceive to be the cause of their sadness or pain.

The irony of this hatred shown by mobs, often to those merely accused as well as to those convicted of violent or shocking crimes, is that it mirrors the very affects which gave rise to the crime itself: hatred and frustration arising from lack of power. To be consumed by the force of such affects entails that one need not consider the causes of the behaviour that result in rape, murder, violence. Since the 'guilty one' is separated out from the rest of the community – exiled – he or she is no longer considered a part of the body that condemns him or her. This is one way in which the social body can absolve itself of responsibility for the acts committed, since between 'the criminal' and 'us' a distance and a difference has been created. It is this fabricated 'difference' that contributes to the marked fascination/repulsion that so many, encouraged by the media, appear to have for serial killers or those convicted of particularly violent or shocking crimes. The frequent finding of such media 'exposés' is that, according to neighbours and acquaintances, the so-called 'monster' was a quiet, polite 'ordinary sort of guy'. This ordinariness adds to, rather than undermines his 'monstros-ity'.[58] The 'spectacular' cruelty of such crimes only serves to mask the underlying banality of a largely unchallenged violence which structures our social relations.

Notes

1 G. Deleuze, *Spinoza: Practical Philosophy*, trans. Robert Hurley, San Fran-cisco, City Lights Books, 1988, p. 126, my emphasis.

2 B. Spinoza, *A Political Treatise*, in *The Chief Works of Benedict de Spinoza*, vol. I, ed. R.H.M. Elwes, New York, Dover, 1951 p. 292. There are several translations of Spinoza's works. The best is *The Collected Works of Spinoza*, trans. E. Curley, Princeton, N.J., Princeton University Press, 1985. Unfortu-nately only volume I has appeared to date. References to the *Ethics* and the *Treatise on the Emendation of the Intellect* will be to Curley's editon. Refer-ences to *A Theologico-Political Treatise* and *A Political Treatise* will be to Elwes' edition of the *Chief Works*. I have used both editions for Spinoza's correspondence.

3 *The Passions of the Soul*, in *The Philosophical Works of Descartes*, vol. I, trans. E.S. Haldane and G.R.T. Ross, Cambridge University Press, 1970, p. 333.

4 See Descartes' letter to Princess Elisabeth in *Descartes: Philosophical Letters*, ed. A. Kenny, Oxford, Clarendon Press, 1970, p. 141.

5 *Ethics*, pt. II, lemma 7, scholium.

6 Ibid., pt. II, postulates on the body, IV.

7 Ibid., pt. II, props. 11 and 13.

8 H. Jonas, 'Spinoza and the Theory of Organism', in M. Grene, ed., *Spinoza: A Collection of Critical Essays*, Notre Dame, Ind., University of Notre Dame Press, 1979, p. 271.

9 *Ethics*, pt. III, prop. 2.

10 Ibid., pt. V, preface.

11 Ibid., pt. II, prop. 49; see also Letter 2 to Oldenburgh, where Spinoza writes: 'will is merely an entity of the reason', in *Chief Works*, vol. I, p. 279.

12 *Ethics*, pt. III, preface.

13 Deleuze, *Spinoza*, p. 102.

14 *Ethics*, pt. II, prop. 13, scholium.

15 Spinoza defines joy as the 'passage from a lesser to a greater perfection'; *Ethics*, pt. III, definition of the affects, II.

16 Spinoza defines sadness as the 'passage from a greater to a lesser perfection'; ibid., definition of the affects, III.

17 G. Deleuze, *Expressionism in Philosophy: Spinoza*, New York, Zone Books, 1990, p. 280.

18 *Discourse on Method*, quoted in J. Blom, *Descartes: His Moral Philosophy and Psychology*, Brighton, Harvester Press, 1978, p. 43.

19 *A Political Treatise*, p. 313.

20 Ibid., p. 294. See also p. 297; and *Ethics*, pt. IV, app., VII and IX.

21 *A Political Treatise*, p. 297.

22 *A Theologico-Political Treatise*, p. 208.

23 *A Political Treatise*, p. 299.

24 For an excellent and systematic account of Spinoza's views on law see: G. Belaief, *Spinoza's Philosophy of Law*, The Hague, Mouton, 1971. I will not discuss ceremonial law here as it is not relevant to the issues at hand. However, see Belaief, pp. 38–41.

25 *Ethics*, pt. II.
26 *A Theologico-Political Treatise*, p. 44.
27 The example which Spinoza most commonly employs to illustrate the nature of this confusion is the 'story of the first man': Adam's 'disobedience' to the 'command' not to eat of the tree of the knowledge of good and evil. (Curiously, Eve is never mentioned in this connection.) Spinoza uses this example in the famous 'letters on evil' to Blijenbergh and again in *A Theologico-Political Treatise*, pp. 62f., and in *Ethics* pt. IV, prop. 68. In Letter 19 to Blijenbergh, Spinoza writes: 'The prohibition to Adam, then, consisted only in this: god revealed to Adam that eating of that tree caused death, just as he also reveals to us through the natural intellect that poison is deadly to us.' (*Collected Works*, vol. I, p. 360.) On these letters see: Deleuze, *Spinoza*, pp. 30–43, and *Expressionism*, pp. 247–8.
28 Belaief, *Spinoza's Philosophy*, pp. 41–2.
29 As Spinoza writes in *A Political Treatise*, 'liberty . . . does not take away the necessity of acting, but supposes it' (pp. 295–6).
30 *A Theologico-Political Treatise*, pp. 58, 59.
31 The notion of an arbitrary will is consistently rejected at all levels of Spinoza's thought: god, or nature, is not separate from that which it wills, human being does not will separately from its various understandings, and the sovereign cannot will laws separately from its understanding of what the civil body must affirm in order to persevere in its existence.
32 H. Cairns, *Legal Philosophy from Plato to Hegel*, Baltimore, Johns Hopkins University Press, 1949, p. 289. See also Belaief, *Spinoza's Philosophy*, pp. 25–6.
33 *A Political Treatise*, p. 310.
34 Belaief, *Spinoza's Philosophy*, p. 25, emphasis in original.
35 Ibid., p. 52. See also A. Negri, *The Savage Anomaly*, trans. Michael Hardt, Minneapolis, University of Minnesota Press, 1991, where he insists on the distinction in Spinoza's texts between *potentia* and *potestas* – a distinction usually lost in English translations, though not in French and Italian – in terms of 'constitution' versus 'command'.
36 *A Political Treatise*, p. 311.
37 Ibid., p. 312.
38 Belaief, *Spinoza's Philosophy*, p. 104.
39 Ibid., p. 106.
40 Ibid., p. 77.
41 Ibid., p. 83.
42 Spinoza makes his views on this clear in *A Theologico-Political Treatise*, where he writes that people are distinguishable 'by the difference of their language, their customs and their laws; while from the two last – i.e. customs and laws – it may arise that they have a peculiar disposition, a peculiar manner of life, and peculiar prejudices' (p. 232).
43 Y. Yovel, in *Spinoza and Other Heretics: The Adventures of Immanence*, Princeton, N.J., Princeton University Press, 1989, p. 14, draws attention to this point in the following terms:

> What to do about the multitude is the general problem underlying [*A Theologico-Political Treatise*] and spelled out in both its parts. The general answer is to reshape the cognitive and emotive power governing the multitude – what Spinoza calls *imaginatio* – as an external imitation of *ratio*, using obedience to authority in order to enforce and institutionalize the results.

However, because Yovel fails to grant any notion of historical growth – either intensive or extensive – to Spinoza's idea of reason, he fails to see that *A Theologico-Political Treatise* concerns itself with that which the *Ethics* assumes: the *development* of a rational community.

44 See *Ethics*, pt. IV, prop. 67, demonstration.

45 As Spinoza observes in *A Political Treatise*, 'rewards of virtue are granted to slaves, not freemen' (p. 382).

46 This question is the specific focus of Chapter 9.

47 *A Theologico-Political Treatise*, pp. 258–9; see also *Treatise on the Emendation of the Intellect*, §§14 and 15.

48 Y. Yovel, *Spinoza and Other Heretics*, p. 6.

49 Ibid., p. 177.

50 For example, that proposed by A. MacIntyre in *After Virtue: A Study in Moral Theory*, London, Duckworth, 2nd edn., 1985. Note the role of his notion of practice and the centrality of practices to tradition and virtue; for example, p. 220, pp. 239–40, p. 273. Iris Marion Young offers a cogent account of the oppressive aspects of communitarianism, especially for women, in *Justice and the Politics of Difference*, Princeton, N.J., Princeton University Press, 1990.

51 This failure to address structural causes of crime is very apparent in the 'Massie case' in which Darrow defended a man and his mother-in-law against murder charges after the husband had shot one of the men allegedly involved in a particularly brutal gang rape of his wife. The case is complex and deserves more careful treatment than I can offer here, but it is important to note that the woman who was raped was all but 'invisible' in Darrow's long defence speech. Further, in a postscript to the case, Darrow is credited with talking the 'family' (presumably, this included the wife?) out of pressing charges against the other men allegedly involved in the gang rape. See A. Weinberg, ed., *Attorney for the Damned*, London, MacDonald, 1957.

52 Letter 25 to Oldenburg, in *Chief Works*, p. 306.

53 Letter 42 to Tschirnhausen, in *Chief Works*, p. 392.

54 As reported in the *Sydney Morning Herald*, 30 October 1993.

55 Ibid.

56 See C. Pateman, *The Sexual Contract*, Cambridge, Polity Press, 1988, for an interesting, if controversial, reading of the marriage contract.

57 *Ethics*, pt. IV, app., XIV–XVI.

58 On this phenomenon, see B. Massumi, 'Everywhere You Want To Be: Introduction to Fear', in *The Politics of Everyday Fear*, ed. B. Massumi, Minneapolis, University of Minnesota Press, 1993, pp. 4–5.

9 Power, ethics and sexual imaginaries

In a recent book which explores the connections between Spinoza's politics and metaphysics, Antonio Negri asserts that '[t]he horizon of power is the only metaphysical horizon possible. But since this is true, only ethics . . . can adequately investigate it.'[1] For those who argue (or merely assume) that where power is, ethics is not, Negri's words must seem paradoxical.

Certainly, some feminists hold that power and freedom are opposed concepts and that ethical relations are possible only between free and equal persons. On their view, power is associated with repressive regimes and oppression whereas freedom is associated with liberation from such power. More will be said about this opposition between power and freedom below. Many early 'second wave' feminists saw the path to liberation as one which begins with the exploration of 'everyday consciousness', or 'consciousness-raising'. Paying attention to the context in which such political techniques were developed may be useful to the present.

Conditions of illusion

Over twenty years ago both Sheila Rowbotham and Juliet Mitchell wrote that their experiences of male chauvinism in male-dominated leftwing groups contributed to the development of their feminist consciousness. Marxist theory had little to contribute to the analysis of the specific oppression that women (in any social formation) experience as *women*. Works by Sartre, Reich, Fanon, Laing and Freud on the individual, the family and sexuality were mobilized by these feminist theorists to supplement the class-based analyses of society provided by Marxist thought. Nevertheless, socialist politics did have a marked effect on the shape of early 1970s feminist theory and practice. This is evident from the reliance of 1970s feminist *theory* on a notion of 'patriarchal ideology' as well as on the *practice* of 'consciousness-raising.'

In 1973, Rowbotham asked: 'How could I understand the manner in which society communicated itself through to the individual consciousness? How does individual consciousness translate itself back into a social movement?'[2] Since women's lived experience had little input into traditional political or social theory, the task as Rowbotham saw it was to '*translate* these strange phenomena of female life as we now live it into the language of theory'.[3] The practice of consciousness-raising was seen to be a crucial step in this 'translation' of lived experience into theory. The notion of consciousness-raising was often understood to involve the *transcendence* of ideology, where ideology was understood as the false, imaginary or illusory consciousness of one's real conditions of existence. The immediate or 'everyday' consciousness (often understood as simply 'feelings') that one has of one's existence was thought to be unreliable, contradictory and in need of being raised to the level of rational or objective political analysis. This split between one's 'real' conditions of existence and one's consciousness of those conditions was very prominent in 1970s feminist theory. A popular text of the time, entitled *Conditions of Illusion*,[4] bears on its title page the well-known quote from Marx: 'The call to abandon their illusions about their conditions is a call to abandon a condition which requires illusions.'

The practice of consciousness-raising – which was deployed in a theoretical context where the 'real conditions of existence' were understood to be obscured by the ideologies of both patriarchy and capitalism – functioned to entrench in feminist theory the split between ideology and truth, between illusory or imaginary conditions of existence and the true or real conditions of existence. The additional influence of the political voluntarism of theorists such as Sartre made for a rather interesting, if hybrid, political stance. For example, Rowbotham wrote that, while it was clear that social movements must have 'their own culture', a culture which would be capable of 'project[ing] alternative values', she could not see *how* this could be achieved without 'perpetually creating small, self-defeating, totalizing utopias which served only to exhaust everybody more by trying to live up to an impossibly ideal standard'.[5]

The effect of these theoretical influences was that much feminist theory held the view that public (or at least semi-public) reflection on one's feelings had a potentially transformative effect on those feelings. Private illusions or imaginings took on the status of 'raw materials' for the development of political insights into women's conditions of existence when they were shared and analysed by feminist groups. Feelings, illusions and the imagination were thus seen as that which must be overcome, transformed or transcended in political and social theory. Political theory itself was not acknowledged as having its own imaginary component. Why was the practice of consciousness-raising ultimately politically ineffective? Why has the notion of 'ideology' virtually disappeared from contemporary feminist writing? Here I wish to focus on the manner in which these two questions are interconnected. It is the power of feelings and the imagination, particularly in the context of ethical relations between the sexes, that I wish to address in this chapter.

Embodied knowledge

My starting point will not be the puzzle of how we get beyond 'the conditions of illusion', which cause us to misinterpret our 'real conditions of existence.' Rather, this chapter will explore the contribution that a Spinozistic perspective can make to thinking through ethical relations between the sexes. Spinoza's introduction to *A Political Treatise* recalls the sentiments expressed by Rowbotham concerning the utopian nature of much political theory. He writes:

> Philosophers conceive of the passions which harass us as vices into which men fall by their own fault, and therefore, generally deride, bewail, or blame them, or execrate them, if they wish to seem unusually pious. And so they think they are doing something wonderful, and reaching the pinnacle of learning, when they are clever enough to bestow manifold praise on such human nature, as is nowhere to be found, and to make verbal attacks on that which, in fact, exists. For they conceive of men, not as they are, but as they themselves would like them to be. Whence it has come to pass that, instead of ethics, they have generally written satire, and that they have never conceived a theory of politics, which could be turned to use, but such as might be taken for a chimera, or might have been formed in Utopia.[6]

In contemporary philosophy, Spinoza is almost invariably presented, along with Descartes and Leibniz, as one of the three great rationalists of the seventeenth century. Although it is certainly the case that for him reason is the greatest power available to human beings, his notion of reason, unlike Descartes, is immanent and embodied. Yovel puts this point well. He argues that

> [for Spinoza] knowledge is more a mode of being than of having, not something we possess but something we *are* or *become*. As Monique Schneider notes, in attaining knowledge we do not gain an acquisition, as if something new were added to the inventory of our possessions, but rather we exist differently.[7]

Hence the three sorts of knowledge (imagination, reason and intuition) that Spinoza outlines in part II of the *Ethics* should be understood not simply as different forms of consciousness or 'knowing' but also as different forms of being. To know something by the first kind of knowledge, that is, imagination, is to exist in a particular way in relation to one's context. This, in turn, will affect one's ability to act as well as one's capacity to be acted upon. On the Spinozist view, imagination is the source of various illusions and superstitions, such as those propagated by anthropocentric religions. He speaks of such misconceptions as 'scars of our former bondage' which 'disfigure' our understanding of ourselves and our context.[8] It is the imagination that gives rise to the illusions of free will and contingency.

Spinoza rejects contingency, arguing that what we take to be contingent in fact signals our partial or distorted knowledge. All that is is governed by necessity, and reason, or the second kind of knowledge, understands things truly when it understands this necessity. Our imaginative and passionate capacities are no more or less necessary to our nature on this view than is our capacity to reason. Spinoza likens the necessity of passions in human life to that of storms, winds, cyclones and floods in the rest of nature. Such apparent disturbances do not disrupt, but rather follow the laws of nature which are always and everywhere the same. Our passions, no less than cyclones, have causes through which we may understand them.

Some have understood the necessity which governs Spinoza's view of existence to involve a fatalistic and pessimistic picture of human agency, which could yield only a politics of resignation or quietism. I think this is a mistaken reading since such necessity provides the condition of possibility for free human action, if not free will. Without necessity, human freedom would remain as chimerical as the assumed freedom of the infant who believes he freely wants milk or the drunkard who believes he freely speaks his mind.[9] Put differently, human freedom would amount to little more than the false assumption that, because we are conscious of our appetites, we must also be their cause. This is a crucial aspect of Spinoza's account of human psychology and the imagination: the 'illusion of consciousness'[10] encourages the habit of mistaking the 'will' as the origin of our affects, that is, we 'experience' the affect but are often ignorant of the chain of causes which determine that affect.

Much of the character of interpersonal relations may be analysed in terms of such mistakes: I believe I love A because of her fine qualities; I hate B because of his odious qualities; I fear C because of her jealous nature, and so on. Each of these responses locates the cause of my passion or affect (love, hate, fear) in my consciousness of the effect which the object A, B, C has on me. The pairs love–hate and joy–sadness may be understood as signs of that which I take to empower or diminish me. Amelie Rorty has defined the passions or affects as: 'the ideational indicants of bodily thriving or declining', along with the important observation that such affects are relational and dynamic:

> Thoughts and passions alike are individuated in a field of forces. Each individual is so constituted as to attempt to perpetuate and enhance his nature, in relation to other individuals . . . a person's thoughts and passions are the traces – the expressions and reflections – of all this activity.[11]

What individuates a particular individual is its desire or *conatus* to maintain itself in its power of existing for as long as it can. The 'field of forces' in which it strives to maintain itself is made up of things that can empower or destroy it. The striving or 'essence' of each thing is to seek out, as far as possible and in so far as the individual's understanding allows, those things which enhance its power of existing and to avoid those which harm it.

The affects have no less influence in political relations than they do in interpersonal relations. Politico-ethical judgements on classes of people are frequently affective in nature: X pities indigenous peoples because of their colonized conditions of life; Y fears Germans because they are nationalistic; Z hates men because they are violent. The 'good–bad' morality operating in these cases locates the value – goodness or badness – in the object or class rather than in the *relation* between the object or the class and the person undergoing the affect. Any social or political theory that does not address the affective sphere will be, as Spinoza claimed above, a politics fit only for a utopia. Political theory cannot afford to treat the affective aspects of human relations as mere errors or 'illusions', that is, as those relations from which the political theorist must abstract in her theorizing. On the contrary, as Antonio Negri asserts, Spinoza begins with the passions and the imagination because these are 'the only effective reality from which the analysis of the concrete can proceed. Politics is not the realm of what 'ought' to be done; rather, it is the theoretical practice of human nature seen in its effectual capacity.'[12] It is in this sense that politics may itself be seen as 'the metaphysics of the imagination',[13] that is, as the metaphysics of the specifically human constitution of the world; not as an 'ought' but as an 'is'. Negri is here echoing Spinoza's own rejection of the notion that human being is in nature as 'a dominion within a dominion'.[14] Human nature in its affective, political or ethical dimensions does not depart from or transcend nature but rather is an immanent 'expression' of that nature. It would be incoherent, then, for a Spinozist political theorist to want to put aside the passions and the imagination and to construct a politics based solely in reason.

In so far as the political realm is concerned with the governance of ourselves and others, the organization of our needs and resources, our rights and obligations, it is quintessentially concerned with the passions and the imagination. As such the political is not simply that realm which is to be constituted but is also constitutive of human historical reality. To understand that reality, and the avenues for free action which are possible for us, given our constitution in and through history, means grasping the phenomenology through which power, or the capacity to affect and be affected, is experienced as value. Negri is right to insist on the passional as central to the ethico-ontological project of the *Ethics*.

> Insisting on the ethicality of the mode means living within its phenomenology . . . The ethics could not be constituted in a project, in the metaphysics of the mode and reality, if it were not inserted into history, into politics, into the phenomenology of single and collective life: if it were not to derive new nourishment from that engagement.[15]

It is in these terms that part III of the *Ethics* should be understood. In parts I and II Spinoza has laid the groundwork for the startling claim that opens part III: 'I shall consider human actions and appetites just as if it were a question of lines, planes, and bodies.'[16] Of course, he does much more than this – he offers a genealogical account of our consciousness of our power to affect and be affected in ways that cause joy or sadness, that is, in ways that involve an increase or decrease in our feeling of power. The more our actions emanate from within us rather than outside us, the more powerful and free we are and the more we experience joy. The capacity to act, rather than be acted on, to express one's own nature rather than merely reflect or react to the nature of another, is an expression of one's freedom, power, virtue or *conatus*. Throughout the progress of the *Ethics*, these terms come to stand in a synonymous relation to each other.[17]

In contrast to the voluntarist tradition, Spinoza's notion of power is not opposed to freedom, nor is freedom opposed to necessity. Rather, necessity is the condition which allows the possibility of becoming conscious of our power or, put differently, of our freedom to act. As Spinoza writes in *A Political Treatise*, 'liberty . . . does not take away the necessity of acting, but supposes it.'[18] There is, of course, a qualitative difference between the feeling of an increase in power and a genuine increase in power. Many of our affects give rise to feelings of power that may be largely imaginary. Yet, these imaginary feelings of an increase in our power may indeed increase our power to act though this is likely to be in an erratic and unreliable way. Such joyful affects may easily be reversed and hence become sad and debilitating affects.

Lust, love and freedom of mind (in a political frame)

Differences between one human individual and the next may amount to *qualitative* as well as quantitative differences in power. This would be one possible way in which one could describe differences between men and women. Given that, for Spinoza, the mind is the idea of the body, it is arguable that, in so far as men and women are bodily different, such differences would have their parallels in the specific kinds of pleasures and pains of which each type of body is capable.[19] This may provide support for Simone de Beauvoir's claim that men and women have their own specific sensualities.[20] The 'essentialism' of Spinoza's ontology, if we can call it that, pertains to the power of acting and enjoying peculiar to each. He is quite explicit about the specificity of the joys and pains of this or that individual:

> Both the horse and the man are driven by lust to procreate; but the one is driven by an equine lust, the other by a human lust. So also the lusts and appetites of insects, fish, and birds must vary. Therefore, though each lives content with his own nature, by which he is constituted, and is glad of it, nevertheless that life with which each one is content, and that gladness, are nothing but the idea, or soul, of the individual. And so the gladness of the one differs in nature from the gladness of the other as

much as the essence of the one differs from the essence of the other. Finally, it follows that there is no small difference between the gladness by which a drunk is led and the gladness a philosopher possesses.[21]

Gladness – or the power of being affected by joy – which arises through either drinking alcohol or engaging in philosophy, is a power of enjoyment that is unlikely to be markedly different simply by virtue of one's biological sex. One may acknowledge this without thereby denying that historical conditions can, and do, inhibit some and facilitate other sorts of activity purely on the basis of one's designated sex.[22] In addition, social conditions construct different social and political significances *of the same activity* for the sexes. Such historical and sociopolitical conditions can, and do, affect the range of capacities and powers that women and men are able to express. A person's capacity to affect and to be affected are not determined solely by the body she or he is but also by everything which makes up the context in which that body is acted upon and acts. When the term 'embodiment' is used in the context of Spinoza's thought it should be understood to refer not simply to an individual body but to the *total* affective context of that body.

Spinoza's 'essentialism' is thus not likely to provide anything approaching a justification for ontological sexual difference since individuals are as much formed by their context as by their own constitution. Hence, a man and a woman from a similar historical and political context may have much more in common than two women or two men from radically different contexts. The politics of both class and race resist the too easy reduction of humanity to the category of sexual difference.[23] Indeed, it is arguable that the notion of ontological sexual difference belongs to a system of classification (genus, species, kind) that is quite foreign to Spinoza's thought. As Deleuze makes clear, Spinoza defines beings

> by their *capacity for being affected*, by the affections of which they are capable, the excitations to which they react, those by which they are unaffected, and those which exceed their capacity and make them ill or cause them to die. In this way, one will obtain a classification of beings by their power; one will see which beings agree with others, and which do not agree with one another, as well as who can serve as food for whom, who is social with whom, and according to what relations.[24]

However, Spinoza's view of embodiment and power carries with it the corollary that all human relations are ethically structured. One primary sphere of ethical relations between the sexes will be sexual relations. In keeping with Spinoza's rejection of final causes, he does not attempt to explain sexual desire teleologically.[25] The desire or love which we feel for an other can arise for any number of reasons. Anyone and anything can become an object of desire provided the context is one in which we feel an increase in power (or joy) in the experience of the combination of that body with our own. As Alexandre Matheron explains, Spinoza's rejection of final causes allows for 'sexuality without taboo'.[26] The sexual relation, in so far as it gives rise to joyful feelings, is good. Spinoza's monistic view of human being dictates that what increases the power of action of the body also increases the power of action of the mind.[27] Hence bodily pleasures are as important for the well-being of the individual as is the cultivation of reason. As Spinoza observes '[n]othing forbids our pleasure except a savage and sad superstition', and the rational no less than the passionate person is enjoined by him

> to refresh and restore himself in moderation with pleasant food and drink, with scents, with the beauty of green plants, with decoration, music, sports, the theater, and other things of this kind, which anyone can use without injury to another. For the human Body is composed of a great many parts of different natures, which constantly require new and varied nourishment, so that the whole Body may be equally capable of all the things which can follow from its nature, and hence, so that the Mind also may be equally capable of understanding many things.[28]

In fact, the activity of body and mind are one and the same. However, sexual desire, in so far as it is a passion, is as likely to become a source of pain or sadness as it is to give rise to pleasure or joy. This is because, like other passions that arise from our modal constitution, we are passive in relation to its power to affect us. This is particularly so for sexual passion that is 'lustful'. Lustful sexuality tends to desire the possession of the object. As such the desired object becomes a constant source of anxiety, hope and fear, since actual possession of the object is not possible. The passions of hope and fear are particularly singled out by Spinoza as 'sad' passions which seriously deplete our power of acting.

However, Spinoza also speaks of love between free individuals or love from freedom of mind. This is where 'the love of each . . . is caused not by external appearance only, but mainly by freedom of mind'.[29] Spinoza's conception of 'freedom of mind' is not an easy one to grasp.[30] My under-standing of his meaning, in the context of love between the sexes, is that love 'from freedom of mind' is based not merely on physical attraction but on an understanding of why one is attracted to this person and an active affirmation of such attraction when it is a genuinely empowering one. Such love would have as its basis a knowledge of oneself, of the other, and of the necessity which governs the context of the relation between the two. Presumably, too, each should strive to maintain an 'agreement in power', that is, each should seek to maintain the harmony that promotes the joyful affects of both.[31]

The view of love relations presented in the *Ethics* is extremely interest-ing and deserves consideration in its own right. In the two excellent papers mentioned above, Rorty and Matheron offer persuasive reasons why these views are of interest in the present. However, neither Rorty nor Matheron give sufficient attention to the political and historical context in which these relations are lived out. In particular, neither pays sufficient attention to the implications for love relations between the sexes of the fact that these take place in a patriarchal society that has a history of excluding women from political participation.[32] What effect does this have on the ability of each, the man and the woman, to love from freedom of mind? What effect does this history have on the ability of each to maintain a harmonious relation, that is, a relation which involves an agreement in power?[33]

To consider this question in Spinoza's own terms, we need to place the philosophy of the *Ethics* in a political frame. Without doubt, one can read the *Ethics* as a philosophy of power that offers a fluid and immanent ethics of joyful and life-enhancing encounters, rather than a transcendent morality which dictates dry duties and encourages a suspicion of the body, pleasure and laughter.[34] And it would seem that Spinoza offers an ethic for anyone who can understand it and is prepared to put in the effort – certainly, it is not a path which all will want or be able to follow; he does, after all, close the *Ethics* with the advice that 'all things excellent are as difficult as they are rare'. However, it is necessary to draw attention to an unacknowledged assumption which is crucial to the coherence of the *Ethics*.[35] The *Ethics* assumes a particular social and political context; it is not addressed to those who are in a state of nature – where conceptions of right or virtue are meaningless – nor to those who live under tyrannical governments. Rather, the *Ethics* is addressed to free and rational members of a democratic body politic. The importance of this assumption was not lost on Spinoza himself. He ceased work on the *Ethics* between 1665 and 1670, in order to address the issues of religion and politics in the *Theologico-Political Treatise* and, later, in the unfinished *Political Treatise*. While the sexual relation has political consequences for both sexes, the history of the 'political problem' posed by sexual difference is a different 'problem' for women than it is for men.

As Matheron points out, Spinoza sees two main problems associated with sexual passion.[36] The first concerns the individual: sexual passion runs the risk of inhibiting one's power to act and to think. The second is political: sexual passion gives rise to competition (implicitly, competition between men) and so promotes discord in the social body. Presumably, this is why, in *A Political Treatise*, in the section on democracy, Spinoza excludes women from political participation. Given his view that the 'true aim of government is liberty'[37] and his view that democracy is the form of government that is 'the most natural, and the most consonant with individual liberty',[38] it is peculiar, to say the least, to see him arguing for the exclusion of half of humanity from the attainment of political liberty.[39]

The reason Spinoza offers for such exclusion is that women are not independent beings but rather are under the authority of men. To his credit, he does at least ask 'whether women are under men's authority by nature or institution'.[40] He answers that women are under men's authority by nature since 'women have not by nature equal right with men'.[41] This is a perplexing view for Spinoza to hold. Elsewhere he warns against treating entire classes of people as possessing intrinsic class-based traits or qualities. For example, in *A Theologico-Political Treatise* he argues against racial or national sterotypes by stating that 'nature forms *individuals*, not peoples'.[42] His point is that dispositions, ways of life and prejudices that distinguish classes of people are the result of specific laws and customs, not nature.[43] In the *Political Treatise* Spinoza cites the case of the Amazons from Justin's *Histories* alongside the comment that if men were ruled by women then they would be 'so brought up, that they [could] make less use of their abilities',[44] without noting that this is arguably the historical situation of women: that is, that women have been so brought up that we can make less use of our abilities. What is the cause of Spinoza's blindness to the historical situation of women? Here I wish to venture a tentative diagnosis by considering a further argument he offers for the exclusion of women from citizenship. He writes:

> But if we further reflect upon human passions, how men, in fact, generally love women merely from the passion of lust, and esteem their cleverness and wisdom in proportion to the excellence of their beauty, and also how very ill-disposed men are to suffer the women they love to show any sort of favour to others, and other facts of this kind, we shall easily see that men and women cannot rule alike without great hurt to peace.[45]

This argument is very odd indeed.[46] It argues for women's political exclusion not on the basis of the qualities or predispositions of women, but rather on the basis of men's predispositions. Moreover, it is an argument that is unacceptable in the context of Spinoza's own political philosophy. Men have all sorts of passions about all sorts of things that the body politic is not obliged to consider. Men may be greedy, querulous, ambitious, and so on, all of which may lead to upsetting the peace. However, in none of these cases does Spinoza consider it appropriate for the political realm to accommodate such passions. On the contrary, if men cannot be masters of their own passions then laws and the power of political society will be their masters for them. Why is the 'lust' of men for women exempted from the standard political solution to the fact that passions divide men, pull them in contrary directions and make them enemies to one another?

Spinoza's exclusion of women from political participation is like 'a scar' which 'disfigures' Spinoza's philosophy. It is a 'scar', if you like, on the body of his work. If it were simply the case that Spinoza, limited by his historical situation, could not think through the implications of his own thought, then we might well respond with a shrug and nevertheless enjoy those parts of his work that are interesting or useful to the present. Unfortunately, Spinoza's views on women and politics are far from exceptional.

The exclusion of women from political society is a 'scar' upon the entire corpus of Western political thought. If we are to understand how this 'scar' continues to mark current relations between the sexes, then a promising place to begin is with the imagination and the passions.

The imagination, Spinoza tells us, has a tendency to form wild generalizations:

> If someone has been affected with joy or sadness by someone of a class, or nation, different from his own, and this joy or sadness is accompanied by the idea of that person as its cause, under the universal name of the class or nation, he will love or hate, not only that person, but everyone of the same class or nation.[47]

This proposition warrants careful consideration in the context of the ideas which each sex forms about the other. In earlier chapters, I argued that the mainstay for one's sexed identity is knowledge of the first kind, that is, imagination, concerning the opposite sex.[48] While each sex entertains its own 'imaginings' about the other sex,[49] such imaginings have asymmetrical implications given the historical predominance of men as producers of public culture and theory.

Sexual imaginaries

Women, as a class, have provided thought for far too long with images or metaphors for whatever vice or virtue a thinker took it upon himself to illustrate. Women are thoroughly inscribed in the imagination of our culture and its history. This affects the quality of life of actual women in a multiplicity of ways: some relatively trivial (for example, sexist advertising) and others not so trivial (for example, the treatment women often receive from the law). This is our historical given, and feminist thought must engage with it if it is not (unwittingly or otherwise) to reproduce it. Earlier chapters have suggested that an understanding of the political and ethical present requires that we undertake a genealogy of the sexual imaginary.

This project must acknowledge the Spinozistic insight that *modes of knowing are also modes of being*. If knowledge is a mode of being rather than having, then the failure of the voluntarist politics that I sketched at the beginning of the chapter is inevitable. If our beliefs, opinions and imaginings are not 'possessions' of which we can take an inventory then it is not surprising that we cannot discard them by an act of will. However, under specific historical conditions, it is open to us to examine at least some beliefs and to question the bases for the continued investment that we and/or others may have in them. An investigation of what brings us joy or sadness, and why, may alter what we are and what could bring us joy or sadness in the future. Of course, one could do worse than offer this as an account of much that is presently taking place under the general rubric of feminist theory.[50]

I am inclined to agree with Spinoza (more, apparently, than he agrees with himself) that nature does not form classes or peoples and that the prejudices, predispositions and peculiarities of such collectivities have their origin in laws and customs and particular 'ways of life', that is, in embodied beliefs and habits. A sexual ethics that is not utopian needs to consider people as they are now; historical men and women whose passions and imaginings about each other have been formed, at least in part, by past and present social and political institutions. There is no 'beyond' of these 'conditions of illusion'; rather, the human condition *is* a condition of illusion.

If one returned, as a novice practitioner of a genealogy of the sexual imaginary, to the reasons for the differential political treatment of women offered by Spinoza, what would one find? As a first attempt, what I find is a paradox in his reasoning. It is precisely the fact that women are not full members of the body politic that allows men to exert their so-called natural right. If women were full members of a body politic then equal political right would supersede instances of unequal natural right. Further, those passions that disrupt civil peace, such as men's sexual passions, would then be dealt with by the guardians of civil peace. There is nothing surprising in this claim – at least, not at the level of traditional political theory. These are precisely the kinds of change that social contract theorists tell us that men hoped to effect in their relations with other men by the institution of political society. In contemporary terms it may be more correct to say that these are the conditions of civil society to which any rational person would consent.[51]

This paradox in Spinoza's reasoning is a paradox endemic to much reasoning on the relations between the sexes. It is not peculiar to the seventeenth-century imagination or to political theory or to philosophical speculations on women. Women in Western democracies literally embody this paradox. It is a paradox at the heart of all the major institutions of contemporary liberal democratic societies. Such a claim cannot be demonstrated in general terms. I intend to draw together the various themes of this chapter by an analysis of recent incidents involving some members of the Australian judiciary, which attracted a good deal of media attention.

Rough handling

In 1992, in the Supreme Court of South Australia, comments made by Justice Bollen when advising the jury on a marital rape case[52] caused a public outcry. His words have ensured him notoriety for years to come in feminist and other circles. His opening remarks to the jury included the following advice:

I must warn you to be especially careful in considering evidence in a case where sexual allegations have been made. *Experience has taught the judges* that there have been cases where *women* have manufactured or invented false allegations of rape and sexual attack.[53]

Presently, I will have something to say about Bollen's view of 'experience' as a teacher and his judgement that it is appropriate to treat 'women' as a class. His view of what counts as 'acceptable persuasion' (leading to intercourse) rather than force or coercion (leading to rape) is captured in these words:

Of course, you may run into considering in this case the question of, shall I say, persuasion. There is, of course, nothing wrong with a *husband*, faced with his *wife's* initial refusal to engage in intercourse, in attempting, in an acceptable way, to persuade her to change her mind, and that may involve a measure of *rougher than usual handling*. It may be, *in the end*, that *handling and persuasion* will persuade the wife to agree. Sometimes it is a fine line between not agreeing, then changing of the mind, and consenting.[54]

The extensive reporting of this case in the media caused such a furore that in 1993 the Court of Criminal Appeal in South Australia was under considerable pressure to reassure the public that Bollen's comments were not representative of judicial attitudes toward women. The Court of Criminal Appeal considered two questions of law arising from Justice Bollen's comments:

firstly, whether it was an error of law to warn the jury of the danger of false allegations in a sexual case . . . and secondly whether the direction as to persuasion 'in an acceptable way' involving 'rougher than usual handling' constituted an error of law.[55]

On the first question the court ruled that a direction to a jury which 'has a tendency to characterize the complainant in a sexual case as a member of a *"class of suspect witness"* will be erroneous in law'.[56] However, on the question of 'rougher than usual handling', the Chief Justice argued that Justice Bollen's comments, considered in context, 'accurately conveyed to the jury the law applicable to the issues which they had to consider relating to consent and the effect of persuasion'. He noted further that 'wooing and persuasion are not unlawful'.[57]

In the same year that these pronouncements were made by the Criminal Court of Appeal, two other incidents made national headlines. In the first a Supreme Court judge from the state of Victoria stated that a schoolgirl who was raped was 'not traumatized' because she was unconscious at the time of the rape. Justice O'Bryan made these remarks when passing sentence on a rapist who had beaten the 17-year-old girl unconscious, raped her and then slit her throat.[58]

The widespread reporting of these judicial attitudes towards the crime of rape, as well as the normative attitudes towards women and heterosexuality which they reveal, triggered a spate of radio and newspaper stories on judges, their backgrounds and their familial and professional profiles. These stories appear to have had an effect on the self-awareness of some judges when passing sentence in rape cases. One judge felt the need to defend judicial perceptions of relations between the sexes. Judge Bland felt it necessary to support indirectly Justice Bollen's remarks in the following terms:

> despite criticism that has been directed at judges lately about violence and women, [and] men acting violently to women during sexual inter-course, it does happen, in the *common experience* of those who have been in the law as long as I have anyway, that 'no' often subsequently means 'yes'.[59]

What do these various cases tell us about the sexual imaginary that under-lies these judgements? The function of the notion of 'experience', in both Justice Bollen's and Judge Bland's comments, warrants some analysis. 'Experience', as an unanalysed 'primitive', plays a crucial justificatory role in these judges' perceptions of relations between the sexes. There is no place in their judgements for multiple and perhaps contradictory 'experiences' of the same event; and no awareness of the manner in which their own experience is inescapably perspectival in nature. Yet the meaning of many social interactions is contested precisely at the level of the way in which these interactions may be 'experienced' differently by the parties involved.

These cases return us to the issues which opened this chapter. Row-botham's question – 'How could I understand the manner in which society communicated itself through to the individual consciousness?' – resonates in the present context. How can one begin to unpack the apparent simpli-city of a term such as 'experience'? When those in positions of consider-able institutional power – such as judges – fall back on 'experience' as a basis for their judgements, the consequences for those who do not share such 'experience' are extreme. In Australia, Canada and the United States of America, some members of the judiciary are taking these issues ser-iously. In many jurisdictions, in all three countries, judicial education programmes on 'gender awareness' have been, or are being, introduced. Most of these programmes could be described as a sort of 'consciousness-raising' for judges but for one crucial difference: it is not their conscious-ness of their own lives that is 'raised' but their consciousness of the lives of others. Such programmes are an important starting point in making the law and its representatives more accountable to the communities which they serve. However, some of the insights from Spinoza's views on knowl-edge and the imagination reveal problems with the way in which these educational programmes are conceived.

An indication of the sorts of technique that are being used in promoting gender awareness in the judiciary may be gained from the account offered by the Chief Justice of Western Australia, David Malcolm.[60] Malcolm intends to introduce in Australia judicial education programmes similar to those in Canada and the United States. He describes one such programme in British Columbia which dealt with issues relating to indigenous peoples as well as sexual assault. The educational techniques used in this programme

> included the re-enactment of a sexual assault trial with the actual Judge and counsel assisted by actors, a television documentary and the exposure of the Judges to discussions with the victims of sexual assaults, native elders and other members and representatives of native groups. The re-enactment of the sexual assault trial was *climaxed by the victim running hysterically from the courtroom screaming, 'None of you will ever understand'*. While a number of Judges *did not like the experience* to which they were exposed in the programme, the general opinion was that it should be repeated.[61]

I have no doubt that such techniques spring from the best of motives. However, if the aim is to educate judges about gender awareness, it is not clear what is to be gained from a woman – who has been raped and who has been through a gruelling rape trial – repeating what was certainly a traumatic experience for the supposed edification of judges. 'Hysterics' in the courtroom are, after all, hardly novel.

The reasoning of these contemporary legal reformists has much in common with John Rawls' *A Theory of Justice*. A brief comparison of some key shared assumptions will help to clarify what I see as the problem with these judicial educational programmes. Susan Moller Okin, who believes that Rawls' theory (with feminist revisions) can have radical consequences for thinking about the nature of a just society, succinctly describes the gist of his view as follows:

> Although Rawls is clearly aware of the effects on individuals of their different places in the social system, he regards it as possible to hypothesize free and rational moral persons in the original position who, *temporarily freed from the contingencies of actual characteristics and social circumstances*, will adopt the viewpoint of the 'representative' human being. He is under no illusions about the difficulty of this task: it requires a 'great shift in perspective' from the way we think about fairness in everyday life. But with the help of the veil of ignorance, he believes that we can 'take up a point of view that everyone can adopt on an equal footing', so that 'we share a common standpoint along with others and do not make our judgements from a personal slant'. The result of this rational impartiality or objectivity, Rawls argues, is that, all

being convinced of the same arguments, agreement about the basic principles of justice will be unanimous.[62]

Moller Okin is sceptical of the idea that any particular person can take the stance of the 'representative human being' largely because she does not concede that gender is the sort of 'characteristic' which one can subtract from one's total viewpoint. However, she defends the potential of Rawls' theory by stating that those critics who claim that his notion of the 'original position' depends on a disembodied concept of the self are mistaken. Rather, Moller Okin argues,

> [t]hose in the original position cannot think from the position of *nobody* . . . rather, [they] think from the perspective of *everybody*, in the sense of *each in turn*. To do this requires, at the very least, both strong empathy and a preparedness to listen carefully to the very different points of view of others.[63]

Moller Okin's view, no less than those of the legal reformists, assumes that one can 'think from' the position of each person. She thus denies the radical, and sometimes unbridgeable, difference which may exist between one individual and the next. Her notion of embodiment appears to be limited to the integrity of a single human body, that is, a person's embodiment is limited to her or his unique occupation of space, within a single epidermal surface. However, one's embodiment, as Spinoza's account of human being shows, includes in a crucial and inescapable sense one's beliefs, habits and entire context. New beliefs, including knowledge concerning others, cannot be acquired like possessions. Aspects of the thought of the legal reformists, Rawls and Moller Okin treat our 'social imaginaries' in a manner which shows up a residual commitment to the notion of a 'false consciousness' that can be overcome by revealing the 'true conditions of existence'. But this opposition between ideology and truth, or imaginary versus real conditions of existence is misleading and unhelpful.

The *limits* to empathizing with, and gaining an understanding of, the specific and total contexts of the lives of those with whom the law deals must be acknowledged. To fail to acknowledge the necessarily limited understanding that a given person can glean about the lives of those who are very differently situated is to do such persons a serious violence. Considerable caution is required in thinking that one can 'know' (in the sense that one knows that $2 + 2 = 4$) how the differently embodied experience themselves or their situation. This is precisely to believe that one can step outside the social imaginary and see the truth, clearly and without distortion. This is the old dream of raising oneself above the 'conditions of illusion'. Arguably, what one may 'see' is at best the system of beliefs, the 'imaginary', if you like, of the other.

If it is the consciousness of the judges that requires 'raising' then it is appropriate to make the lives, experiences and beliefs of the *judges* an object of analysis. This would be to examine their beliefs not simply in relation to the *object* of those beliefs but in relation to the *subject of those beliefs*, that is, the embodied context of the judges themselves. The assumption of those who promote the present educational programmes is that judges can gain 'experience' of the lives of those whom they judge while their own lives, their own particular 'ways of being', remain private or 'sacrosanct'. I am not suggesting that we should subject the lives of the judiciary to wholesale scrutiny. This would not only be impractical, it would also be unwise. A more obvious response to the poor treatment that women often receive at the hands of the judiciary is to ensure that the experiences of women are represented at all levels of legal, social and political life. If Spinoza's views on knowledge and imagination are correct, the only means to ensure genuine representation, given our history, is the presence of women from various walks of life.

The ethical problem concerning the legal treatment meted out to women (and others whose 'ways of being' are not represented in positions of institutional influence) is a political problem. It is a problem that high-lights the historical and embodied nature of our ethical relations. The effects of women's historical exclusion from citizenship do not vanish once women are enfranchised. There is a multiplicity of embodied habits, customs and laws which continue to bear the scars of that exclusion. The removal of formal bars to women's sociopolitical representation does not amount to full participation in legal and political institutions, since those institutions have histories that continue to function in ways that deplete women's powers of action. As far as the present is concerned, there are some (and these 'some' are disproportionately represented in institutional positions of influence, such as the judiciary) who unreflec-tively endorse and perpetuate a sexual imaginary in which women embody the paradox of being considered as *both* free and rational members of a democratic political body *and* beings under the 'natural' authority of men.

Notes

1 A. Negri, *The Savage Anomaly*, trans. M. Hardt, Minneapolis, University of Minnesota Press, 1991, p. 156.
2 S. Rowbotham, *Woman's Consciousness, Man's World*, Harmondsworth, Penguin, 1973, p. 24.
3 Ibid., p. 45, my emphasis.
4 S. Allen, L. Sanders and J. Wallis, eds., *Conditions of Illusion*, Leeds, Feminist Books, 1974.
5 Rowbotham, *Woman's Conciousness*, p. 25, my emphasis.
6 B. Spinoza, *A Political Treatise*, in *The Chief Works of Benedict de Spinoza*, vol. I, ed. R. H. M. Elwes, New York, Dover, 1951, p. 287. There are several translations of Spinoza's works. The best is *The Collected Works of Spinoza*, trans. E. Curley, Princeton, N. J., Princeton University Press, 1985. Unfortunately only volume I has appeared to date. References to the *Ethics* will be to Curley's

142 *Imaginary bodies*

translation. References to *A Theologico-Political Treatise* and *A Political Treatise* will be to Elwes' edition of the *Chief Works*.

7 Y. Yovel, *Spinoza and Other Heretics: The Adventures of Immanence*, Princeton, N. J., Princeton University Press, 1989, p. 159, emphasis in original. Although Yovel concedes that reason is embodied and immanent, he does not think that it is historical. On this see my comments in Chapter 8, note 43. Compare Yovel's view with Negri's: 'Reason neither transcends nor alters the body. It completes it, develops it, fills it' (*Savage Anomaly*, p. 166).

8 See *A Theologico-Political Treatise*, p. 6.

9 See *Ethics*, pt. III, prop. II, scholium.

10 G. Deleuze, in *Spinoza: Practical Philosophy*, San Francisco, City Lights Books, 1988, writes: 'consciousness is inseparable from the triple illusion that *constitutes* it, the illusion of finality, the illusion of freedom, and the theological illusion' (p. 20, emphasis in original).

11 A. Rorty, 'Spinoza on the Pathos of Idolatrous Love and the Hilarity of True Love', in R. C. Solomon and K. M. Higgins, eds., *The Philosophy of (Erotic) Love*, Lawrence, University Press of Kansas, 1991, p. 354.

12 A. Negri, *Savage Anomaly*, p. 186.

13 Ibid., p. 97.

14 *Ethics*, pt. III, Preface.

15 A. Negri, *Savage Anomaly*, p. 84

16 *Ethics*, pt. III, preface.

17 Ibid., pt. IV, definition 8.

18 *A Political Treatise*, pp. 295–6

19 See G. Lloyd, 'Woman as Other: Sex, Gender and Subjectivity', *Australian Feminist Studies*, no. 10 (1989).

20 De Beauvoir is surprisingly Spinozistic on this point. In the conclusion to *The Second Sex* she writes:

there will always be certain differences between man and woman; her eroticism, and therefore her sexual world, have a special form of their own and therefore cannot fail to engender a sensuality, a sensitivity of a special nature. This means that her relations to her own body, to that of the male, to the child, will never be identical with those the male bears to his own body, to that of the female, and to the child; those who make much of 'equality in difference' could not with good grace refuse to grant me the possible existence of differences in equality.

(*The Second Sex*, trans. H.M. Parshley, Harmondsworth, Penguin, 1975, p. 740.)

21 *Ethics*, pt. III, prop. 57, scholium.

22 Perhaps Michèle Le Dœuff's *Hipparchia's Choice: An Essay Concerning Women, Philosophy, etc.*, trans. Trista Selous, Oxford, Blackwell, 1991, has shown this most clearly. Note, however, that her argument does not rely on any commitment to *ontological* sexual difference.

23 In Australia many indigenous women are becoming more vocal about what they see as white feminists' 'gender essentialism'. For example, Larrisa Behrendt, in 'Aboriginal Women and the White Lies of the Feminist Movement: Implications for Aboriginal Women in Rights Discourse', *Australian Feminist Law Journal*, vol. 1 (1993), p. 35, argues that theorists such as Catharine MacKinnon 'isolate gender from other power relationships such as race, class and sexual preference. Such essentialist discourse suppresses the complexities within the categories of 'man' and 'woman.''

24 Deleuze, *Spinoza*, pp. 45–6, emphasis in original. See also p. 127: 'In short, if

we are Spinozists we will not define a thing by its form, nor by its organs and its functions, nor as a substance or a subject.'

25 It is not possible, from a Spinozistic perspective, to explain socially dominant sexual behaviour or preference in functional or teleological terms. Thus, those theories that posit the necessity of the reproduction of the species as an *explanation* for heterosexuality are disallowed. On this see A. Matheron, 'Spinoza et la Sexualité', *Giornale Critico della Filosofia Italiana*, ser. 4, vol. 8 (1977) pp. 442–6. Many thanks to Paul Patton for his informal translation of this paper.

26 Ibid., p. 454

27 *Ethics*, pt. II, prop. 13, scholium.

28 Ibid., pt. IV, prop. 45, corollary 2, scholium.

29 Ibid., pt. IV, app., XIX and XX.

30 An adequate treatment of Spinoza's notion of 'freedom of mind' would take us too far from our present topic. In the notoriously difficult part V of the *Ethics*, he uses it as a synonym for 'blessedness'. An interesting path, which could be explored elsewhere, is the part that love between 'free' women and men could play in the attainment of the third and highest kind of knowledge: intuition. On this see *Ethics*, pt. IV, app., IV. Since, for Spinoza, knowledge is embodied and the attainment of the second and third kinds of knowledge is dependent on the existence of certain social conditions, it is arguable that a society marked by 'unfree' relations between the sexes will produce knowledge that is 'inadequate'. Several feminist epistemologists have put this argument in other terms.

31 See *Ethics*, pt. IV, prop. 32: 'Things that are said to agree in nature are understood to agree in power (by IIP7), but not in lack of power, or negation, and consequently (see IIIP3S) not in passion either.' Matheron comes to a similar conclusion when he writes that free men and women have as their 'fundamental aim' both knowledge and truth. Hence free men and women would seek the 'parallel development of their mental and physical abilities' and seek to 'promote concord' among themselves and, where possible, with others. See Matheron, 'Spinoza', p. 454.

32 It is the historical difference between men's and women's capacities and powers and the effect of this difference on the heterosexual relation that is the focus of this chapter. However, Spinoza's notion of sexuality and desire would bear thinking through in the context of same-sex love relations. Certainly same-sex relations would not present the *same* problems as heterosexual relations and perhaps harmony, understood as an agreement in power, would be easier to achieve in the former.

33 Take the example of a man and a woman of similar capacities who desire to share an equitable and so harmonious life. If the woman fares worse professionally than the man does because of sexual discrimination, what affect will this have on the harmony which both have endeavoured to achieve? Contemporary arrangements concerning child care will be likely to be of crucial importance here.

34 This is Deleuze's reading, *Spinoza*, esp. chs. 2 and 3.

35 Ironically, it is this same assumption which results in the ultimately contradictory nature of Spinoza's thought: the contradiction between the historically given and the ethical drive or impulse. It is this contradiction which Negri refers to as 'the savage anomaly'. E. Balibar, in 'Spinoza, the Anti-Orwell: The Fear of the Masses', in *Masses, Classes, Ideas*, London, Routledge, 1994, p. 3, describes Spinoza's thought as 'aporetic' and 'a complex of contradictions without a genuine solution'. Both philosophers agree, however, that the anomalous and aporetic nature of Spinoza's thought is what draws us to him.

Concerning the contemporary fascination with Spinoza, see also Deleuze, 'Spinoza and Us' in *Spinoza*.
36 See Matheron, 'Spinoza', pp. 452f.
37 *A Theologico-Political Treatise*, p. 259.
38 Ibid., p. 207.
39 Women are indeed a 'political problem' for Spinoza. The unfinished *Political Treatise* abruptly breaks off precisely at the point of the political exclusion of women *as a class*. As Balibar says, it is tempting to say that 'we watch him [Spinoza] die before this blank page' ('Spinoza, the Anti-Orwell', p. 26).
40 *A Political Treatise*, p. 386
41 Ibid., p. 387
42 *A Theologico-Political Treatise*, p. 232, my emphasis.
43 Spinoza writes that people are distinguishable 'by the difference of their language, their customs and their laws' and that the laws of a people may give rise to 'a peculiar disposition, a peculiar manner of life, and peculiar prejudices' (*A Theologico-Political Treatise*, p. 232).
44 *A Political Treatise*, p. 387
45 Ibid., p. 387.
46 I am reminded here of Le Dœuff's comments on the peculiar phenomenon of those – otherwise careful and systematic thinkers – who offer absurd and patently inadequate arguments when their subject is women: 'What is irritating is that the usual standards of philosophical work are commonly abandoned by all writers once women are the topic' (*Hipparchia's Choice*, p. 70).
47 *Ethics*, pt. III, prop. 46.
48 This is a theme of many of the essays in this collection.
49 While I think it is the case that each sex participates in an 'imaginary' concerning the other sex, I am inclined to agree with Judith Butler who questions 'the integrity of either a masculine or a feminine imaginary' (J. Butler, *Bodies that Matter*, New York, Routledge, 1993, p. 262).
50 I take it that this is the general thrust of much recent feminist scholarship that seeks to interrogate the notion of 'experience' and the way that notion has functioned in feminist politics and theory. See the papers by J. Butler and J.W. Scott in *Feminists Theorize the Political*, ed. J. Butler and J.W. Scott, New York, Routledge, 1992.
51 Perhaps the 'classic' articulation of this view in contemporary contractarian thought is John Rawls' *A Theory of Justice*, Cambridge, Mass., Harvard University Press, 1971. Note, however, that Rawls shares aspects of Spinoza's sexual imaginary, that is, Rawls too treats the family as a 'pre-political' association or 'natural' institution, thus ruling out of court considerations of justice and fairness between the sexes. I will have more to say on Rawls below.
52 Marital rape is a criminal offence in South Australia.
53 Quoted in T. Threadgold, 'Critical Theory, Feminisms, the Judiciary and Rape', *Australian Feminist Law Journal*, vol. 1 (1993), p. 18, my emphasis.
54 Ibid., p. 19, my emphasis.
55 Quoted in B.A. Hocking, 'The Presumption not in Keeping with *Any* Times: Judicial Re-appraisal of Justice Bollen's Comments Concerning Marital Rape', *Australian Feminist Law Journal*, vol. 1 (1993), p. 152.
56 Ibid., p. 155. It should be noted that, in spite of the finding of an error in law by the Court of Criminal Appeal, this finding had no effect on the husband's acquittal of the charge of rape.
57 Ibid., p. 155.
58 Reported in *The Age*, on 13 May 1993, quoted in Threadgold, 'Critical Theory', p. 20.

59 Reported in the *Sydney Morning Herald*, 7 May 1993, quoted in Hocking, 'The Presumption', p. 158, my emphasis.
60 D. Malcolm, 'Women and the Law: Proposed Judicial Education Programme on Gender Equality and Task Force on Gender Bias in Western Australia', *Australian Feminist Law Journal*, vol. 1 (1993), pp. 139–51.
61 Ibid., p. 140, my emphasis.
62 S. Moller Okin, *Justice, Gender and the Family*, New York, Basic Books, 1989, p. 105, my emphasis.
63 Ibid., p. 101, emphasis in original.

Epilogue

Let me open the Epilogue with the passage from Spinoza on the imagination with which the Preface closed:

> an imagination is an idea which indicates the present constitution of the human body ... For example, when we look at the sun, we imagine it to be about 200 feet away from us. In this we are deceived so long as we are ignorant of its true distance; but when its distance is known, the error is removed, not the imagination [since this imagination is] not contrary to the true, and do[es] not disappear on its presence.[1]

Spinoza insists that this proposition holds true for all those imaginings that arise from the affective relations between my body and any other body with which I enter into a relation. Hence, his point is pertinent not only to natural science or astronomy, but holds good for my relations with bodies of all kinds, whether they be individual human bodies or corporate social bodies. The nature of my imaginary grasp of these bodies will depend upon how they affect me – do they increase or diminish my power of acting? Do they cause me pleasure or pain? Just as there is a vast difference between the sun *per se* and the sun *as it affects my present bodily constitution* (does it warm me? burn me?), so too can one distinguish between the general nature, constitution or powers of a body and the particular manner in which that body affects me. However, as Spinoza pointed out, an understanding of the nature of another body, including the powers that it possesses independently of its relation to me, does not *remove* the affect that it produces in me, that is, such understanding does not cancel out any imaginary relation which I may have towards it.

Many of the essays in this volume may be seen as attempts to think through this view of the imagination and imaginary relations between bodies, in the context of philosophical accounts of sexual difference. Often enough, such accounts are rooted in historically dominant sexual imaginaries, which include disturbing assumptions about the appropriate political, ethical and legal treatment to which women are entitled. One does not need to subscribe to a 'conspiracy theory' in order to argue that men who occupy positions of institutional power will share some 'imaginings' about women. This is not because they 'conspire' against women in order to protect their privileged positions. Rather, and as many sociological studies have shown, they share similar 'imaginings' about women because they share types of relation to women, for example, as mothers, wives, secretaries. The manner in which 'women', here understood as a 'type' or 'class', stand in relation to these men is likely to be as dependent and subordinate servicers of their needs. Such men may never have encountered women to whom they were socially, professionally or economically subordinate. The problem of the power of the imagination as it operates between the sexes is not that men have 'strange' ideas about women, whereas women have more realistic ideas about men. The problem, as I see it, is that dominant masculine sexual imaginaries are politically, legally, economically and socially legitimated through existing networks of power, whereas women's imaginings about men are not (see Chapter 3). Such legitimation entrenches sexual imaginaries that tell us only about the affective relation in which men stand to women. They tell us nothing about the various powers and capacities which women possess independently of their power to affect, or be affected by, men.

Those who occupy positions of social, economic and political power, such as members of the judiciary, politicians or heads of business corporations, have considerable direct and indirect influence on the lives of many women. Such socially or politically powerful persons will almost certainly believe, in the abstract, that women are entitled to the franchise, are (rightly) covered by the 'rule of law' and (rightly) enjoy a formal equality with men in the market place. Nevertheless, the affective relation in which such men are likely to stand to significant women in their lives will unavoidably affect their general attitudes toward women understood as a 'type' or 'class.' It is here that Spinoza's insight into the resilience of the imagination becomes important to sexual politics.

Spinoza certainly argues that human passions drive each in a different direction in contrast to reason which unites different persons. However, the imagination is capable of forging alliances between people on those occasions when their imaginings correspond. It is, after all, to the power of the imagination that Spinoza turns in order to offer an account of the socially binding nature of various superstitions, including religion.[2] In Chapters 3, 8 and 9 I tried to investigate the operation of sexual imaginaries in the context of sexual ethics, politics and law, respectively. One of the things I tried to show is the utterly paradoxical nature of certain aspects of present liberal democracies in which widely held and institutionally sanctioned views concerning women's equal rights and entitlements sit alongside widely held and institutionally sanctioned notions of women's natural subordination to men. My response to this paradox is that it may be at least epistemically (if not in economic or political terms) approached by *combining* a study of the social and sexual imaginaries in which we live with the formal sociopolitical equality to which all citizens are entitled.

Here we would need to ask: are the legal duties and obligations of a 'wife' in conflict with the rights of a citizen? Is wife-beating an offence which is distinguishable from assaulting a 'fellow' citizen? Is a husband who rapes his wife guilty of a different sort of offence from one who rapes a 'fellow' citizen? Of course, in contemporary liberal democracies, women *are* citizens, and the distinction drawn above, between 'wife' and 'citizen', should not be a significant one.[3] Yet these questions still deserve to be taken seriously – why is that? That these questions make sense at all is itself an indication of the paradoxical nature of female citizenship.[4]

One of the challenges confronting feminist theory is how to account for the manner in which these dominant sexual imaginaries become fundamental to social imaginaries. In Chapters 2 and 7 I tried to link the psychoanalytic notion of the body image, or imaginary body, with a political imaginary that posits an image of the unified and independent 'leviathan' or body politic. While I do not think that social and political imaginaries can be *reduced* to sexual imaginaries, it is an important task for feminist theory to show the complicity of these various imaginaries. I maintain that such complicity may be shown without thereby supporting an essentialist notion of sexual difference. Chapter 6 critically considered attempts by Carole Pateman, Andrea Dworkin and Catharine MacKinnon to draw connections between sexual, political and legal 'imaginaries'. Each of these theorists, I argued, too readily accepts dominant notions of male and female sexual embodiment as the origin of social and political relations between the sexes. In various sections of this book (especially Chapters 6, 7, 8 and 9) I have argued for a genealogical approach to the manner in which sexual difference becomes socially, politically and ethically significant. I see this approach as one which is capable of opening the present to different ways of being a woman or a man, along with different ways of negotiating that difference.

A genealogy of sexual and social imaginaries inevitably raises questions concerning sociability. What types of sociability are realizable for us in the present? This question is of central concern in Chapters 7 and 8. Spinoza's monistic and immanent theory of being is of particular interest here since he offers an account of knowledge in which both reason and imagination are collectively embodied. Rationality is not a transcendent capacity of a disembodied 'mind' but an immanent power of active nature. Neither reason nor law come to us 'from above' but rather develop immanently from our collective situations. Ironically, it is precisely because philosophers often fail to acknowledge the embodiedness of reason and knowledge that their own (embodied) imaginings play such a large part in their 'reasoned' accounts of politics, morality and justice. The specificity of human embodiment should be understood not simply in terms of sexual or racial specificity, but also in terms of the *historical* specificity of human embodiment which provides a basis of commonality for all those who share, however inequitably, a present *as being their present*. It is this fact of embodiment that makes our present situation 'ours' and one which only 'we' can address. Those who make up any particular sociability are literally embodied elements of the historical conditions which make that form of sociability possible.

This view of human social and political being is one which is bound to see social and political power as immanent in the field of social relations. This in turn necessitates the rejection of any morality which would conceive of itself as a transcendent set of rules with the power to impose itself on an independently existing social terrain. Spinoza does not offer a moral theory of this sort, which amounts to a wish list, dreamed up 'outside' power relations. Rather, he offers an ethics of power, where power is conceived as determined capacity for action. In this sense, what he offers sits well with a genealogy of our sexual and social present, where genealogy is understood as a critical history of the present which seeks to understand what we have been, what we are now and, on this basis, what it is possible for us to become. Put differently, ethics is concerned with knowledge concerning that which we are and the type of sociability in which we participate. I have offered some suggestions concerning how we might go about an ethical appraisal of our present in Chapters 8 and 9.

The path taken by these essays has tended to move away from dualistic understandings of sexual difference (sex/gender) and towards understanding differences as constituted through relatively stable but dynamic networks of relational powers, capacities and affects. Spinoza's immanent and monistic theory of being is attractive to me because it allows one to theorize the interconnections between sexed bodies and other body complexes, such as the body politic or other institutional assemblages (the law, for example). It is only within these complex assemblages that sexed bodies are produced as socially and politically meaningful bodies. How would a Spinozist theorize the sex/gender distinction?[5] Since Spinoza maintains that there can be no causal relation between mind and body (since both are modifications of the attributes of a single substance, or nature), sex, in some sense, must be gender, though 'expressed' or made manifest through the attribute of extension rather than thought. This amounts to saying that sex is a particular extensive 'organization' of the material powers and capacities of a body, whereas gender would amount to the affective powers and affects of such a body. On this reading of the sex/gender distinction, gender is both a power and an affect of a certain modification of the attribute of extension.[6]

This understanding introduces a good deal of dynamism into the categories 'sex' and 'gender' since both the extensive (bodies) and the intensive (minds) are conceived by Spinoza as complex fields of interconnecting powers and affects. Hence, both sex and gender, as parallel descriptions of modified nature, will be definable in relational terms only. A particular extensive organization of bodies will be paralleled by certain intensive powers and capacities. However, given that there is no causal relation between the attributes, the sex of a body does not and cannot cause its gender. When I wrote Chapter 1, I did not explicitly have Spinoza 'in mind'. However, it seems that the argument of that chapter is consistent with a Spinozist reading of sex and gender. In this sense, these essays loop back on themselves. For, if we understand gender as the powers, affects and dispositions that *are* the intensive parallel of a certain extensive organization of sexed bodies, then gender can indeed be understood in terms of the imaginative grasp that we have on the specificity of our sexual and historical embodiment.

Notes

1 *Ethics*, pt. IV, prop. 1, scholium.
2 See *A Theologico-Political Treatise*.
3 It is, of course, true that large numbers of women are not citizens of any polity. Here I am concerned to draw out the paradox of female citizenship *simpliciter*. In actual polities the situations of women are much more complex than I can show in this context. Consider, for example, the situation of indigenous women who formally may be citizens of the polity which has colonized them.
4 Carole Pateman has written about the conceptual difficulties involved in female citizenship in *The Sexual Contract*, Cambridge, Polity, 1988 and in *The Disorder of Women*, Cambridge, Polity, 1989.
5 See G. Lloyd, 'Woman as Other: Sex, Gender and Subjectivity', *Australian Feminist Studies*, no. 10 (1989).
6 The 'Spinozism' of both Deleuze and Foucault is obvious in this context. The account offered by Deleuze and Guattari of the extensive and intensive axes of the 'plane of immanence' in *A Thousand Plateaus* and Foucault's account of sexuality in *The History of Sexuality I* resonate with Spinoza's account of mind and body.

Bibliography

Abray, J., 'Feminism in the French Revolution', *American Historical Review*, no. 80, 1975.

Allen, S., Sanders, L. and Wallis, J., eds., *Conditions of Illusion*, Leeds, Feminist Books, 1974.

Althusser, L., 'Ideology and Ideological State Apparatuses', in *Lenin and Philosophy, and Other Essays*, London, New Left Books, 1977.

Bacon, W. and Landsdown, R., 'Women who Kill Husbands: The Battered Wife on Trial', in O'Donnell, C. and Craney, J., eds., *Family Violence in Australia*, Melbourne, Longmans-Cheshire, 1982.

Balibar, E., 'Spinoza, the Anti-Orwell: The Fear of the Masses', in *Masses, Classes, Ideas*, trans. James Swenson, London, Routledge, 1994.

Barrett, M., *Women's Oppression Today*, London, Verso, 1980.

Behrendt, L., 'Aboriginal Women and the White Lies of the Feminist Movement: Implications for Aboriginal Women in Rights Discourse', *Australian Feminist Law Journal*, vol. 1, 1993.

Belaief, G., *Spinoza's Philosophy of Law*, The Hague, Mouton, 1971.

Bell, D., and Napurrula Nelson, T., 'Speaking about Rape is Everyone's Business', *Women's Studies International Forum*, vol. 12, no. 4, 1989.

Benjamin, J., 'The Bonds of Love: Rational Violence and Erotic Domination', in H. Eisenstein and A. Jardine, eds., *The Future of Difference*, Boston, G.K. Hall, 1980.

Blom, J., *Descartes: His Moral Philosophy and Psychology*, Brighton, Harvester Press, 1978.

Bordo, S., *The Flight to Objectivity: Essays on Cartesianism and Culture*, Albany, SUNY, 1987.

——— *Unbearable Weight: Feminism, Western Culture and the Body*, Berkeley, University of California Press, 1993.

Bourdieu, P., *The Logic of Practice*, trans. Richard Nice, Stanford, Stanford University Press, 1990.

Braidotti, R., 'The Ethics of Sexual Difference: The Case of Foucault and Irigaray', *Australian Feminist Studies*, no. 3, 1986.

——— 'The Politics of Ontological Difference', in T. Brennan, ed., *Between Feminism and Psychoanalysis*, Routledge, London, 1989.

——— *Patterns of Dissonance: A Study of Women in Contemporary Philosophy*, Cambridge, Polity Press, 1991.

Brennan, T., *History After Lacan*, London, Routledge, 1993.

Brown, W., 'Feminist Hesitations, Postmodern Exposures', *differences*, vol. 3, no. 1, Spring 1991.

Butler, J., *Gender Trouble: Feminism and the Subversion of Identity*, New York, Routledge, 1990.

—— *Bodies That Matter: On the Discursive Limits of ' Sex'*, New York, Routledge, 1993.

Caine, B., Grosz, E., and de Lepervanche, M., eds., *Crossing Boundaries*, Sydney, Allen & Unwin, 1988.

Cairns, H., *Legal Philosophy from Plato to Hegel*, Baltimore, Johns Hopkins University Press, 1949.

Calvino, I., *Invisible Cities*, London, Picador, 1979.

Carrigan, T., 'Of Marx and Men', *Gay Information*, no. 11, 1982.

Chodorow, N., *The Reproduction of Mothering*, Berkeley, University of California Press, 1978.

—— 'Gender Relations and Difference in Psychoanalytic Perspective', in A. Jardine and H. Eisenstein, eds., *The Future of Difference*, Boston, G.K. Hall, 1980.

Cixous, H., 'The Laugh of the Medusa', in E. Marks and I. Courtivron, eds., *New French Feminisms*, Amherst, University of Massachusetts Press, 1980.

—— 'Sorties', in E. Marks and I. Courtivron, eds., *New French Feminisms*, Amherst, University of Massachusetts Press, 1980.

—— 'Castration or Decapitation?', *Signs*, vol. 7, no. 1, 1981.

Daly, M., *Gyn/Ecology: The Metaethics of Radical Feminism*, Boston, Mass., Beacon Press, 1978.

De Beauvoir, S., *The Ethics of Ambiguity*, Secaucus, N.J., Citadel, 1975.

——*The Second Sex*, Harmondsworth, Penguin, 1975.

Deleuze, G., *Spinoza: Practical Philosophy*, trans. Robert Hurley, San Francisco, City Lights Books, 1988.

—— *Expressionism in Philosophy: Spinoza*, trans. Martin Joughin, New York, Zone Books, 1990.

Deleuze, G. and Guattari, F., *A Thousand Plateaus: Capitalism and Schizophrenia*, trans. B. Massumi, Minneapolis, University of Minnesota Press, 1987.

Descartes, R., *Descartes: Philosophical Letters*, ed. A. Kenny, Oxford, Clarendon Press, 1970.

—— *The Philosophical Works of Descartes*, vol. I, trans. E.S. Haldane and G.R.T. Ross, Cambridge, Cambridge University Press, 1970.

—— *'Discourse on Method' and the 'Meditations'*, Harmondsworth, Penguin, 1985.

Deutsch, F., ed., *On the Mysterious Leap from the Mind to the Body*, New York, International Universities Press, 1973.

Di Stefano, C., 'Masculine Marx', in M.L. Shanley and C. Pateman, eds., *Feminist Interpretations and Political Theory*, Cambridge, Polity Press, 1991.

Dinnerstein, D., *The Mermaid and the Minotaur*, New York, Harper & Row, 1977.

Diprose, R., *The Bodies of Women: Ethics, Embodiment and Sexual Difference*, London, Routledge, 1994.

Diprose, R. and Ferrell, R., eds., *Cartographies: Poststructuralism and the Mapping of Bodies and Spaces*, Sydney, Allen & Unwin, 1991.

Dworkin, A., *Intercourse*, London, Secker & Warburg, 1987.

Eder, D.L., 'The Idea of the Double', *Psychoanalytic Review*, vol. 65, no. 4, 1978.

Eisenstein, H. and Jardine, A., eds., *The Future of Difference*, Boston, G.K. Hall, 1980.

Firestone, S., *The Dialectic of Sex*, London, Paladin, 1970.

Flax, J., 'Mother–Daughter Relationships: Psychodynamics, Politics and Philosophy', in H. Eisenstein and A. Jardine, eds., *The Future of Difference*, Boston, G.K. Hall, 1980.

Foucault, M., *Discipline and Punish: The Birth of the Prison*, trans. Alan Sheridan, London, Allen Lane, 1977.

—— 'Nietzsche, Genealogy, History', in *Language, Counter-Memory, Practice*, ed. D. Bouchard, Ithaca, Cornell University Press, 1977.

—— *The History of Sexuality*, vol. I, London, Allen Lane, 1978.

—— *Herculine Barbin*, New York, Pantheon, 1980.

—— *Power/Knowledge*, ed. C. Gordon, Brighton, Harvester Press, 1980.

—— 'Nietzsche, Freud, Marx', *Critical Texts*, vol. 3, no. 2, Winter 1986.

Freud, S., 'Beyond the Pleasure Principle', in *The Standard Edition of the Complete Psychological Works of Sigmund Freud*, vol. XVIII, ed. J. Strachey, London, Hogarth Press, 1978.

—— *Civilization and its Discontents*, The Pelican Freud Library, vol. 12, Harmondsworth, Penguin, 1985.

—— 'The Ego and the Id', in *The Standard Edition of the Complete Psychological Works of Sigmund Freud*, vol. XIX, ed. J. Strachey, London, Hogarth Press, 1978.

—— 'Fetishism', in *The Standard Edition of the Complete Psychological Works of Sigmund Freud*, vol. XXI, ed. J. Strachey, London, Hogarth Press, 1978.

—— 'Fragment of an Analysis of a Case of Hysteria ("Dora")', in *The Standard Edition of the Complete Psychological Works of Sigmund Freud*, vol. VII, ed. J. Strachey, London, Hogarth Press, 1978.

—— *The Future of an Illusion*, The Pelican Freud Library, vol. 12, Harmondsworth, Penguin, 1985.

—— 'Infantile Genital Organisation', in *The Standard Edition of the Complete Psychological Works of Sigmund Freud*, vol. XIX, ed. J. Strachey, London, Hogarth Press, 1978.

—— 'The Interpretation of Dreams', in *The Standard Edition of the Complete Psychological Works of Sigmund Freud*, vol. VI, ed. J. Strachey, London, Hogarth Press, 1978.

—— Letter 52 to Fliess, in *The Standard Edition of the Complete Psychological Works of Sigmund Freud*, vol. II, ed. J. Strachey, London, Hogarth Press, 1978.

—— *Moses and Monotheism*, The Pelican Freud Library, vol. 13, Harmondsworth, Penguin, 1985.

—— 'On Narcissism: An Introduction', in *The Standard Edition of the Complete Psychological Works of Sigmund Freud*, vol. XIV, ed. J. Strachey, London, Hogarth Press, 1978.

—— 'Notes upon a Case of Obsessional Neurosis', in *The Standard Edition of the Complete Psychological Works of Sigmund Freud*, vol. X, ed. J. Strachey, London, Hogarth Press, 1978.

—— 'An Outline of Psychoanalysis', in *The Standard Edition of the Complete Psychological Works of Sigmund Freud*, vol. XXIII, ed. J. Strachey, London, Hogarth Press, 1978.

—— 'Project for a Scientific Psychology', in *The Standard Edition of the Complete Psychological Works of Sigmund Freud*, vol. I, ed. J. Strachey, London, Hogarth Press, 1978.

—— 'Some Psychological Consequences of the Anatomical Distinction between the Sexes', in *The Standard Edition of the Complete Psychological Works of Sigmund Freud*, vol. XIX, ed. J. Strachey, London, Hogarth Press, 1978.

—— 'A Special Type of Object-Choice Made by Men', in *The Standard Edition of the Complete Psychological Works of Sigmund Freud*, vol. XI, ed. J. Strachey, London, Hogarth Press, 1978.

—— 'Splitting of the Ego in the Process of Defence', in *The Standard Edition of the Complete Psychological Works of Sigmund Freud*, vol. XXIII, ed. J. Strachey, London, Hogarth Press, 1978.

—— *Totem and Taboo*, The Pelican Freud Library, vol. 12, Harmondsworth, Penguin, 1985.

—— 'The Unconscious', in *The Standard Edition of the Complete Psychological Works of Sigmund Freud*, vol. XIV, ed. J. Strachey, London, Hogarth Press, 1978.

Freud, S. and Breuer, J., 'Studies on Hysteria', in *The Standard Edition of the Complete Psychological Works of Sigmund Freud*, vol. II, ed. J. Strachey, London, Hogarth Press, 1978.

Fuss, D., *Essentially Speaking: Feminism, Nature and Difference*, New York, Routledge, 1989.

Gallagher, C. and Laqueur, T., eds., *The Making of the Modern Body*, Berkeley, University of California Press, 1987.

Gallop, J., *Feminism and Psychoanalysis*, London, Macmillan, 1982.

—— *Thinking Through the Body*, New York, Columbia University Press, 1988.

Gatens, M., 'Dualism and Difference: Theories of Subjectivity in Modern Philosophy', Ph.D. diss., University of Sydney, 1986.

—— 'Feminism, Philosophy and Riddles Without Answers', in C. Pateman and E. Gross, eds., *Feminist Challenges: Social and Political Theory*, Sydney, Allen & Unwin, 1986.

—— *Feminism and Philosophy: Perspectives on Difference and Equality*, Cambridge, Polity Press, 1991.

Gilligan, C., 'In a Different Voice: Women's Conceptions of Self and Morality', in H. Eisenstein and A. Jardine, eds., *The Future of Difference*, Boston, G.K. Hall, 1980.

Greer, G., *The Female Eunuch*, London, Paladin, 1971.

Grimshaw, J., *Feminist Philosophers: Women's Perspectives on Philosophical Traditions*, Brighton, Harvester, 1986.

Gross, E., 'Philosophy, Subjectivity and the Body: Kristeva and Irigaray', in C. Pateman and E. Gross, eds., *Feminist Challenges*, Sydney, Allen & Unwin, 1986.

Grosz, E., *Sexual Subversions*, Sydney, Allen & Unwin, 1989.

—— *Jacques Lacan: A Feminist Introduction*, London, Routledge, 1990.

—— 'A Note on Essentialism and Difference', in S. Gunew, ed., *Feminist Knowledge: Critique and Construct*, London, Routledge, 1990.

Haraway, D., *Primate Visions: Gender, Race and Nature in the World of Modern Science*, New York, Routledge, 1989.

Harding, S., *The Science Question in Feminism*, Milton Keynes, Open University Press, 1986.

Hobbes, T., *Leviathan*, Harmondsworth, Penguin, 1968.

Hocking, B.A., 'The Presumption not in Keeping with *Any* Times: Judicial Reappraisal of Justice Bollen's Comments Concerning Marital Rape', *Australian Feminist Law Journal*, vol. 1, 1993.

Hoy, D.C., 'Deconstructing Ideology', *Philosophy and Literature*, vol. 18, no. 1, April 1994.

Hume, D., *An Enquiry Concerning the Principles of Morals*, ed. L.A. Selby-Bigge, Oxford, Clarendon Press, 1975.

Irigaray, L., 'Women's Exile', Ideology and Consciousness, no. 1, 1977.

—— 'This Sex Which is Not One', in E. Marks and I. Courtivron, eds., *New French Feminisms*, Amherst, University of Massachusetts Press, 1980.

—— *This Sex Which is Not One*, Ithaca, Cornell University Press, 1985.

—— *Speculum of the Other Woman*, Ithaca, Cornell University Press, 1985.

——— *An Ethics of Sexual Difference*, trans. C. Burke and G.C. Gill, Ithaca, Cornell University Press, 1993.

Johnston, C., 'Radical Homosexual Politics', *Gay Information*, nos. 2–3, 1980.

Jonas, H., 'Spinoza and the Theory of Organism', in M. Grene, ed., *Spinoza: A Collection of Critical Essays*, Notre Dame, Ind., University of Notre Dame Press, 1979.

Kirby, V., 'Corporeal Habits: Addressing Essentialism Differently', *Hypatia*, vol. 6, no. 3, Fall 1991.

——— 'Corpus Delicti: The Body at the Scene of Writing', in R. Diprose and R. Ferrell, eds., *Cartographies: Poststructuralism and the Mapping of Bodies and Spaces*, Sydney, Allen & Unwin, 1991.

Lacan, J., 'Some Reflections on the Ego', *International Journal of Psychoanalysis*, vol. 34, 1953.

——— *Ecrits*, London, Tavistock, 1977.

——— 'The Mirror Stage as Formative of the Function of the I', in *Ecrits*, London, Tavistock, 1977.

Laing, R.D., *The Divided Self*, Harmondsworth, Penguin, 1965.

Landes, J., *Women and the Public Sphere in the Age of the French Revolution*, Ithaca, Cornell University Press, 1988.

Laplanche, J., *Life and Death in Psychoanalysis*, Baltimore, Johns Hopkins University Press, 1976.

Laplanche, J. and Pontalis, J.B., *The Language of Psychoanalysis*, London, Hogarth Press, 1983.

Le Dœuff, M., 'Women and Philosophy', *Radical Philosophy*, no. 17, 1977.

——— *The Philosophical Imaginary*, trans. C. Gordon, London, Athlone, 1989.

——— *Hipparchia's Choice: An Essay Concerning Women, Philosophy, etc.*, trans. Trista Selous, Oxford: Blackwell, 1991.

Lloyd, G., *The Man of Reason: 'Male' and 'Female' in Western Philosophy*, London, Methuen, 1984.

——— 'Woman as Other: Sex, Gender and Subjectivity', *Australian Feminist Studies*, no. 10, 1989.

Locke, J., *Two Treatises of Government*, London, Cambridge University Press, 1967.

Lyotard, J. F., 'One of the Things at Stake in Women's Struggles', *Substance*, no. 20, 1978.

——— *The Postmodern Condition*, Manchester, Manchester University Press, 1984.

MacIntyre, A., *After Virtue: A Study in Moral Theory*, London, Duckworth, 2nd edn., 1985.

——— *Three Rival Versions of Moral Enquiry*, London, Duckworth, 1990.

Mackenzie, C., 'Simone de Beauvoir: Philosophy and/or the Female Body', in C. Pateman and E. Gross, eds., *Feminist Challenges*, Sydney, Allen & Unwin, 1987.

MacKinnon, C., *Feminism Unmodified: Discourses on Life and Law*, Cambridge, Mass., Harvard University Press, 1987.

———'Sexuality, Pornography and Method: "Pleasure Under Patriarchy"', *Ethics*, vol. 99, no. 2, 1989.

Maclean, I., *The Renaissance Notion of Woman*, Cambridge, Cambridge University Press, 1980.

McMillan, C., *Women, Reason and Nature*, Oxford, Basil Blackwell, 1982.

Mahon, M., *Foucault's Nietzschean Genealogy: Truth, Power and the Subject*, Albany, SUNY Press, 1992.

Malcolm, D., 'Women and the Law: Proposed Judicial Education Programme on

Gender Equality and Task Force on Gender Bias in Western Australia', *Australian Feminist Law Journal*, vol. 1, 1993.

Mannoni, M., *The Child, his Illness and Others*, Harmondsworth, Penguin, 1970.

Marcus, S., 'Fighting Bodies, Fighting Words: A Theory and Politics of Rape Prevention', in J. Butler and J.W. Scott, eds., *Feminists Theorize the Political*, New York, Routledge, 1992.

Marks, E., and Courtivron, I., eds., *New French Feminisms*, Amherst, University of Massachusetts Press, 1980.

Massumi, B., 'Everywhere You Want To Be: Introduction to Fear', in B. Massumi, ed., *The Politics of Everyday Fear*, Minneapolis, University of Minnesota Press, 1993.

Matheron, A., 'Spinoza et la Sexualité', *Giornale Critico della Filosofia Italiana*, ser. 4, vol. 8, 1977.

Merleau-Ponty, M., 'The Child's Relations with Others', in *The Primacy of Perception*, ed. J.M. Edie, Evanston, Ill., Northwestern University Press, 1964.

——— *The Phenomenology of Perception*, London, Routledge & Kegan Paul, 1970.

Milkman, R., 'Women's History and the Sears Case', *Feminist Studies*, vol. 12, Summer 1986.

Mill, J. S., *On Liberty*, Harmondsworth, Penguin, 1976.

——— 'On the Subjection of Women', in *Essays on Sex Equality*, ed. A. Rossi, Chicago, University of Chicago Press, 1970.

Miller, C. and Swift, K., *Words and Women*, New York, Anchor Doubleday, 1977.

Millett, K., *Sexual Politics*, London, Abacus, 1971.

Mitchell, J., *Psychoanalysis and Feminism*, Harmondsworth, Penguin, 1974.

——— *Women's Estate*, Harmondsworth, Penguin, 1971.

Moi, T., *Sexual/Textual Politics*, London, Methuen, 1985.

Moller Okin, S., *Women in Western Political Thought*, Princeton, N. J., Princeton University Press, 1979.

——— *Justice, Gender and the Family*, New York, Basic Books, 1989.

——— 'John Rawls: Justice as Fairness – For Whom?', in M.L. Shanley and C. Pateman, eds., *Feminist Interpretations and Political Theory*, Cambridge, Polity Press, 1991.

Morgan, S., *My Place*, Fremantle, Fremantle Arts Centre Press, 1987.

Mouffe, C., 'Feminism, Citizenship and Radical Democratic Politics', in J. Butler and J. W. Scott, eds., *Feminists Theorize the Political*, Routledge, New York, 1992.

Negri, A., *The Savage Anomaly*, trans. Michael Hardt, Minneapolis, University of Minnesota Press, 1991.

Nehamas, A., *Nietzsche: Life as Literature*, Cambridge, Mass., Harvard University Press, 1985.

Nicholson, L., ed., *Feminism/Postmodernism*, New York, Routledge, 1990.

Nietzsche, F., *Thus Spoke Zarathustra*, Harmondsworth, Penguin, 1976.

——— *On the Advantage and Disadvantage of History for Life*, trans. Peter Preuss, Indianapolis, Hackett Publishing Co., 1980.

——— *Beyond Good and Evil*, New York, Vintage Books, 1989.

——— *On The Genealogy of Morals*, New York, Vintage Books, 1989.

Oakley, A., *Sex, Gender and Society*, London, Temple Smith, 1972.

Pateman, C., 'The Fraternal Social Contract', paper delivered to the Annual American Political Science Association, Washington, D.C., 1984.

——— *The Sexual Contract*, Cambridge, Polity Press, 1988.

——— *The Disorder of Women*, Cambridge, Polity Press, 1989.

Patton, P., 'Nietzsche and the Body of the Philosopher', in R. Diprose and R.

Ferrell, eds., *Cartographies: Poststructuralism and the Mapping of Bodies and Spaces*, Sydney, Allen & Unwin, 1991.

———— 'Politics and the Concept of Power in Hobbes and Nietzsche', in P. Patton, ed., *Nietzsche, Feminism and Political Theory*, New York: Routledge, 1993.

———— ed., *Nietzsche, Feminism and Political Theory*, New York, Routledge, 1993.

———— 'Metamorpho-logic: Bodies and Powers in *A Thousand Plateaus*', *Journal of the British Society for Phenomenology*, vol. 25, no. 2, 1994.

———— 'Deleuze and Desire: Desire as Power', paper delivered at the *Forces of Desire* Conference at the Humanities Research Centre, ANU, 13–15 August 1993.

Plaza, M., ' "Phallomorphic Power" and the Psychology of "Woman" ', *Ideology and Consciousness*, no. 4, 1978.

Rajchman, J., 'Ethics After Foucault', *Social Text*, 13/14, 1986.

Rawls, J., *A Theory of Justice*, Cambridge, Mass., Harvard University Press, 1971.

Rich, A., 'Motherhood: The Contemporary Emergency and the Quantum Leap', in *On Lies, Secrets and Silence*, London, Virago, 1980.

———— 'Women and Honour: Some Notes on Lying', in *On Lies, Secrets and Silence*, London, Virago, 1980.

———— *Blood, Bread and Poetry*, London, Virago, 1987.

Riley, D., *Am I that Name? Feminism and the Category of 'Women' in History*, London, Macmillan Press, 1988.

Rorty, A., 'Spinoza on the Pathos of Idolatrous Love and the Hilarity of True Love', in R.C. Solomon and K.M. Higgins, eds., *The Philosophy of (Erotic) Love*, Lawrence, University Press of Kansas, 1991.

Rousseau, J.-J., *The Social Contract*, Harmondsworth, Penguin, 1968.

———— *Emile*, London, Dent & Sons, 1972.

Routh, C.R.N., *Who's Who in History*, vol. II: *England 1485 to 1603*, Oxford, Basil Blackwell, 1964.

Rowbotham, S., *Woman's Consciousness, Man's World*, Harmondsworth, Penguin, 1973.

Sartre, J. P., *Portrait of the Anti-Semite*, London, Secker & Warburg, 1948.

———— *Being and Nothingness*, London, Methuen, 1977.

Sawicki, J., 'Foucault and Feminism: Toward a Politics of Difference', in M.L. Shanley and C. Pateman, eds., *Feminist Interpretations and Political Theory*, Cambridge, Polity Press, 1991.

Saxonhouse, A., 'Aristotle: Defective Males, Hierarchy, and the Limits of Politics', in M.L. Shanley and C. Pateman, eds., *Feminist Interpretations and Political Theory*, Cambridge, Polity Press, 1991.

Schilder, P., *The Image and Appearance of the Human Body*, New York, International Universities Press, 1978.

Scott, J.W., 'Deconstructing Equality-versus-Difference: Or the Uses of Poststructuralist Theory for Feminism', *Feminist Studies*, vol. 14, no. 1, Spring 1988.

———— 'Experience', in J. Butler and J.W. Scott, eds., *Feminists Theorize the Political*, New York, Routledge, 1992.

Shanley, M.L., and Pateman, C., eds., *Feminist Interpretations and Political Theory*, Cambridge, Polity Press, 1991.

Spelman, E., 'Woman as Body: Ancient and Contemporary Views', *Feminist Studies*, vol. 8, no. 1, 1982.

———— 'The Politicization of the Soul', in S. Harding and M.B. Hintikka, eds., *Discovering Reality*, Dordrecht, Reidel, 1983.

Spender, D., *Man-Made Language*, London, Routledge & Kegan Paul, 1980.

Spinoza, B., *Ethics*, in *The Chief Works of Benedict de Spinoza*, vol. II, ed. R.H.M. Elwes, New York, Dover, 1951.
—— *A Political Treatise*, in *The Chief Works of Benedict de Spinoza*, vol. I, ed. R.H.M. Elwes, New York, Dover, 1951.
—— *A Theologico-Political Treatise*, in *The Chief Works of Benedict de Spinoza*, vol. I, ed. R.H.M. Elwes, New York, Dover, 1951.
—— *Ethics*, in *The Collected Works of Spinoza*, vol. I, trans. E. Curley, Princeton, N.J., Princeton University Press, 1985.
Spivak, G. C., 'Displacement and the Discourse of Woman', in M. Krupnick, ed., *Displacement: Derrida and After*, Bloomington, Indiana University Press, 1986.
Stoller, R.J., *Sex and Gender*, London, Hogarth Press, 1968.
—— *The Transsexual Experiment*, London, Hogarth Press, 1975.
Tapper, M., '*Ressentiment* and Power: Some Reflections on Feminist Practices', in P. Patton, ed., *Nietzsche, Feminism and Political Theory*, New York, Routledge, 1993.
Threadgold T., 'Critical Theory, Feminisms, the Judiciary and Rape', *Australian Feminist Law Journal*, vol. 1, 1993.
Weinbaum, B., *The Curious Courtship of Socialism and Feminism*, Boston, Mass., South End Press, 1978.
Weinberg, A., ed., *Attorney for the Damned*, London, MacDonald, 1957.
West, D., 'Spinoza on Positive Freedom', *Political Studies*, vol. 41, no. 2, 1993.
Whitford, M., *Luce Irigaray: Philosophy in the Feminine*, London, Routledge, 1991.
Wollstonecraft, M., *Vindication of the Rights of Woman*, Harmondsworth, Penguin, 1975.
Yeatman, A., *Postmodern Revisionings of the Political*, New York, Routledge, 1993.
—— 'Feminism and Power', *Women's Studies Journal*, vol. 10, no. 1, 1994.
Young, I.M., *Justice and the Politics of Difference*, Princeton, N.J., Princeton University Press, 1990.
Yovel, Y., *Spinoza and Other Heretics: The Adventures of Immanence*, Princeton, N.J., Princeton University Press, 1989.
—— *Spinoza and Other Heretics: The Marrano of Reason*, Princeton, N.J., Princeton University Press, 1989.

Index

85–8, 95, 104, 126, 135, 148; theory of difference 4, 5, 31; theory of the 1970s 37, 51, 62, 125, 126
fetishism 33, 34, 88
Filmer, R. 79
Firestone, S. 17, 51, 68
Flax, J. 32
forgetting 77, 84, 89 n5, 102
Foucault, M. 52, 54, 58, 66–7, 69, 70, 78, 83
fraternity 54, 79–81
free will 110–13, 117, 127; *see also* determinism
freedom 90, 100, 105, 111–16, 125, 128, 130–3, 142 n10, 143 n30
Freud, S. 5, 8, 10–13, 30, 31, 33–4, 40, 41, 43, 52–3, 79, 83, 86, 103–4, 125

genealogy 76, 77, 87, 88, 99–105, 130, 135–6, 148–9; as critical history, 76, 101, 104
gestalt 32–5, 38, 70
Gilligan, C. 32
Greer, G. 6

habit xi, xv n13, 31, 111, 117–19, 128
habitus x, xi, xv n11
Harding, S. 32
Hawke, R. J. 26–7
Hegel, G. W. F. 31–2, 79
Heidegger, M. 77
Helsby, S. 118–19
Hobbes, T. xii, 21–2, 25, 51, 53, 79, 82, 96–7, 100, 113, 114
Hoy, D. C. x
humanism 7, 15, 66; anti- 51–2
Hume, D. viii, 97

identity 6, 9, 32, 33, 36, 77, 95, 110, 135; gender 5, 6, 14, 20, 39
ideology viii–x, 16, 17, 35, 63–6, 70, 125–6; and truth 67, 126, 140
imaginaries viii, xi, xiv, 126, 130; legal 148; philosophical viii, ix; political xiii, 126, 148; sexual x–xiv, 125, 135–6, 138, 141, 144 n49, 146–8; social viii–xiii, 140, 148
imaginary bodies viii, x, 3, 11–14, 16, 70, 72, 82, 146, 148
imagination viii, x, xiii, xiv, 126–9, 135, 136, 138, 146–7; and reason 113, 127, 129, 141, 148

immanence 103, 108, 117, 127, 129, 133, 148–50; *see also* transcendence
individualism xii, 15, 96, 99, 104–5, 111, 117
interpretans/interpretandum 83–4
intra- and intersexual 37–9, 41, 42, 44
Irigaray, L. viii, ix, 38, 42–3, 52, 72, 73

Jonas, H. 110
justice 96, 98, 115, 117, 140, 144 n51, 148; and injustice 112; theory of 139

Kant, I. 79, 99, 101, 103
knowledge ix, 12, 40, 49, 84, 110–16, 132, 138, 140, 149; as imagination 113, 127, 135, 141, 148; as intuition 113, 127, 143 n30; as reason 113, 127–8, 148; embodied 127–30, 135, 143 n30

La Mettrie, J. 53
Lacan, J. vii, viii, 11, 31, 33–4, 40, 43, 69–70, 72
Laing, R. D. 32, 125
Laplanche, J. 11
law, the x, xiii, 17, 27, 43, 63, 78, 108–17, 122 n24, 135, 137, 138, 140, 147, 148, 149; ceremonial 113; civil 113, 115, 116, 120; as command 113–15; divine 113; family 119; of the Father 34; human 113; as knowledge 113–15; natural 110, 113; of non-contradiction 33;
laws 22, 25, 97, 99, 115–21, 134, 136, 141; of nature 110–13, 128
Le Dœuff, M. vii, ix–xii, 62
Leibniz, G. W. 127
liberalism 4, 7, 26, 60–6, 115
Lloyd, G. xii, 50
Locke, J. 53, 79, 100
love 31, 35, 37, 40, 111, 128, 130–5
lust 130–4
Lyotard, J. F. 54

MacIntyre, A. 77, 99, 103
MacKinnon, C. 78, 87, 148
Malcolm, D. 139
Man x, 24
Marcus, S. 82
Marx, K. 126
Marxism x, 3, 4, 15, 16, 19 n32, 60–7, 125
masochism 13, 35–6, 40